THE SPIRIT OF CHINA

The Spirit of
China

DAVID BURNETT

MONARCH
BOOKS
Oxford, UK and Grand Rapids, Michigan, USA

Published by Monarch Books
an imprint of
Lion Hudson plc
Wilkinson House, Jordan Hill Road,
Oxford OX2 8DR, England
Email: monarch@lionhudson.com
www.lionhudson.com/monarch

ISBN: 978-1-85424-751-3

First edition 2008

Acknowledgments
Unless otherwise stated, Scripture quotations are taken from the
Holy Bible, New International Version, © 1973, 1978, 1984 by the
International Bible Society. Used by permission of Hodder & Stoughton
Ltd. All rights reserved.

A catalogue record for this book is available from the British Library.

CONTENTS

PREFACE

Looking out of my window, I can see the modern buildings across the road that are part of the large estate in which I live. The apartments, like mine, have large, bright windows and a little balcony ideal for hanging out the washing. Most apartments have air-conditioning units for the summer, when temperatures can reach 40 degrees. The well-tended communal gardens have palms growing among the many trees. Cars line up in neat rows ready for the daily commute. This is China in the twenty-first century, but it is only part of the story.

Outside the walls of the estate lie the busy streets of a rapidly growing city. Buses, lorries, taxis and cars jostle for space amidst the bicycles that have for so long been China's favoured means of transport. Cities are rushing to build new roads and flyovers for the rapidly growing number of private cars. Subways, communal spaces, shopping malls and superstores are now all part of city life.

The booming cities of China are, however, still only a part of the wider picture. Urban population amounts to only some 20 per cent of the total population, and while many urbanites are enjoying the benefits of economic growth, many in the rural areas struggle to cope. Although China has seen tremendous economic growth since the 1980s, that growth is unequal. Multimillionaires live in luxurious homes while rural peasants struggle in the fields. China is a vast land and one with great diversity. I am aware that a single volume like this cannot adequately describe the complex situation that is modern China.

In recent years many books have been produced on the history of China, and this volume does not seek to compete with them. The aim here focuses on how Chinese religious ideas and practices have developed and changed over the millennia. Only by understanding this broader picture can one come to understand the complex spiritual and religious situation that is now found in modern China.

What is happening in China will continue to affect the whole world in this century. It is therefore necessary for every Christian to be aware of the many factors that have shaped twenty-first-century China. I hope this book will provide the reader with an introduction to the spirit of China.

David Burnett
China

Chapter 1

THE PEOPLE OF THE YELLOW EARTH

*From the origins of Chinese civilization
to the Qin dynasty (221 BC)*

The origins of the Chinese civilization remain one of the most uncertain and confusing stories in world history. Archaeological studies discovered the famed 'Peking Man' in the 1920s, which is considered to be the best-documented example of *Homo erectus*. Human beings (*Homo sapiens*) are believed to have inhabited the region in the Stone Age period of 100,000 to 10,000 BC, and by about 5,000 BC agricultural communities had emerged in many of the river valleys, and with them a growth in technology and practical skills.

Myths of time

Most peoples of the world have myths and stories of origins. These are usually stories of a supreme being who created the universe, and of founding figures who gave rise to the particular tribe or clan. These are not to be understood as attempts at drafting some primitive history or science, but as expressions of a quest for meaning and understanding of their world and life itself. In this sense they often establish a framework from which later religious ideas emerge and grow. This chapter explores the emergence of the earliest ideas that were to form the foundations of the Chinese civilization.

Traditional Chinese views about the origins of China are

framed in myths and legends. Today, when you enquire about the Chinese creation myth, you will probably be told the story of Pangu. This has been depicted in many ways, but will have the following form.

In the beginning there was darkness and chaos ruled. Within the darkness there formed a vast egg, and this was subject to the *Yin* (female, passive) and *Yang* (male and active). Inside the egg the giant Pangu came into being, and he stretched his huge limbs and in so doing broke the egg. The lighter parts of the egg floated upwards to form the heavens, and the denser parts sank downwards, to become the earth. Between the sky and earth was Pangu, who every day grew ten feet taller as the sky rose ten feet and the earth became ten feet thicker. After 18,000 years Pangu dissolved, and his head became the mountains, his breath the wind, his left eye the sun and his right eye the moon. His limbs became the four corners of the world, his blood the rivers and his flesh the soil.

Derk Bodde, in his study of early Chinese myths, argues that the legend of Pangu is the only one that can in any way be called a creation story.[1] Even then it appears to have been an obscure story, which did not come to prominence until much later. It is likely that outsiders, in their assumption that all civilizations have an explanation of the creation of the world, asked what was the equivalent Chinese legend. When the Chinese realized what outsiders were seeking, the Pangu story became the most convenient reply.

Bodde goes on to argue that the Pangu legend may have even been imported into China, because the story has similarities with other creation myths. In the Vedic tradition of India the primordial being is Purusa, who is sacrificed.[2] This theory, however, has never received much support in China, and more recently Chinese scholars have tried to prove the indigenous nature of the myth of Pangu. Professor Qin Naichang, head of the Guangxi Institute for Nationality Studies, has found that the mythology is closely related to the Miao people's culture even today. 'They still celebrate a traditional Pangu Festival, tell centuries-old tales, sing lyrics and stage operas about the god,' he said. 'Many villages, mountains and grottoes have been named after Pangu.' The research team also found an ancient Pangu Temple in the city of Laibin.[3]

The myth continues that *Yin* and *Yang* gave birth to the Heavenly Emperors, who gave way to the Earthly Emperors, believed to be the ancestors of the Chinese rulers. The first three Emperors were Fu Xi, Shen Nong and Huang Di.

The myths relating to Fu Xi associate him with his sister Nu Wa, and together they are often represented as two dragons with tails intertwined. According to legend, he was carried in his mother's womb for twelve years before birth. He taught people how to hunt, fish, domesticate animals and tend their flocks. He instituted marriage and taught people how to devise tools to split wood, kindle fire and cook food. He devised the mysterious trigrams, which evolved from markings on tortoise shells. These trigrams served as the basis for mathematics, medicine, divination and geomancy and as clues to the secrets of creation, such as the evolution of nature and its cyclic changes. He was considered to be the first real ruler. Nu Wa is mostly known for patching up heaven after its disruption.

The second sovereign was Shen Nong, the Divine Farmer. He is credited with inventing the wooden plough and teaching people the art of agriculture. By experimenting with various plants, he discovered which ones were useful and which were harmful or poisonous. He was absorbed deeply in the study of herbs in order to find remedies for the diseases among his people. He was very successful in his investigations. He was regarded as 'The Prince of Cereals' by the farmers, and the classic book *Shen Nong's Botany (Shen Nong Ben Cao Jing)* is still in use at present. He also expanded the system of eight trigrams into sixty-four hexagrams.

The third sovereign was Huang Di, who was considered to be the ancestor of the Chinese nation. He is said to have had full command of the language while still an infant. Huang Di invented the wheel and made carts, and improved communication by building roads, bridges and ships. He discovered the art of making pottery, instructed the people how to build houses, and composed a calendar for farming. He made musical and astronomical instruments. The soldiers of his army used bows, arrows and swords provided by him. He led an army to fight Chiyou, the leader of barbarian tribes in Zhuolu (modern Hebei Province), where he captured and slew him. With the overthrow of Chiyou he became established as the most powerful chieftain of the region. He appointed wise ministers to help him in the reforms. Under his administration, precious stones, gold and copper were introduced to serve as money. His consort, Lady Xi Ling, is credited with developing the art of sericulture – the raising of silkworms and the methods of silk production. She also taught people the art of weaving. Huang Di is said to have governed for about a hundred years, and died after a glorious reign.

These stories illustrate that the Chinese account of origins focuses on a series of great beings whose inventions transformed the Chinese step by step from a primitive people to a great civilization. As such, the story of the Chinese civilization is presented as a single-stranded narrative that can be traced back through a succession of rulers to Pangu. The Chinese are therefore seen as one people in one great land.

The land of China

Geography helped to shape the foundations of Chinese civilization in various ways. To the west is the Tibetan Plateau that rises out of the Sichuan basin to over 4,000 metres, and to the north-west is the Gobi Desert. These form a natural barrier that separates the region from the rest of the Eurasian landmass. This isolation had important consequences, as China was separated by over 3,000 miles from the emerging civilizations of India and the Fertile Crescent. It also marked China out as a vast area comparable in size to the whole of Europe or the USA. The distance from Shanghai on the eastern coast to Chengdu in the west is almost as great as the distance from Warsaw to Paris. The land is interlaced with river valleys separated from each other by mountain ranges, and it was in these river valleys that the first human settlements were established.

Two great river systems emerge in the Tibetan Plateau and flow eastwards. The Yellow River (*Huang He*) rises in the Kunlun Mountains in Qinghai Province and turns sharply through the Gobi Desert before flowing southwards through the hilly area of loess earth that turns the water yellow with silt. The river then turns eastwards to traverse the alluvial plains until it empties into the sea. During the winter dry season the Yellow River is slow-moving and silt-laden, but with the summer rains it often becomes a raging torrent. Further to the south the mighty Yangzi River (*Changjieng*) rises in the Tibetan highlands and continues round the southern rim of the Sichuan Basin before cutting through the world-famous gorges. As it leaves the gorges it now meets the great dam that tames the mighty river before it continues to flow eastwards over the plains for over 1,200 kilometres.

The two river systems have different soil, topography and rainfall. The north tends to be colder and flatter. Loess is a fine, wind-blown earth that is both fertile and easy to work, even with primitive tools. Loess can be compressed to form bricks for making walls and buildings. The soil is alkaline, making it suitable for crops like wheat and millet. These crops required the use of manure from domesticated animals, but as a result the land was much more productive than its equivalent in the Roman Empire. Loess, however, can dehydrate quickly, and during dry periods crops would fail and famine would result. If there was too much rain, the structural stability of loess created severe flooding. Over the centuries farmers have constructed dykes to keep the river in its course. Nevertheless, down through history many millions of Chinese have died as a consequence of these hazards, and to this day natural catastrophes remain a political liability.

The area drained by the Yangzi is warmer and wetter than that of the Yellow River. The river carries a much greater volume of water, which makes it suited to rice cultivation, and it has the potential for growing two crops a year. The Yangzi and many of its tributaries are navigable, which provided means of transport and trade. These differences resulted in a north–south divide that was significant throughout the history of China.

Not only was there a regional distinction between north and south, but there was also a divide between east and west. In the west, in what is now Shaanxi and Gansu Provinces, the Yangshao culture flourished between about 5,000 and 3,000 BC. Here burials were generally simple and pottery was decorated with geometric designs. Towards the east, along the coast, there was a different style. One of the most spectacular aspects of this is the so-called Longshan culture (3300–2250 BC), especially known for its jade objects.

Soon after the beginning of the second millennium BC, the diverse neolithic communities in the north of China began to form into more complex bronze-age societies. This was marked not only by the use of metalwork, but also by the domestication of the horse, increased technology and social stratification. One of the first civilizations was called Xia. Little was known about it, and until fairly recently, most historians thought that its existence was a myth. However, recent archaeological evidence has proven the existence of the Xia, which probably descended from the

Longshan culture. Even though no known examples of Xia-era writing survive, they almost certainly had a writing system that was a precursor of the Shang Dynasty's 'oracle bones'.

Although these early civilizations did exist, it was with the formation of the Shang dynasty that Chinese civilization moved onto the pages of recorded history. This shall be taken as our starting point, as it was from this time that something entirely new began to emerge.

The Shang dynasty (c. 1700–1100 BC)

The name 'Shang' refers to a town that was the early capital of the Shang dynasty – a line of twenty-nine kings (*wang*) who ruled over a small but strategic state. The Shang state covered the central and lower part of the Yellow River and controlled an area about the size of modern France, but its influence spread well beyond its territorial limits. The Shang had successive capitals, and several large settlements have been discovered, including Anyang and Zhenzhou. Their walled towns were not like the compact urban communities found in Mesopotamia and the Indus Valley of that time. At the centre of their towns were large palaces, temples and elevated altars, and then around these were industrial areas occupied by potters, bronze workers, stone carvers and other artisans. Beyond these were smaller houses built partly below ground level. All the buildings were made of stamped earth. The Shang economy was based upon intensive cultivation of the fertile soil. People kept cattle, pigs and dogs. Warfare was common and from earliest times the Shang were regularly at war with surrounding peoples.

It was around 1300 BC that the first known writing appeared in Shang civilization – writing that developed more than 3,000 characters, partly pictorial and partly phonetic. Most of their written records have disappeared because they were written on strips of bamboo that have disintegrated. However, inscriptions on bronze and on the oracle bones still survive, giving us specimens of the very first Chinese writings. The writing system was originally pictographic, which fairly closely resembled the meaning of the word. The picture for 'sun', for instance, was a circle with a dot in the centre. This pictographic form developed into the more complex ideographic writing that characterizes Chinese contemporary writing.

The Shang are best known for their work in bronze. Shang artists made fine pottery and bronze vases of different shapes, which often stood on three legs. Shang potters produced hard-paste and glazed pottery, which was fired at very high temperatures. This, along with works of art made from ivory and jade, illustrates the high level of Shang technology.

There is only a little evidence of the Shang state organization, but it shows an effective political system. Each Shang town had its own king and the succession was patrilinear. The nobles ruling the Shang cities recognized the *Shang Di* ('High Lord') as the head of the confederation, because his powers were considered to be ordained by heaven. The Emperor of Shang was recognized as both a religious and a military leader.

Heaven and earth

Shang religion, as David Keightley suggested, can be pictured as two triangles, one on top of the other.[4] The 'heavenly' realm is populated by the deified ancestors of the imperial family, with *Shang Di* at the apex having authority over the dynasty. At the apex of the lower, or 'earthly' triangle was the king. The concentration of political power in his person was justified by his ability to communicate with the ancestors through divination and the influence of sacrifice.

The connection between the two realms was reciprocal. The king depended on the ancestors for prosperity, the ancestors depended on the king's grain offerings, animal and even human sacrifices. The obligations within the family included, therefore, the ancestors. Failing in one's duties to the ancestors could bring all kinds of disaster on a family. All of these divine and semi-divine figures, from *Shang Di* to a family's ancestors, required sacrifices, but little is known of the nature or the frequency of these sacrifices. Only the king could sacrifice to *Shang Di*, and it is likely that *Shang Di* was the 'national god' of the Shang kings, who was subsequently elevated as the Shang themselves became more dominant in the region.

Religious and political power was therefore conceived as part of a single continuum. Kingly rule and sacred power were linked through the doctrine of the 'Mandate of Heaven', which was an idea propagated by the founders of Zhou, who were to follow the Shang, as will be discussed later.

Sacrifice

Shang sacrifice included human beings who were offered at the consecration of buildings and other ceremonial events. Slaves and prisoners of war were often sacrificed by the hundreds when a king died and was buried in the multilevel tomb. Some of them would be beheaded first with ceremonial bronze axes. Kings would frequently have wives and even good friends sealed into the tomb to accompany them in death.

At the centre of the chamber a deeper pit was dug, apparently as a gateway to the underworld. This gateway was protected by a sacrificial burial of armed warriors. Later dynasties replaced the humans with terracotta figures, resulting in the famed underground army of the First Emperor. Found buried with the Shang kings were their personal ornaments and spears with bronze blades and the remains of bows and arrows. Also buried with the kings were horses and chariots for transporting soldiers to battle, dogs, and servants.

Divination

The Shang kings communicated with their ancestors not only through sacrifices, but also by divination. The most common subjects for divination were questions about what were suitable sacrifices, whether *Di* would assist the king in a military campaign, reasons for the failure of agriculture or natural disasters, the significance of dreams, or whether *Di* approved of a particular site for building a new settlement.

The most popular method of divination used by the Shang involved the diviner applying a red-hot metal rod to a turtle shell or the shinbone of a cow. The resulting heat fractures were interpreted as auspicious (*ji*), inauspicious or neutral regarding the question that had been presented. After the prognostication was made, a record of the procedure was inscribed onto the bone, including the date and name of the diviner. On a few occasions the eventual outcome of the event in question was added to the bone. Over 100,000 inscribed bone fragments from the late Shang period have been discovered, most of them in pits, where they were most likely stored as official records.

Shang religion was concerned with maintaining a harmony between the realm of the gods and ancestors and the profane world. Harmony was the explicit aim of all Shang religion, but the purpose was to promote the well-being of society. The king's role was the crucial pivot linking heaven (*tian*) and earth (*di*). These themes were to continue throughout the history of Chinese religion.

To the east, north and south of the Shang civilization were those whom the Shang saw as barbarians, including the farming people along the Yangzi River. Shang kings sent out armies to repulse invaders, and the kings went beyond their domains to plunder and to capture foreign peoples needed for sacrifice to their gods. Uncovered tombs of kings from the Shang period indicate that they could put into the field as many as 5,000 soldiers.

The Zhou and the 'Mandate of Heaven'

The Zhou were a small but culturally distinct people whose civilization was less developed than that of the Shang. While the Shang exhausted themselves in foreign campaigns, the Zhou established alliances with the other quasi-independent states. In 1045 BC, when the twenty-ninth Shang king, Di Xin, was occupied by a war against tribal people to the south-east, the Zhou and their allies saw this as an opportunity to move against him. The Shang army was routed at the battle of Muye and Di Xin committed suicide.

The Zhou kings acquired a territory ten times bigger than that previously ruled by the Shang. They claimed that all lands belonged to heaven, and as they were the sons of heaven, all lands and all people were their subjects. As the land area they had conquered was vast, the Zhou king divided these lands into regions and assigned people with the authority to rule each region. They usually chose a close family member, a trusted member of their clan, or the chief of a tribe that had been allied with them against the Shang. As the Zhou were located in the middle of the smaller regions, this gave rise to a term that was eventually to be the name that the Chinese use for their country – 'the Middle Kingdom' (*Zhongguo*). Through this system of hegemony the Zhou were able to maintain peace and stability for several hundred years.

The earliest account of the origins of the Zhou is found in the ancient text *The Historical Record* written by a Han historian some 400 years later. This tells of the lifestyle of the Zhou and their migration. They had considerable contact with the earlier Shang civilization and borrowed many of their ways. Bronzes have been found in Zhou areas that are faithful copies of Shang models, while others were adapted to the Zhou lifestyle. Although the Zhou criticized their predecessors, they admired their works of art and enriched their own civilization by adopting many of their ways.

There is more archaeological evidence about early Zhou religion than about the Shang, and this shows notable changes. The Zhou ended human sacrifice at burials, which probably showed a change in the understanding of the nature of death. The practice of accompanying the deceased in death continued, but on a considerably smaller scale. The practice of divining with bones and shells changed to one that involved the interpretation of randomly selected sets of broken and unbroken lines, which was eventually to become formalized in the *Book of Changes (I-Ching)*.

Although all sections of society believed in gods and ancestors that caused problems, there were different emphases to their beliefs. It is possible to distinguish the beliefs of the elite from those of the ordinary people. What was of particular significance to the elite was a moral connotation to the term *Tian* that had political repercussions. Although the early Zhou worshipped *Shang Di* of the Shang kings, they also worshipped *Tian* ('Heaven'). It is likely that *Tian* was worshipped before they conquered the Shang, and the two terms were regarded as synonymous. However, *Shang Di* denoted a more personal deity while *Tian* was a more ambiguous term. *Tian* may have initially been a personal deity, but it was perceived also as the abode of the gods and ancestors. *Tian* therefore was used in a personal sense as referring to God, or the realm of God, or the sky above.

As was seen in the discussion of Shang divination, there was little association between the behaviour of the king and the moral requirements of *Shang Di*. The Zhou, however, considered their dynasty to be linked to an innate moral order, such that the king could only rule as long as he retained the favour of heaven. If a king neglected his duties, heaven would show displeasure by sending natural disasters. If the king failed to heed these warnings, heaven would withdraw his mandate. Social unrest and disorder would increase and eventually heaven would select a new person upon whom to bestow a mandate to rule. Moral values therefore became part of the natural order and history was read as a mirror of the will of heaven.

This idea of a 'Mandate of Heaven' (*Tianming*) became the cornerstone for their political legitimacy. It answered the question of why the great Shang dynasty had come to an end. For the Zhou, their rulers were the link between heaven and earth, and the emperor's virtue ensured a proper harmony between the two sides. They saw their conquest of the Shang as a result of a moral legitimacy to succeed. They cited the weaknesses and excesses of the late Shang kings, accusing them, among other things, of over-indulgence in alcohol. The Zhou were 'chosen' because of their good conduct, as revealed in the *Book of Poetry*:

> Great is God.
> Beholding this lower world in majesty,
> He surveyed the four quarters (of the world),
> Seeking for someone to give settlement to the people.
> These two (earlier) dynasties
> Had failed to satisfy him with their government;
> So throughout the various states,
> He sought and considered,
> For one on which he might confer the rule.
> Hating all the (other great) states,
> He turned his kind regards on the West,
> And there gave a settlement (to King Tai).[5]

This idea became a central part of Chinese thought until modern times and also prepared for the tradition of humanism in Chinese thought.

One historical event particularly illustrates this mandate. A tyrannical king named Li Wang, who ruled from 878 to 841 BC, is said to have departed from the way of virtue by hiring a sorcerer to kill his critics. The King bragged that any hint of slander against him had stopped because the people had become afraid to talk even. However, the Duke of Shao, a nobleman, pointed out that the King was merely damming up the resentment, but he could not prevent the flow of water. Three years later King Li was expelled by the nobles, who chose two of their own to rule until the crown prince Xuan was installed. Incursions from the north occurred during most of the forty-five-year reign of Xuan that began in 827 BC.

Tian was not considered to be tied to any nation, but was omnipresent. As such, *Tian* acquired the status of an impartial judge who could transmit moral concerns to secular rulers. The Zhou, however, drew their moral principles not from divine revelation, but from lessons of historical precedent. These principles included sincerity, consciousness of moral conduct, service to the people, diligence in government, honouring good people and abstention from alcohol.

In contrast to the elite, the beliefs of the peasants of Zhou were closely tied to the agricultural cycle and the struggle to cope with everyday life. Rather than being concerned with the abstract notion of *Tian*, they were more concerned with a great variety of local gods, spirits and ghosts. Some of the more troublesome were hungry ghosts, thorn demons and water gods. There were also the gods of mountains and rivers and the earth god (*tu shen*). None of these spiritual beings was considered immortal and neither were they particularly concerned with human morality. Sacrifices were, however, offered in order to gain their favours.

The shaman (wu)

Religious specialists best regarded as shamans were employed by the state and by individuals. They were expected to fulfil certain functions, and failure in an assignment was often punishable by death. During the Zhou dynasty, the duties of the shamans included calling the spirits, interpreting dreams, reading omens, rain-making, healing and celestial divination.

Shamans invited the spirits to visit the mortal realm and offered themselves as a place for the spirits to stay temporarily. The visitation of the spirit generally began with a dance, which put the shaman in a trance and allowed the spirit to enter the shaman's body. This is different from possession, in which the spirit enters the body of the possessed, which then causes the trance. The shaman's trance is the state of consciousness necessary for the visitation, rather than the result of the visitation. As Eliade asserts, this is the hallmark of a shamanic experience, making shamans different from psychic mediums and sorcerers whose magic is based on possession.

A second duty of the shaman was the interpretation of dreams. Dreams were considered to be carriers of omens, and one of the shaman's tasks was to interpret these messages from the spirits. In ancient China, the dream was also linked to the journey of the shaman to other realms. The ceremony of summoning the soul of the dead was conducted by a shaman called 'the dream master'. This suggests that although the dreams of non-shamans were messages from the spirits, they were not under the dreamer's control, whereas the dreams of the shaman were journeys to other realms of existence in which the shaman was in full control of the dream journey.

A third function was the reading of omens by observing the changes in nature, predicting the course of events, and deciding whether it was auspicious or not to engage in a certain activity. Thus, shamans in the Zhou dynasty were adept in the knowledge of the *I-Ching* (the classic work of divination known as the *Book of Changes*) and were the forerunners of the diviners.

It was also the task of the shaman to pray for rain. The rain-making ceremony involved dancing and singing. The Chinese word for 'spirit' (*ling*) consists of three radicals: one meaning 'rain', another (showing three mouths), 'chanting', and the third, 'shaman'. Often, the shaman would be exposed to the sun, using his or her suffering to 'persuade' the sacred powers to send rain. Although the specifics of the ceremony have changed down the years, praying for rain has continued to be an integral part of Chinese religious ritual, and today the ceremony is performed by Daoist priests.

A fifth duty was that of healing. In the earliest times, this was primarily the responsibility of the shamaness. We are told that, in the healing ceremony, she grasped a green snake in her right hand and a red snake in her left hand and climbed into the mountains to gather the herbs that would restore life and health to a sick or dying person. The ancient Chinese believed that illness was the result of malevolent spirits invading the body; it was therefore logical that the task of healing should fall on the shoulders of the shaman, who had the ability to deal with both good and malevolent spirits.

The shaman acted as a healer in summoning back the soul of a sick person. In a poem entitled 'Summoning the Soul' the shaman pleads for the soul of the departed to return:

O soul, come back! In the east you cannot abide.
There are giants there a thousand fathoms tall,
Who seek only for souls to catch,
And ten suns that come out together,
Melting metal, dissolving stone...
O soul, come back! In the south you cannot stay,
There the people have tattooed faces and blackened teeth;
They sacrifice flesh of men,
And pound bones to paste...
O soul, come back! For the west holds many perils;
The moving sands stretch on for a hundred leagues...
And you will drift there for ever,
With nowhere to go in that vastness...

O soul, come back! In the north you may not stay,
And the snowflakes fly
For a hundred leagues and more...
O soul, come back! Climb not to the heavens above.
For tigers and leopards guard the gates...
O soul, come back! Go not down to the Land of Darkness,
Where the Earth-God lies, nine-coiled,
With dreadful horns...
O soul, come back! Return to your old abode.[6]

During the latter part of the Zhou dynasty, celestial divination was very popular. It was believed that, given harmony
in the skies, there would be peace, prosperity and harmony
on earth. The key to peace and prosperity lies in following
the Celestial Way, or the will of heaven, and for the Celestial
Way to be followed, the meaning of celestial phenomena
must be interpreted; thus, shamans were employed in the
court to observe the skies and interpret celestial events.

The historical texts also show that the shamans were
employed for invoking curses. One such practice was called
ku and originally signified the concoction of a poison. It is
hardly surprising that such practices led to criticism of the
shamans, especially by the scholars.

Cosmology

Cosmology is the attempt to conceptualize the nature of the
cosmos. The term for cosmology in Chinese is *yu-zhou-
kuan*, or 'the concept of *yu* and *zhou*'. The two characters
literally mean 'eaves' and 'ridge-pole' – in other words, they
are parts of the roof. They mark out space and time, and so
cosmology may be explained as a people's awareness in
space and time.

By the time of the Zhou dynasty some profound elements of Chinese thought had been established. *The Book
of Changes (I-Ching)* illustrates the thinking of the period,
and has continued to have a pervasive and stimulating

influence on Chinese thought. *I-Ching* is a book of divination texts, apparently embodying Zhou divination methods and concepts, but at the same time, it presents a remarkable cosmology.

It has already been mentioned that the ancient Chinese did not have a distinct creator myth like those of many other ancient peoples. Even the account of Pangu suggests a view of the world in which the wind, water, mountains, the sun, the moon and so on are part of the primordial nature. These elements are therefore perceived as worthy of veneration because they were all, at one time, part of the man who founded the earth and kept the sky from growing back onto it. Mote has described ancient Chinese cosmology as 'organismic':

> The genuine Chinese cosmology is that of organismic process, meaning that all the parts of the entire cosmos belong to one organic whole and that they interact as participants in one spontaneously self-generating life process.[7]

This differs strikingly from the Semitic tradition out of which have emerged Judaism, Christianity and Islam. The organismic cosmology does not have a creator as in the Genesis account, with creation *ex nihilo* by the will of God. There are therefore no absolute laws because there is no ultimate authority on which they can be based. There is nobody to punish law-breakers, except the government, either in this life or after death. Similarly, human death is perceived as merely a return to the earth, just like Pangu's death.

The early Chinese accepted the view that spiritual beings existed, but somehow they existed apart from normal human life. The landscape had always been seen as filled with fearsome spirits, local deities and hungry ghosts. If no ultimate Creator was acknowledged, there was no impulse towards monotheism. The belief in gods and spirits meant that Chinese popular religion has been considered a primitive form of polytheism. This has resulted in a more pragmatic element in Chinese thought than found in other societies. There was, however, an essential harmony and balance that was fundamental to the cosmic whole.

Such an organismic cosmology means that there can be no parts wrongly present. Everything that exists belongs, so evil as an active force cannot exist. Evil cannot be personified as Satan or devils in conflict with forces of good. F. W. Mote comments:

> The late Dr Hu Shih, eminent historian of Chinese thought and culture, used to say with sly delight that centuries of Christian missionaries had been frustrated and chagrined by the apparent inability of Chinese to take sin seriously.[8]

The consequences of such an understanding of evil stress the necessity of personal and social constraints. This can be understood in the distinction between shame and guilt cultures. Guilt cultures tend to emerge from a cosmology of a creator who knows a person's motive, while shame cultures depend more upon outward actions. Chinese cosmology therefore requires some authority to establish social and ethical norms to produce a stable and peaceful society.

Though the elite and peasants had different emphases in their beliefs, they did not hold radically distinct world-views and all were familiar with the multitude of spiritual beings that could bring calamity on individuals and families. The emphasis of the elite upon the moral aspect of *Tian* and its expression in the 'Mandate of Heaven' were major developments that were later to produce a more complex and sophisticated philosophy that characterizes Chinese society.

The end of Zhou

In 771 BC, King Yu was killed by invading barbarians, and this resulted in the division of the Zhou dynasty. The acceptance of a capital in the east marked the beginning of the so-called Eastern Zhou period. Nevertheless, the Zhou court continued to exercise at least a nominal hegemony for another 500 years, even though the period became known as that of 'the warring states'. As will be seen in the following chapter, this period was to produce a golden age of Chinese thought.

During the neolithic period several cultures emerged in China, and mutual interactions enriched them all. Although the Shang emerged as the greatest force, they did not develop a common national identity, and the Shang supreme deity remained one that was tribal, with no hint of being a universal deity. The Zhou could not claim cultural superiority as had the Shang, but the Zhou organized a political and cultural coalition that eventually served as the foundation of a nation sharing a common Chinese culture. Hsu and Linduff comment:

> The most notable change was the emergence of the notion of a universal supreme being. The Zhou aristocracy claimed that Heaven was a universal god, concerned with the welfare of all people in the world, beyond the limits of any nation. The Zhou kings, like the rulers of previous dynasties, reigned because they received the Mandate of Heaven, and they could lose the throne if their performance did not satisfy heaven. Thus, Zhou kingship was founded on the pretence of legitimacy, which in turn depended on accountability to a universal Supreme Being who guided the world of human beings on a moral course.[9]

Karl Jaspers suggests that this period in the middle of the first millennium BC was one in which the ancient world experienced a new set of values that transcended the mundane order.[10] In China, this so-called 'Axial Age' (about

500 BC) resulted in the emergence of Confucianism and other philosophical schools.

Sanxingdui

In 1986, a surprising discovery was made at Sanxingdui, a site in south-western China on a tributary of the Yangzi about 40 kilometres from the modern city of Chengdu in Sichuan Province.[11] Outside the walls of an ancient city, workers from a local brick factory discovered two large pits filled with sixty elephant tusks, more than fifty life-size bronze heads, twenty bronze masks, gold and silver objects, ritual vessels, jades and, astonishingly, the first and only life-size human figure known from bronze-age China. No ancient texts identify with any certainty this previously unknown culture, which is roughly contemporary with the tomb of Fu Hao. The pits were not graves, as they contain no trace of human skeletons. The fact that many of the objects had been burned before burial suggests that they could have been offerings to deities or ancestral spirits.

The Sanxingdui finds are exciting, but they remain enigmatic. No texts have been found, nor is there any mention of this culture in the records of other countries. Analysis of lead and other elements in the bronzes indicates sources similar to those of other cultures along the lower reaches of the Yangzi River. It could be that competing states learned bronze-making from the Shang, and this stimulated their economic development. It is generally believed that at least 3,000 years ago an ancient Ba culture existed in an area in south-west China, with Sichuan Province as its centre. In 221 BC, General Sima Cuo of the Qin State led his army to conquer the Shu State in western Sichuan Province (see Chapter 4). He advanced his troops onward, attempting to take the Ba State in the middle reaches of the Yangzi River. Several months later, the Ba State came to an end under converging attacks by Qin and Chu.

The sculptures at Sanxingdui may have been substitutes for actual human sacrifice. It is also possible that the statue and bronze heads are images of the spirits or deities worshipped by the people of Sanxingdui, who may have buried them to prevent their most sacred objects from falling into the hands of invaders. The remarkable images have large ears or protruding eyes, which are thought to mean the deities could hear and see over long distances. At this point, however, the unique culture that produced these artefacts still remains something of a mystery.

More discoveries are being found throughout China. In February 2001, Jinsha was accidentally discovered in the western suburbs of Chengdu during real-estate construction. It is located about 50 kilometres from Sanxingdui. The site flourished around 1000 BC and shares similarities in burial objects with the Sanxingdui site. Ivory, jade artefacts and objects of bronze, gold and carved stone were found at the site. Unlike the site at Sanxingdui, Jinsha did not have a city wall.

These discoveries show that the history of the Chinese people comes not from a single source, but from many sources. These were to come together to form the rich heritage of the Chinese civilization.

Further reading
Mote, F. W., *Intellectual Foundations of China*, New York: McGraw Hill, 1993. An excellent introduction to early Chinese thought.

Hsu, Cho-Yun and Linduff, K. M., *Western Chou Civilization*, New Haven: Yale University Press, 1988.

Keightley, D. N., *Sources of Shang History: The Oracle Bones Inscriptions of Bronze Age China*, Berkeley: University of California, 1978. A leading American historian of the Shang period describes the art of deciphering Shang oracle bones.

Keightley, D. N., *The Ancestral Landscape: Time, Space, and Community in Late Shang China*, Berkeley: University of California, 2000. Describes how Shang culture has been deduced from the oracle bones and other archaeological evidence.

Chang, K. C., *Art, Myth and Ritual: The Path to Political Authority in Ancient China*, Cambridge: Harvard University Press, 1983. A good introduction to the Shang and Zhou periods by a leading archaeologist.

Websites

Sangxingdui. A website of the museum near Chengdu housing the collection of Sangxingdui. http://www.china.org.cn/e-sanxingdui/index.htm

Jinsha. A new website showing some of the artefacts of Jinsha. It includes the famous gold 'sun bird' that inspired a contemporary Chinese musical. http://www.chinaculture.org/gb/en_chinaway/2006-10/18/content_87105.htm

World History. A site initially set up in 1997 by Frank Smitha providing a good range of resources on world history. A useful introduction to the global context of Chinese history. http://www.fsmitha.com/h1/ch06.htm

Chapter 2
EARLY CONFUCIAN TEACHING
The Eastern Zhou period (770–221 BC)

The decentralized rule of the Western Zhou had from the beginning carried the potential of regional lords becoming more powerful and rebelling against the lordship of the Zhou. In 771 BC, for increased security the capital was moved east from the Wei River valley to the modern city of Luoyang, located just south of the Yellow River in the middle of the central plains. Although the Zhou kings still retained a ritual function as intermediaries with heaven, militarily and politically they were losing power. Finally, in 256 BC the regional kings refused to recognize the sovereignty of the Zhou king.

This period of the Eastern Zhou (771–256 BC) is usually divided into two halves. The first is called 'the Spring and Autumn Period' after a book entitled *The Spring and Autumn Annals* that provides a history of the period from 722 to 481 BC, and the second half is called 'the Warring States Period' (403–221 BC), because of the increased level of wars and conflicts. Whereas in the earlier period the armies were small and battles lasted only a day, during the Warring States Period military conflict became what modern strategists would call 'total war'. Massive armies as large as half a million soldiers were not uncommon, and this resulted in long battles and sieges.

Regional warlords competed in building strong and loyal armies, which required increasing economic production to ensure a broader base for tax collection. To effect these economic, military and cultural developments, the regional lords needed ever-increasing numbers of skilled, literate officials and teachers, the recruitment of whom was based on merit. Commerce was stimulated through the introduction of coinage and technological improvements. Iron came into general use, making possible not only the forging of weapons of war but also the manufacture of farm implements. Public works on a grand scale were undertaken, such as flood control, irrigation projects, and the construction of canals. Enormous walls were also built around cities and along broad stretches of the northern frontier.

This age of warfare and unrest was to stimulate intellectual thought that was to have a profound effect on Chinese society. So many different philosophies developed during the late Spring and Autumn and early Warring States periods that the era is often known as that of the 'Hundred Schools of Thought'. From these schools came many of the great classical writings on which Chinese practices were to be based for the next two and a half millennia. Many of the thinkers were itinerant intellectuals who, besides teaching their disciples, were employed as advisers to one or another of the various state rulers on the methods of government, war and diplomacy. The three most important schools, from a historical standpoint, were Confucianism, Daoism and Legalism.

The 'School of the Literati', which is often called Confucianism in the West, was certainly to become the most influential. Confucius and his followers made the first efforts to formulate a new philosophy based on the old traditions and promote a path to peace and harmony, and the written legacy embodied in the Confucian Classics was to become the basis for the order of traditional society. The origin of the English word 'Confucianism' can be traced back to the Jesuit missionaries of the sixteenth century. They were the first Europeans to encounter the 'School of the the Literati', as they called them, and translated the tradition into a religious '-ism'. What is meant by the term is actually more a tradition rooted in Chinese culture and nurtured by Confucius rather than a new religion founded by him.

The tradition of *ru*

Confucius (551–479 BC) represents a tradition known as *ru* that came to mean something equivalent to 'scholar'. As we have seen, prior to the Shang civilization it was the shaman who took the ritual lead in the community. During the Shang period the rituals were only semi-religious, and the harmony of the human and spirit worlds began to have a more pragmatic basis. Ritual came to be more philosophically conceived as something that contributed to the harmony of the cosmos. As Mote points out, the functions of the *ru* were similar to what might have been performed by priests in other societies.[1] The *ru* were the experts of the written culture, and of the particulars of the elaborate rituals that governed the official and private conduct of the ruling aristocracy. Compared to the victorious soldiers of Zhou, the *ru* of the Shang were gentle and yielding, but their learning made them indispensable to the Zhou. The *ru* therefore served the new rulers as subservient civil servants with a variety of functions.

First, the *ru* ordered the ceremonial concerning the ancestors and spirits, and especially the ancestors of the ruling clans. Since the Zhou 'Mandate from Heaven' to rule the people was held by the clan and involved responsibilities to royal ancestors, the legitimacy to rule was closely associated with the ancestral cult of the clan. Second, to fulfil their duties, *ru* had to study astronomy and keep accurate records in order to predict rains and droughts. The calendar was the supreme royal prerogative, and failure could lead to disharmony by threatening the Heavenly Mandate. Third, from this came their knowledge of historical data and their command of specialist books. The *ru* were masters of music and dance, were aware of their own refinements and manners, and believed their own worth resided in a cultivated and noble etiquette that distinguished them from the peasants and warriors.

Confucius was descended from the remnants of the Shang and must have felt some of the continuing Shang–Zhou demands. However, he managed to draw together the intellectual aspects of the Shang and Zhou cultures to form what was to become the Chinese way of life.

The life of Confucius

Confucius was born in 551 BC in what was at that time the state of Lu, near the present city of Qufu. His family name was Kong, and his personal name was Qiu. As an adult he was often called by the honorific name *Kongzi*, meaning 'Teacher Kong' or 'Master Kong'. His name was Latinized by seventeenth-century Jesuit missionaries, who used the honorific title *fuzi*, so he became known as *Kongfuzi* or 'Confucius'.

The state of Lu had been the domain of the Duke of Zhou, and it prided itself on its links to the great age of the Zhou dynasty. The family had known some eminence in the nobility, but declined as a result of the political uncertainties of the age. Confucius was ambitious to make a career in government, but was not suited to the life of a courtier, with its endless use of flattering words to those in political power. He was too frank, and this made him a difficult person to have in court. He was also very intelligent and learned, which made him increasingly frustrated. He finally left his minor office at the Lu court and began to wander among the neighbouring states, of which there were about seventy in existence during his time. He hoped to find some enlightened ruler who would value his wisdom and accept him as his teacher.

Confucius travelled in a convoy of carriages accompanied by some of his disciples. He was always welcomed by the princes of the states he visited, and his party were treated as honoured guests, but during ten years of wandering he found no one open to his teaching. In 485 BC he therefore returned to Lu, a disappointed old man. He gathered around him another group of disciples, but was saddened by the sudden death of his only son and, soon afterwards, by that of his favourite disciple, Yen Hui. Confucius himself died in the fourth month of 479 BC.

By the estimate of his contemporaries and even himself, Confucius achieved little during his lifetime. He had taught as an official for forty years, always hoping that a time would come when he could take up his real life's work. After the years of wandering he realized that being a teacher was the most he would ever achieve. However, his quest for involvement in the world situation meant that his teaching had a practical edge that was to become significant in the following centuries of the history of the Chinese people.

As far as we know, Confucius was the first self-conscious philosopher in the Chinese tradition. The best record we have of his teaching is a collection of his sayings known in Chinese as *Lunyu* ('Sayings'), and in English as the *Analects*. Although many others would come after him, it was he and his school that dominated China's social conservatism, characterized by a strong ethical awareness. The learning of *ru* became one of the defining characteristics of Chinese culture. It is not surprising, therefore, that following the excesses of the Cultural Revolution (1966–76), when many statues of Confucius were defaced or destroyed, universities in modern China have now proudly erected new statues to the great philosopher.

The Classics

One feature that distinguishes Confucianism from other traditions of the time was its commitment to the study and transmission of the ancient classical literature. Confucius was a great editor of and commentator on the Classics. Since the Han dynasty, most scholars have believed that there were no Classics proper before Confucius – only court letters, popular poems, religious and philosophical deliberations, various rituals and descriptions of historical events. Confucius is believed to have collected these together and rearranged them with suitable comments. Thus he fixed the diverse texts into what amounted to an official canon. This view has been accepted as the orthodox story by most of the dynasties following Han. However, there is an alternative view that Confucius merely undertook some slight rearrangement of some previous, older texts for the sake of his students. Five unrelated texts were put together during the Warring States Period, and it was these that became the core of Confucian teaching.

The Five Classics

The Five Classics (*Wu Jing*) have been considered as the faithful record of the ancient culture, including all aspects of its politics, history, philosophy, religion and poetry. First, the *Yijing* or *I-Qing* (*The Book of Changes*) is a manual of divination composed of two parts, the text and the commentaries. The text (*jing*) is from a much earlier period and deals with the patterns of six lines known as hexagrams. The hexagrams are composed of six broken lines (– –) and/or unbroken lines (—). The second part of the book is ten commentaries, called 'The Ten Wings', which are traditionally credited to Confucius.

The second text is the *Shijing* (*The Book of Poetry*). It is a collection of writings originating from the ancient Zhou dynasty and the middle of the Spring and Autumn Period. It is believed that Confucius selected 305 from more than 3,000 poems in order to make one book that would be useful for teaching. Each of the 305 poems is known by a phrase found in its opening words. Each poem is also preceded by a short passage which explains its content and main points. The poems fall into four parts: 160 poems about local customs, 74 about the festivals of local states, 31 about the kingdom of Zhou, and 40 hymns of praise and liturgies.

Following *The Book of Poetry* is the *Shang Shu*. *Shang* means 'above' or 'ancient' and *shu* means 'book', so literally the title means 'a book about ancient things'. It is the earliest known book of history, and it has for 2,000 years served as the basis of Confucian historiography. The book records the history of the three ancient dynasties: the Xia, the Shang and the Zhou. It is written in the form of conversations between the kings and their ministers. For a long time this has been considered the most important of the Classics.

The fourth Classic is the *Li Ji*, usually translated as *The Book of Rites*. It deals with the principles of conduct, including those for public and private ceremonies. Like many of the other Classics, many copies were destroyed in the fire of the Qin Emperor during the third century BC (see Chapter 4). During the Han dynasty the book was re-compiled from various sources, and two versions resulted. One has eighty-five chapters and the other forty-nine.

The last of the Five Classics is the *Chun Qiu* (*The Spring and Autumn Annals*). It is an historical work recording political and economic history for the period from 722 to 481 BC. It is a chronicle of the State of Lu, which was the home state of Confucius, and so he is considered to be the writer.

The Four Books

During the period from the Han dynasty to the Tang dynasty (c. 200 BC – AD 900), the Five Classics were the main texts for Confucian studies and for the state examination. This changed during the Song Dynasty with the resurgence of Confucianism in the twelfth century, when greater emphasis was placed upon 'The Four Books' (*Si Shu*). These were considered to be the necessary ladder for scholars who wanted to learn the way of the Sages. They are compilations of the sayings of Confucius and Mengzi and of commentaries by followers on their teachings.

These are arranged according to their length and depth. Thus, the shortest of the four is the first. The *Da Xue* (*The Great Learning*) is believed to be the work of one of Confucius' disciples, Zengzi (505–432 BC). It aims to teach people about the Great Way, and explains what a person should do if he wants to govern the whole world well. This is not achieved through arms or force, but by moral strength and virtue. The book therefore provides eight steps to follow, namely: investigating things, extending knowledge, making the will sincere, rectifying the heart, cultivating the character, controlling the family, governing the state, and bringing peace to the world.

The second book is the *Zhong Yong* (*The Doctrine of the Mean*). This contains philosophical utterances arranged systematically with comments and expositions by Confucius' disciples. If *The Great Learning* considers how to govern the world, *The Doctrine of the Mean* is an exploration of the way to cultivate one's own character. In order to follow this way, one has to keep one's mind sincere. Sincerity (*cheng*) enables people to extend and develop their nature, so that a sage can stand between Heaven and Earth.

The *Lunyu*, which is the third book, is usually called *The Analects* in English and is a collection of maxims by Confucius that form the basis of his moral and political philosophy. This is the primary source by which we know Confucius and his teaching. The book comes in 20 sections with a total of 500 paragraphs. It was not until about a hundred years after the death of Confucius that the book was finally compiled by his disciples. The edition that we have today did not come into being until the third century AD. It is therefore a matter of some debate as to how much of the original teaching of Confucius is actually contained in the *Analects*. Arthur Waley, in the introduction to his famous translation, writes: 'I have used the term "Confucius" throughout this book in a conventional sense, simply meaning the particular early Confucian whose ideas are embodied in the sayings.'[2]

The *Analects* of Confucius provide the closest approach to understanding the real Confucius. The archaic nature of the language and the rudimentary arrangement of the material not only give the text a sense of authenticity, but they also add to the problems for a modern reader. As we shall see through the progression of this book, these original ideas have been reworked by following generations to make them appropriate for their own times.

The fourth book is *Mengzi*, or *The Book of Mengzi*, which obviously contains the teachings of Mengzi (372–289 BC). Mengzi was one of the greatest Confucian scholars during the Warring States Period. The book is comprised of seven sections, each with two parts. The book argues with representatives of other traditions and expounds the theories of the original goodness of human beings, and the unity of humans with heaven.

The Way of Confucius

Confucius' solution to the problems resulting from the breakdown of Zhou authority was that peace could be restored by reviving the virtuous moral character (*de*) of the ruling class. He believed that it was to this inner moral character that heaven responded, not the outward ritual or military power. Society could best be transformed from the top downward. Confucius assumed that there are three powers of the universe: *tian* (heaven), *di* (earth) and *ren* (humans). These three powers work together so that heaven generates, earth nourishes and humans perfect. These three powers must work together for there to be harmony.

The nature of *tian* is traditionally defined as the 'supreme ultimate', but it should not be compared with the

Christian notion of heaven, apart from being above the material world. *Tian* functions as the ultimate reality, to which humans are answerable with respect to fulfilling their destiny. As Yao writes:

> There is no doubt that Heaven is the focal point where all Confucian beliefs converge and that Confucians take Heaven as their ultimate spiritual authority. As the transcendental Being, Heaven is believed to have the power to determine the course of the natural and the human world, although the majority of the later Confucians look askance at an absolute creator or anthropomorphic Lord (*di*), preferring the ultimate enforcement of Natural Law. In the mind of Confucians, Heaven is the transcendental power that guarantees harmony between the metaphysical and the physical, between the spiritual and the secular, and between human nature and human destiny.[3]

Although Confucian teaching does not have the concept of a transcendent creator God, it has a notion of heaven that has a religious quality. Heaven is not only the creator of life, the supreme governor of the cosmos, but it is also a just administrator of human affairs. Heaven is not revered as the source of some ultimate salvation, but with awe in that heaven is the final sanction for humanity. Thus, heaven signifies morality, and to follow the way of heaven is to lead a virtuous life.

A key teaching of Confucius is therefore the perfection of human conduct by engaging with and maintaining relationships with other people in a wider social context. In an age of continuing warfare, his quest was for a way in which people could live in harmony. There is therefore no place for the life of a recluse as found in the Indian tradition. What we have is therefore an ethical philosophy based on religious consciousness.

Dao

The teaching of the *Analects* can be explained by looking at a number of key Chinese characters found in the text. One of the most important is that of 'The Way' (*dao*), but Confucius never explicitly defined what he meant by this. The character *dao* originally meant 'path' or 'road'. It is a way by which people may travel in order to reach a certain goal. In the *Analects* the term has an ethical connotation, meaning the way a person must travel because it has been ordained by heaven. It is the way a person must follow if they are to attain human perfection. As we shall see in the following chapter, the notion of *dao* is also used in the teaching of Daoism, but in a somewhat different way.

Virtue

A second key character is *ren*. Before Confucius, *ren* meant 'kindness' and 'generosity', especially that of a social superior to an inferior. Confucius saw it as a cardinal virtue – that is, the perfection of what it means to be a human being. It is a quality of life that may be understood as being humane, as expressing loving-kindness to other people. The nearest thing that we can find to a definition of *ren* in the *Analects* is the answer to a question from Fan Chi. The Master answers, 'Love others' (*Analects* 12:22). This quality of life (*ren*) can only be achieved by strenuous moral effort.

According to Confucius, all people act according to their nature, which is bestowed by heaven. This is like the raw material that needs to be cultivated by self-effort so as to attain mastery over self. Self may be too aggressive or too submissive, too extrovert or too introvert, too insensitive or too sensitive. Through self-cultivation one should seek to achieve a life of courtesy, faithfulness, diligence and kindness. In the *Analects*, Confucius summarizes the principle of *ren* in this statement, often called 'The Silver Rule': 'Do not do to others what you would not like them to do to you' (*Analects* 15:23).

Christians will recognize that Jesus summarizes his teachings in a similar way: 'Love the Lord your God with all your heart, with all your soul, and with all your mind. This is the first and greatest commandment. And the second is like it: Love your neighbour as yourself' (Matthew 22:37–39). Confucius believed that in order to truly achieve the character of the true gentleman, one must look within oneself. In contrast, Jesus sets all his teaching first around a relationship with God, and only then can one ever truly love one's fellow man.

Filial piety

A third key character is *Xiao* (or *Hsiao*) meaning 'filial piety' or 'respect for parents and elders'. In the pre-Confucian literature the duty of filial piety is a recurring theme. In all nomadic or agricultural communities the extended family and the wider clan structure are essential to cope with the struggles of life. Confucius recognized the importance of the virtues of filial piety and brotherly affection in contributing to good government and social harmony. To him, filial piety meant more than to ensure that one's parents are well provided for or helping them with their work. It is to live and act in such a way that the parents have no cause for anxiety apart from the possibility of ill health.

The family has therefore always been the centre of loyalty for individuals in China. Children are taught to have filial piety towards their parents and to respect senior members of the extended family. Members of the family were even responsible for each other's behaviour, and infraction of the law by one member would bring punishment to all the other members. Such consequences meant that the family would impose strict internal discipline on its members, a response welcomed by rulers.

Families in China also function as a collective security system, which provides for the sick, disabled and unemployed. In the West, parents are responsible for the upbringing of their children, but children are not necessarily obliged later to support their parents. In China, however, the obligation is mutual. Parents are responsible for the upbringing of their children and the children are obliged to take care of their parents in their old age. This is not just a moral issue, but was required by law. In modern China this is a matter of great concern for young people, with the increasing proportion of the elderly in society.

Central to Confucius' teaching were the five great relationships:

- Ruler–subject.
- Father–son.
- Husband–wife.
- Elder–younger brother.
- Friend–friend.

In each of the relationships, the superior member (ruler, father etc.) has the duty of benevolence and care for the subordinate member (subject, son etc.). In return, the subordinate member has the duty of obedience and cooperation.

Cultivation of self

According to Confucius, the perfection of the self could only be attained by the cultivation of good manners, so that whatever society a person was in, he would behave with kindness, courtesy and consideration. For this purpose he taught the rules of right conduct and the study of music. This was cultivated by the study of *Li*, a term originally used for religious rituals, but broadened to include all habitual social patterns of behaviour. In this sense, Confucian life becomes a continuing ceremony touching all aspects of life. It was especially expressed in the decorum and etiquette followed in the royal courts.

The result of all this was the notion of a superior person,

a *junzi* (or *chun-tzu*). The original meaning of the term was 'a son of a noble', referring to hereditary aristocracy. Confucius transformed the meaning from family pedigree into that of a person who lives according to the highest ethical standards. In Confucian thought, a *junzi* is a person dedicated to the cultivation of *ren*. Such a person is characterized by self-examination and a love of learning. By learning Confucius meant primarily the study of the cultural traditions handed down from the past and preserved in the ancient texts. He believed the 'Way of Heaven' had been successfully put into practice during the time of the early Zhou kings and had fallen into disuse. It was therefore necessary to study the records of that time and their arts. Thus, the learning of *junzi* was essentially the study of the Five Classics, mentioned earlier, and also learning ritual and music.

The gentleman was also considered to display five virtues: self-respect, generosity, sincerity, persistence and benevolence. His relationships are described as the following: as a son, he is always loyal; as a father, he is just and kind; as an official, he is loyal and faithful; as a husband, he is righteous and just; and as a friend, he is faithful and tactful. One passage in the *Analects* illustrates this:

> The master said, 'Tseng-tzu, my way has only one theme that holds it all together.' Tseng-tzu replied, 'That is so.' When the master went out, the other disciples asked Tseng-tzu what Confucius had meant. Tseng-tzu replied, 'The master's way is simply loyalty and consideration.'   (*Analects* 4.15)

Moral government

Confucius taught that government should be an instrument of social transformation which would create a social environment that would enable individuals to grow in their human potential. People would be transformed by the moral quality of government that influences society as a whole. This moral power is known as *de*, and was considered to be more effective than military force. It was argued that people are attracted to, and inspired by, a moral ruler, and will follow his example without the need for coercion. As Confucius said in a conversation with a government official:

> If you, sir, want goodness, the people will be good. The virtue of a noble person (*junzi*) is like the wind, and the virtue of small people is like grass. When the wind blows over the grass, the grass must bend.   (*Analects* 12:19)

Confucian teaching provided moral principles of family, social and political life. The emphasis was on the ethical character of a ruler, whether of a family or a state. The ethical behaviour of the ruler would determine the ethical and spiritual well-being of the whole of society. It followed that social reforms come from a benevolent ruler, and not from the common people. This assumption might help explain the political situation in China today.

Although textbooks often stress that Confucius was an ethical philosopher and not a religious teacher, that is not altogether correct. That assessment is based on the understanding of religion as being teaching about gods and spirits, about the nature of the after-life and the way of salvation. It is true that Confucius did not explicitly teach about these things, but that does not mean that he did not hold to such religious beliefs. He accepted the ancestor cult as obligatory, and believed in the efficacy of sacrifices and rituals. He was not a founder of a new religion like Mohammed, but he certainly renovated the existing religious beliefs. Heaven was to Confucius the highest world principle, which he considered to be the regulator of the eternal, cosmic moral order. The Confucian system, however, does not seek to answer some key questions: 'Why does the universe exist?' and 'What is the ultimate meaning of existence?'

Confucius died in the year 479 BC at the age of seventy-three, but his ideas continued to have a major influence in Chinese thought and civilization.

Mencius

Mencius (372–289 BC) was a Confucian scholar who made a major contribution to the body of Confucian thought. His real name was Meng Ke, but he was often called Mengzi ('Master Meng'). He and Confucius are the only two Chinese scholars whose Latinized names are still in common use. He was born about a century after the death of Confucius in the state of Zou, which was close to the state of Lu, the birthplace of Confucius. His father is believed to have died soon after his birth and he was brought up by his mother.

Mencius accepted Confucius as his ideal and sought to implement his teachings in order to alleviate the terrible social conditions of his time. Unlike Confucius, Mencius gained the position of adviser to a number of local rulers, but none put his ideas into practice. His major contribution was to frame the ideas of Confucius into a more systematic philosophy with a rational argument. His teaching is compiled in the *Mengzi* (or *Mencius*) mentioned earlier, which is probably the verbatim notes of his own students.

His two major themes were humane government (*ren sheng*) and human nature (*ren xing*). These two themes were to be expounded further by later Chinese scholars. These themes relate to the social context of the period of the Warring States, when there was much social unrest and many rulers were tyrannical. He argued that a ruler's first responsibility was to ensure that his people can feed, clothe and house themselves. It is only then that the ruler can expect the people to serve in his army, and only then can they grow morally. The ruler should therefore treat his subjects as he himself would want to be treated.

In his teaching on *ren sheng* Mencius contrasts the way of 'the true king' with that of a 'despot'. He argues that the despot may achieve some immediate results, but it is actually the moral influence of the true king that will have greater long-term results. As people are inherently good, they are attracted by the moral example of a true king because he serves both their material and spiritual needs. Despotic rule was the loss of the 'Mandate of Heaven' (*Tianming*).

Mencius' second theme was his belief that human nature (*ren xing*) was inherently good. A well-known illustration that he used to argue for this was that of a child about to fall into a well. He argued that no human being could fail to react in some way at the sight of a child in such danger. In all persons, therefore, there is an inherent moral quality. According to Mencius, the four innate sources of this morality are the 'four beings': *ren*, *yi*, *li* and *zhi*. However, these are only 'seeds' that need to be cultivated in order to become the fully-fledged virtues of humanity, righteousness, ritual propriety and wisdom. All people have the potential for the growth of their moral character, and it is this potential that makes them different from animals.

For Mencius, the answer to the question of what is the difference between good and bad people is simply that the former have cultivated their moral character. In another famous analogy, Mencius compares a person who is bad to a naturally wooded mountain that has become bare. Even though shoots continue to sprout in the ground, the grazing of animals and the logging of woodsmen mean that the hill is deforested.[4] Likewise, a person's innately good nature can fail if it is not preserved and nourished. In the modern nature/nurture debate, Mencius would say that all people are good by nature, but this must be cultivated. In contrast, the Christian teaching of original sin states that all people are by nature sinful, and so can't be saved by self-effort. It is only by God's free gift of grace that human beings can be redeemed.

Mencius' position is therefore that a person must be encouraged to cultivate morality. As the family is the first social context, it is the family that should encourage the growth of our innate qualities. This therefore stresses the importance of the family, and this is why filiality (*xiao*) is rated so highly. Later education continues outside the family, and this should expose the student to exemplary sages and teachers who will help the young person. Self-knowledge is equivalent to knowing and serving Heaven, because the goodness of human nature is given by Heaven.

> Mencius said, 'It is the man who has stretched his mind to the full who fully understands man's true nature. And understanding his true nature, he understands Heaven. To guard one's mind and to nourish one's true nature is to serve Heaven. Do not be in two minds about premature death or a ripe old age. Cultivate yourself and await the outcome. In this way you will attain to your allotted span.'[5]

There were to be accretions to the corpus of Confucian thought, both immediately and over the millennia, and from within and outside the Confucian school. Interpretations made to suit or influence contemporary society made Confucianism dynamic while preserving a fundamental system of model behaviour based on ancient texts.

Xunzi

The Mencian interpretation of the teaching of Confucius was not without its critics and rivals. Xunzi, or 'Master Xun' (*Hsun Tzu*), was probably the most influential. He lived from about 310 to about 210 BC, but little is known about him. Like Confucius and Mengzi, he lived in northern China, and was acknowledged as one of the most learned persons of his time. However, unlike his predecessors, he spent most of his working life as a regional administrator in the local government of China. He was therefore the first great Confucian philosopher to have significant influence upon the practical affairs of government.

Xunzi was also the first Confucian scholar to write essays for other people to read. Thus, we have a fuller and clearer explanation of his teachings than for either Confucius or Mengzi. He is therefore the most orderly and understandable Confucian scholar to read. His sharp mind meant that he entered into debate with other philosophical traditions of his time, including the Daoist, Moist and Legalist schools, which will be discussed in the following chapter. P. R. Goldin comments:

> If we know anything about Xunzi at all, we know that he loved ideas. Xunzi is concerned from start to finish with ideas. They are largely practical ideas, but he continuously justifies his pragmatism as he justifies all his other claims: on philosophical grounds.[6]

He is best known for his criticism of Mencius view that human nature (*ren xing*) is essentially good. Xunzi argued that if something has inherent natural qualities, this implies that these will grow spontaneously without the need for cultivation. Thus, the fact that human nature needs to be morally trained means that human nature is not inherently good. Mencius is therefore wrong in his basic assumption.

Although Xunzi agrees with Mencius that all people have the potential to become sages, he is more aware of the difficulties they face. Mencius argued that the process required only self-reflection, but Xunzi argues that more was needed than this. He especially pointed out the external influences of the sages of the past and the character-forming rituals that they devised. The rituals of *li* refine and purify the emotions and senses of the person participating in them. For

Xunzi, becoming a sage was a transforming process, while for Mencius it was only one of self-development.

A third topic of disagreement was that Xunzi did not consider Heaven to have a moral will. Heaven was simply the natural world, with no innate moral character. He wrote at length that people should not seek to interpret natural phenomena as signs to guide rulers and the state. Humans must attend only to the social realm, because any good that does occur is only the result of our deliberate actions. Xunzi therefore takes Confucian thinking to the extreme of a purely naturalist philosophy that Confucius himself would probably not have agreed with. Xunzi did not have great success in convincing people of his views, but in later ages this rational theme emerged to have a place in Chinese thought.

Mozi

It was mentioned earlier that the period of the Warring States (479–221 BC) resulted in a profusion of philosophical schools. Another of these schools was based around the scholar Mozi ('Master Mo') who was born after Confucius died, but before Mencius – that is, around 479–438 BC. It is unlikely that Mo was a family name, as *mo* means the dark mark of a brand or tattoo. For this reason, some writers think that this denotes some kind of distinguishing mark, suggesting that he came from a lower class such as craftsmen or even slaves. This is difficult to confirm, but it would explain why the Moist school was associated more with the middle and lower ranks of society. Even so, Mozi was well educated and must have studied under Confucian teachers. However, he became strongly opposed to many fundamental principles of Confucian teaching, especially with regard to heaven and spiritual beings. He eventually separated from the Confucians, and the resulting Moist school became one of the most important offshoots of Confucian teaching.

Mozi had a strong belief in gods and spirits that was

consistent with the Chinese cosmology of the period. His teaching is unique in the fact that he believed in a supreme being that he called *Tian*. This supreme deity enforced his moral order by punishing evil and rewarding good through a host of secondary spiritual beings who enforced the moral behaviour of individuals and governments.

The Will of Heaven provided the sanction for human behaviour, but it was not the sole cause of events in human lives. For example, once Mozi himself was ill and he explained that his illness was not necessarily the punishment for some bad deed and certainly not the result of blind fate. Illness could result from some natural reason such as the consequences of heat or cold, fatigue or bad food. Although Mozi emphasized the importance of the spiritual realm, he had a realistic view of nature.

His most radical teaching was that Heaven loved all human beings equally and so urged his followers to practise 'universal love'. This love should be manifested in caring for others' material needs and avoiding extravagances that fail to provide for the basic needs of others. He therefore argued against the elaborate rituals and music practised by Confucians. Mozi's ideal of universal love implies an organized, but egalitarian society.

Like Mengzi, his teaching was later compiled into a book that is called by the name of the great teacher. The *Mozi* originally consisted of seventy-one books, of which eighteen are now lost. These books fall into five groups that are considered to present ten key doctrines organized into five pairs.

The first pair is 'Elevating the Worthy' and 'Conforming Upward'. The purpose of government is to achieve a stable social, economic and political society by promulgating a unified system of morality. This task of moral education was to be carried out by encouraging everyone to 'conform upwards' to the good example set by social and political superiors, and by rewarding those who do so and punishing those who do not. Government is to be structured as a centralized, bureaucratic state led by a virtuous monarch and managed by a hierarchy of appointed officials. Appointments are to be made on the basis of competence and moral merit without regard for the candidates' social status or origin.

The second pair is 'Inclusive Care' and 'Rejecting Aggression'. To achieve social order and exemplify the key virtue of *ren*, people must care for other people as much as they care for themselves. Military aggression is wrong for the same reason as theft, robbery and murder. It harms other people in the pursuit of selfish benefit, while ultimately failing to benefit Heaven, the spirits or society as a whole.

The third pair is 'Thrift in Utilization' and 'Thrift in Funerals'. To benefit society and care for the welfare of the people, wasteful luxury and useless expenditure must be eliminated. Seeking always to bring wealth to the people and order to society, the *ren* person avoids wasting resources on extravagant funerals and prolonged mourning, which was the custom in ancient China.

The fourth pair is 'Heaven's Intention' and 'Elucidating Gods'. Heaven is the noblest, wisest moral agent, so its intention is a reliable, objective standard of what is morally right and must be respected. Heaven rewards those who obey its intention and punishes those who defy it, hence people should strive to be humane and do what is right. Social and moral order can be advanced by encouraging belief in gods and spirits who reward the good and punish the wicked.

The final pair is 'Rejecting Music' and 'Rejecting Fatalism'. The humane person opposes the extravagant musical entertainment and other luxuries enjoyed by rulers and high officials, because these waste resources that could otherwise be used for feeding and clothing the common people. Fatalism is not *ren*, because teaching that our circumstances in life are predestined and human effort is useless interferes with the pursuit of economic wealth, a large population and social order.

Moism flourished in many parts of China in the period of Eastern Zhou, when it established what can most simply be regarded as 'states within states'. It formed socialist communities and shifted the focus from the family to the community. Mozi actively promoted peace. When he heard of a king preparing to make war on another state, he would rush to try to dissuade him. The story is told that on one of these peace missions he walked for ten days and nights, and along the way he tore pieces of cloth from his robes to bind his sore feet.

Although Moism represented the interests of peasants and craftsmen, and was beneficial to economic growth, it was essentially disadvantageous to the ruling classes. It was therefore never well received in the course of the feudal rule that lasted 2,000 years in China. With the emergence of the Qin dynasty in 221 BC, Moist communities were shattered even though they sought to defend themselves. Some writers have suggested that the lingering Moist influences were responsible for the idea of 'knights errant' found in the early imperial centuries. These were Robin Hood figures who lived outside the law and sought to defend the poor against tyrants. The popular Chinese film *Hero* is set in such a context.

Moism ran counter to the trends of the age, and the Confucian ideal of the 'superior man' remained dominant. Moism disappeared and contributed little to Chinese civilization until it underwent a curious revival in the nineteenth and early twentieth centuries, when it appealed to Christian missionaries and Chinese modernizers. Missionaries have often used cultural precedents to explain their teaching, and the Moist doctrine of universal love seemed akin to the Christian doctrine. This helped Christian converts understand parables such as that of the Good Samaritan and his practical demonstration of love in caring for a stranger in need.

With the founding of the People's Republic of China, the

feudal system that had long prevailed was destroyed, and Moism once more began to receive attention from the Chinese people. Since China began to carry out the policy of reform and opening to the outside world, Moism has received even wider attention. In Tengzhou Municipality, the home of Mozi, two learned societies have been established: the Shandong University–Tengzhou Municipality Centre for Moist Studies and the China Moist Society. These two institutions have jointly sponsored symposiums on Moism and the First International Seminar on Mozi. The Mozi Museum has also been established with a statue of the sage standing aloft on Tengzhou's soil.

Further reading

Berthrong, John H. and Evelyn, N., *Confucianism: A Short Introduction*, Oxford: Oneworld, 2004.

Dawson, R., *Confucius*, Oxford: OUP, 1989. A short, clear portrayal of the life of Confucius.

Mote, F. W., *Intellectual Foundations of China*, New York: McGraw Hill, 1993. An excellent text on the intellectual context of early China.

Xinzhong Yao, *An Introduction to Confucianism*, Cambridge: CUP, 2000. An excellent historical and topical introduction to Confucian teaching.

Websites

Warring States Project. http://www.umass.edu/wsp/

Confucian Teaching. An interesting site with much information about Confucian teaching. http://www.friesian.com/confuci.htm

Sacred Texts – Confucian. http://www.sacred-texts.com/cfu/

Moist Canon. Part of the free encyclopaedia made available by Stanford University, USA. http://plato.stanford.edu/entries/mohist-canons/

Chapter 3

EARLY DAOISM

The Eastern Zhou period (770–221 BC)

As we have mentioned, Chinese thought is generally considered to consist of two major traditions: Confucian and Daoist. While Confucian thought gives little time to speculation about the spiritual realm removed from daily life, Daoism is fascinated by such speculative thought. However, these competing systems of thought should not be seen merely as opposing truths. As Mott writes:

> Confucianism and Daoism have been complementary, not mutually exclusive, views of life. Confucian optimistic rationalism in its social-mindedness and Daoist pessimistic mysticism in its extreme individualism, mutually contradictory as they can be on the levels of both theory and practice, nonetheless have related to each other like the opposite sides of one coin or the two poles of one axis. Their union as part of one coin or one axis, as aspects of one Chinese civilization, has been more important than hostility between them.[1]

Daoism, or 'Taoism' (using an older mode of transliterating Chinese), has fascinated Europeans since the first contacts with Chinese civilization. Daoist teaching has its roots in the ancient Shang view of the unity of heaven and earth, and the appreciation of beauty. Its main ideas are centred on the 'Way', which embraces the notion of harmony with nature and includes a system of health based upon the view that *Qi* (pronounced 'chee') flows through the body. The Daoist view of life has been shaped by two remarkable texts associated with the inspirational figures of Laozi and Zhuangzi.

Laozi

According to tradition, Laozi (or Lao Tzu) was considered to be the founder of the tradition and a contemporary of Confucius. He would therefore have lived in the fifth century BC. Even though the Chinese Tourist Board exhibits a house said to have been built where Laozi used to live, there is little historical information about his real identity. The traditional account of Laozi's life is based on a biography in chapter 63 of the *Shiji* (*Historical Records*), written around 100 BC by Sima Qian, who identifies Laozi as an archivist named Li Dan, or Lao Dan ('Old Dan'), who worked at the ancient Zhou court. During his life he is supposed to have instructed Confucius on matters of ritual. Scholars today are still divided concerning whether such a person actually lived or is merely a legendary figure.

As Daoist teachings became more popular, the public estimation of Laozi was elevated to that of an immortal with magical powers. Laozi was seen as a manifestation or an incarnation of the *Dao* itself. Even his birth was considered to be a supernatural act. A well-known story tells that Laozi's mother was pregnant with him for seventy-two years, so that when he was finally born he had a white beard and walked with a stick. This is in fact suggested by his name, which can mean 'Old Child' as well as 'Old Master'.

Another well-known story tells that after many years as keeper of the royal archives, Laozi left the Zhou capital to travel west. At the Hangu Pass, the border of the Empire, he was stopped by the gatekeeper, Yin Xi, who recognized him as a great philosopher. He asked him to write down some of his teaching before he left, and Laozi wrote down 5,000 characters that came to be known as the *Daode Jing* (or the *Tao Te Ching*). Then, riding on an ox, he travelled into the west, never to be heard of again. Some accounts say that Yin Xi actually joined him and became his disciple.

Kohn has noted that, with time, the stories about Laozi become more formalized into six distinct parts:[2]

1. Laozi as the Dao creates the universe (creation).
2. Laozi descends as the teacher of dynasties (transformation).
3. Laozi is born on earth and serves as an archivist for the Zhou (birth).
4. Laozi emigrates and transmits the *Daode Jing* to Yin Xi (transmission).
5. Laozi and Yin Xi go west and convert the barbarians to Buddhism (conversion).
6. Laozi ascends to heaven and comes back again to give revelations to Chinese seekers, founding Daoist schools (revelation).

It was only in the later historiographies that the two later parts were added, which probably appealed to Daoists, following the entry of Buddhism into China. Laozi and Yin Xi are said to have travelled west across the desert and settled on a lonely mountain, usually located in Kashmir. It was here that a barbarian king found them during a hunt, and, intrigued by the strangers, he accepted their invitation to a banquet. Laozi brought along a host of heavenly beings, and the frightened king, thinking that they were actually demons, tried to kill Laozi by various means, but failed. The king finally submitted to the authority of Laozi and agreed to install the rules and regulations of Buddhism throughout his kingdom.[3] Buddhism is therefore portrayed as being initiated by Laozi as the most appropriate religion for the people of India.

In contrast, in a later Buddhist polemic, Laozi is presented as a *bodhisattva* (heavenly being) sent by the Buddha to awaken the Chinese people. When he had successfully accomplished his mission, he returned to the west to report to his master, the Buddha. These accounts show the ongoing interaction with Buddhism and the changing picture of the mysterious figure who was to become the Lord Laozi.

It is more likely that Daoism had no single founder, but as the tradition developed the teaching was ascribed to a single source. The text of the *Daode Jing* presents the figure of an old master, but this could simply be a literary device. It is unlikely that a full understanding of the history of Daoism will ever be known, but for convenience Laozi will be referred to as a person in this book, even though he is a semi-fictitious figure.

The Daode Jing

The *Daode Jing* is a short text of 5,000 characters, and is the most widely read Chinese book in the English language. Its ambiguity makes translation difficult, and there are dozens of English versions that differ greatly in form and meaning. For example, the first line of the *Daode Jing* can be translated as 'The Way that can be walked is not the enduring and unchanging Way.' It can also be translated as 'The Way that can be known is not the true Way.' There are several other translations – they all have the same general paradoxical meaning, but are all different. The websites listed at the end of this chapter give two differing styles of translation that the reader may like to explore.

The *Daode Jing* is divided into two parts, for which the two characters of the title provide subtitles. The first part is called *The Book of Dao*, meaning 'way'; the second part is *The Book of De*, which is an elusive term that has been variously translated as 'power' or 'virtue'. The term *Jing* merely means a revered text, so the title may be translated as 'The Classic of the Way and its Power'. The book has been read either as a document of early Chinese culture or as a spiritual text that has universal relevance.

The Dao

The main concept of the *Daode Jing* is *Dao*, which is fundamental to the teachings of both Confucius and Laozi.
However, they understand the term differently. In the *Daode
Jing*, the central message is that to live a meaningful life,
one must live it after the way of nature. *Dao* is the transcendent source of all things, the inexhaustible spring out of
which all life flows. It is the origin of heaven and earth. It
is always good, and evil happens when people or things
move against the flow of *Dao*.

The first few verses of the *Daode Jing* are perhaps the
most quoted and enigmatic statement in religious literature:[4]

> The Way that can be experienced is not true;
> The world that can be constructed is not true.
> The Way manifests all that happens and may happen;
> The world represents all that exists and may exist.
>
> (GNL, verse 1)

The first sentence probably means that ultimate truth is
beyond conceptual thinking. Beyond all relative things is a
nameless reality that is the absolute, unconditioned origin
of the cosmos:

> There is a mystery,
> Beneath abstraction,
> Silent, depthless,
> Alone, unchanging,
> Ubiquitous and liquid,
> The mother of nature.
> It has no name, but I call it 'the Way';
> It has no limit, but I call it 'limitless'.   (GNL, verse 25)

Wu *(non-being)*

Although the *Dao* is considered to be indescribable, its nature is emptiness. This means it is empty of itself and it is not self-important or full of itself. For a wheel to be able to function as a wheel, there must be an empty space at its centre where the axle can fit. For a cup to be able to function as a container, it must have a space inside that can contain the liquid. For a door to function as a door, there must be a space where there is no wall. Things can therefore achieve success, not in spite of their limitations, but because of them. Similarly, for a person to function as a person, they must be empty of self. Emptiness is a virtue.

> Thirty spokes meet at a nave;
> Because of the hole we may use the wheel.
> Clay is moulded into a vessel;
> Because of the hollow we may use the cup.
> Walls are built around a hearth;
> Because of the doors we may use the house.
> Thus tools come from what exists,
> But use from what does not.   (GNL, verse 11)

The virtue of *de* is not moral power, as in Confucian thought, but is the power to do whatever a thing does. *Dao* is spontaneous, and is ever fresh and new. This is illustrated in the image of an 'uncarved block' of wood, which is simple and unmanipulated by human action, and yet has unlimited potential:

> The enlightened possess understanding
> So profound they cannot be understood.
> Because they cannot be understood
> I can only describe their appearance:
> Cautious as one crossing thin ice,
> Undecided as one surrounded by danger,
> Modest as one who is a guest,
> Unbounded as melting ice,

Genuine as unshaped wood,
Broad as a valley,
Seamless as muddy water.   (GNL, verse 15)

The opening passage can be compared with the beginning
of Genesis, where God creates the universe by the act of
speaking. The world is fashioned by creative separations
and divisions as God makes the heaven and the earth. In
the *Daode Jing* there is no creator, no distinctions, and the
focus is a nameless void. There is therefore a marked
contrast between the cosmologies of Christianity and
Daoism. The Chinese word *Dao* is, however, similar to the
Greek word *Logos*, 'the Word'. It has therefore been used in
translating the prologue of John's Gospel: 'In the beginning
was the *Dao*' (John 1:1).

The *Dao* as the ultimate way of nature also has implica-
tions as to how people should live and how societies should
be organized. For the individual, the goal of life is longevity,
which is possible by living in harmony with one's social and
natural environment. The state must seek political unity and
harmony by the least possible degree of coercion. These
goals are best sought by the surprising means of doing
nothing (*wuwei*)! *Wu* means 'not' and *wei* means 'action', but
this does not mean literally doing nothing, but an avoid-
ance of conscious, intentional actions. If, for example, one
wants to grow a tree, it is best to leave the seed alone rather
than continually digging it up to see how it is growing. All
that is necessary is to let it be and to avoid harming it.

The sage
The sage should therefore be very different from other men.
He does not push himself forward, but is sensitive to the
demands of nature. He acts intuitively to each situation:

Therefore a sage has said, 'I will do nothing (of purpose), and
the people will be transformed of themselves; I will be fond of

keeping still, and the people will of themselves become correct. I will take no trouble about it, and the people will of
themselves become rich; I will manifest no ambition, and the
people will of themselves attain to the primitive simplicity.'

(Legge, verse 57)

There are three reasons for preferring spontaneity over
planned action. First, the fact that the *Dao* is ineffable
means that our human cognitive capacity cannot be trusted
to respond appropriately to the changing world. Second,
the natural world does not operate by conscious delibera-
tion, so we should seek to emulate this natural order if we
are to live in harmony with it. Third, the observation of
nature shows that spontaneous action is ultimately more
effective than planned action.

> Man takes his law from the Earth; the Earth takes its law from
> Heaven; Heaven takes its law from the Tao. The law of the Tao
> is its being what it is.   (Legge, verse 25)

The *Daode Jing* contains many illustrations of the principle
that planned action is ultimately self-defeating. One should
be still and content with what one has, and adapt
spontaneously to one's circumstances rather than acting in
accordance with desired goals. The ancient Daoist text
Huai Nan Tzu tells the following story:

> Once upon a time there was a peasant who saved up his money
> for many years until eventually he had enough to buy a horse.
> When he returned home from the market leading his new
> horse his next-door neighbour came in to congratulate him.
> But the peasant, being a good Daoist, replied, 'Who knows
> what's good and what's bad!'
>   During the night his new horse escaped, and all his savings
> were lost. His next-door neighbour came in to commiserate
> with him. But the peasant, being a good Daoist, replied, 'Who
> knows what's good and what's bad!'

The following day the horse returned, bringing with him a wild horse. Quickly the peasant sent his sons out to catch both of them. Now he had two horses. His next-door neighbour came to congratulate him. But the peasant replied, 'Who knows what's good and what's bad!'

The next day his eldest son was out breaking in the wild horse, when he fell off and broke his leg. His next-door neighbour came to commiserate with him. But the peasant replied, 'Who knows what's good and what's bad!'

Shortly after the Emperor's army came around seeking conscripts for the war then taking place, and they would have taken the peasant's eldest son, but since he now had a broken leg, he could go free. His next-door neighbour came to congratulate him. But the peasant replied, 'Who knows what's good and what's bad!'[5]

In the modern world of business plans and SMART goals, the teaching of the *Daode Jing* stands in striking contrast. This is one reason why this little Chinese text has attracted so much attention from Western readers. Benjamin Hoff, in *The Tao of Pooh*, shows that Winnie-the-Pooh has a certain way of doing things that is strangely close to the ancient principles of *Dao*![6] Pooh lives in harmony with life in the Hundred Acre Wood, and he has an effortless spontaneity that makes him such an endearing character.

Government

The *Daode Jing* was written to provide the governing class with a philosophy of how to rule the people. The best government will be the one that governs least, and does not meddle with the affairs of people. It will seek only to prevent harm from being done and will allow society to prosper and flourish in its own way. The goal is that of a small-scale, self-sufficient and low-technology society. It is the ideal alternative society advocated by the Western Romantic tradition:

Let your community be small, with only a few people;
Keep tools in abundance, but do not depend upon them;
Appreciate your life and be content with your home;
Sail boats and ride horses, but don't go too far;
Keep weapons and armour, but do not employ them;
Let everyone read and write,
Eat well and make beautiful things.
Live peacefully and delight in your own society;
Dwell within cock-crow of your neighbours,
But maintain your independence from them. (GNL, verse 80)

One must continually remember that the *Daode Jing* originated from the period of the Warring States when war, conflict and social instability were an integral part of life. The image of a simple society, with everyone content with what they have and no one driven to conquer and explore, would have seemed to be a utopian dream.

The *Daode Jing* has a fascinating form and style that allows the text to be read at various levels. It is not surprising that it has continued to have a profound influence upon Chinese culture and religion. It was a principal source of inspiration for China's poets and artists, and it has spread through every aspect of Chinese life, including the practice of *taiji* shadow-boxing and the other martial arts.

Zhuangzi

Zhuangzi (or Chuang Tzu – 'Master Zhuang'), along with Laozi, is a defining figure in Daoism, and he was certainly a historical figure who lived in the fourth century BC. The historian Sima Qian (c. 145–86 BC) records that Zhuangzi was a native of the town of Meng, south of the Yellow River, where he once served as an official in the 'lacquer garden'. The location of Meng is uncertain, but it was probably in the state of Song. This state did not have much political influence, but its mark of distinction was that it was the place of residence of the descendants of the defeated Shang dynasty. Zhuangzi was one of the great intellectual philosophers of the period, who probed new philosophical depths while having a stimulating literary style.

The text that is known by his name is one of the masterpieces of classical Chinese literature. Zhuangzi probably only wrote the first seven chapters of the present text, which are known as the 'Inner Chapters'. The others were written either by followers or other thinkers with related ideas who expanded on themes in the Inner Chapters. These are divided into fifteen Outer Chapters and eleven Miscellaneous Chapters.

The *Zhuangzi* uses various literary devices to bring across its message, which aims to free the reader from the bondage of conventional values. One device that is used to great effect is the paradoxical anecdote, the nonsensical remark that jolts the thinking of the reader out of the usual rut. This is a device later widely used in Zen Buddhism. Another device was the use of pseudo-logical debates that start off sounding completely rational, and end up in what amounts to gibberish. As we shall see, Zhuangzi also makes use of humour, which was traditionally only sparingly used by most Chinese philosophers. He seems to think that laughter is the best assault against the staid, pompous teaching of his contemporaries.

The central concept of Zhuangzi is that the cosmos is in a continual flux, and *Dao* is the sum total of all natural processes. He emphatically denies that there is any external directing force, and believes that the principle of change is inherent within them. The book commences:

> In the northern darkness there is a fish and his name is Kun. The Kun is so huge, I don't know how many thousand *li* he measures. He changes and becomes a bird whose name is Peng. The back of the Peng measures I don't know how many thousand *li* across and, when he rises up and flies off, his

wings are like clouds all over the sky. When the sea begins to move, this bird sets out for the southern darkness, which is the Lake of Heaven.[7]

Kun means 'fish roe', so Zhuangzi is beginning with a paradox that means that the tiniest fish imaginable is also the largest fish imaginable. The theme is, however, that all things transform themselves.

With this assumption of the nature of the world, Zhuangzi explores the best ways of thinking to guide a person through life. He proposes the need for equanimity in the face of change. One should not sorrow over the transience of things, but delight in the very process of transformation. Change provides new opportunities that should be enjoyed. Zhuangzi tells a story of four friends, one of whom suddenly becomes crippled and disfigured.[8] When asked if he resents the misfortune, he says he does not and that he is looking forward to discovering his transformed body. Another of the friends suddenly falls ill and is about to die. The family quickly gathers round him, crying and weeping. One of the friends tells them to be quiet and not to disturb the transformation.

Zhuangzi also provides an intellectual response to transformation by a critique of cognitive knowledge. How do we know what is really real? He presents this argument in the well-known account of dreaming he is a butterfly:

> Once Zhuang Zhou dreamed he was a butterfly, a fluttering butterfly. What fun he had, doing as he pleased! He did not know he was Zhou. Suddenly he woke up and found himself to be Zhou. He did not know whether Zhou had dreamed he was a butterfly or a butterfly had dreamed he was Zhou. Between Zhou and the butterfly there must be some distinction. This is what is meant by the transformation of things.[9]

All judgments are conditioned by the individual's perspective, and unless we can be freed from this limited perspective we can never have true and unconditioned knowledge. The *Dao* provides the broadest possible perspective, free from the limitations of one's own circumstances. How can this be accomplished? The mind must be emptied of all preconceived ideas and categories, and the mind will respond to things as they are. The expression 'fasting of the mind' (*xinzhai*) is used for this, and it is achieved by 'sitting and forgetting' (*zuowang*), which is a form of meditation.

Zhuangzi sets this teaching in a long dialogue between Confucius and his favourite disciple, Yen Hui:

> Yen Hui said, 'My family is poor. I haven't drunk wine or eaten any strong foods for several months. So can I be considered as having fasted?'
> 'That is the fasting one does before a sacrifice, not the fasting of the mind.'
> 'May I ask what the fasting of the mind is?'
> Confucius said, 'Make your will one! Don't listen with your ears, listen with your mind. No, don't listen with your mind, but listen with your spirit. Listening stops with the ears, the mind stops with recognition, but spirit is empty and waits on all things. The Way gathers in emptiness alone. Emptiness is the fasting of the mind.'
> Yen Hui said, 'Before I heard this, I was certain that I was Hui. But now that I have heard it, there is no more Hui. Can this be called emptiness?'[10]

Zhuangzi is more practical in his teaching than Laozi, and he frequently uses the person of Confucius in his stories. Another well-known story of Zhuangzi summarizes his teaching on the need to 'go with the flow' of life:

> Confucius was seeing the sights at Lu-liang, where the water falls from a height of thirty fathoms and races and boils along for forty *li*, so swift that no fish or other water creature can

swim in it. He saw a man dive into the water and, supposing that the man was in some kind of trouble and intended to end his life, he ordered his disciples to line up on the bank and pull the man out. But after the man had gone a couple of hundred paces, he came out of the water and began strolling along the base of the embankment, his hair streaming down, singing a song. Confucius ran after him and said, 'At first I thought you were a ghost, but now I see you're a man. May I ask if you have some special way of staying afloat in the water?'

'I have no way. I began with what I was used to, grew up with my nature, and let things come to completion with fate. I go under with the swirls and come out with the eddies, following along the way the water goes and never thinking about myself. That's how I can stay afloat.'[11]

The relation between the two founding figures of Daoism is a growing puzzle. Tradition treats Zhuangzi as following Laozi, but all that is known of Zhuangzi is what can be surmised from the text, which hardly confirms the traditional story. On the contrary, along with recent archaeological discoveries, the text makes it as plausible that Zhuangzi was the original Daoist. He may have used Laozi's voice so that he could 'talk down' to Confucius.

Later developments

In later times both the *Daode Jing* and the *Zhuangzi* were to be seen as means for transcending the limitations of human existence. They fostered the arts of alchemy and developed a mystical tradition embellished with stories of wonder-working drugs, immortals and bodily ascension to the heavens. Another important text of this period that encouraged this mystical tradition was the *Neiye* ('Inward Training').

Until recent years this wide-ranging compendium was not considered of importance, but is now considered the forerunner of the longevity practices and meditation that became important in the later Daoist tradition. The 'inward training' to which the title alludes is the training of the body to control the vital energy (*qi*) that makes up the cosmos. Cultivating the flow of *qi* is considered to produce healing and longevity. Miller illustrates the concept:

> If a Daoist were to come across the story of how the god of the Bible breathed life into Adam, he or she would say that the divine creator was transferring *qi* energy to him. In Daoism however, *qi* is not bestowed by some almighty creator, but is simply the natural operation of the universe, the basic pattern of expansion and contraction, the rhythm of the Dao.[12]

Miller divides the history of Daoism into four convenient periods:[13]

1. Proto-Daoism (antiquity to the second century AD), which has been considered in this chapter. This period is called 'proto-Daoist' because we have no knowledge of any formal Daoist religious organization at this time.
2. Classical Daoism (142–907 AD). This period commences in AD 142, when Zhang Daoling established 'The Way of the Celestial Masters', the first organized Daoist religious system. It became the official religion of the Tang dynasty, and can be said to have come to an end with the break-up of that dynasty.
3. Modern Daoism (907–1911 AD). The third phase came from the increasing syncretism between Buddhism and Daoism, which resulted in the emergence of the movement known as 'The Way of Complete Perfection', led by Wang Zhe.
4. Contemporary Daoism (1911 onwards). The advent of Western colonial influence in the nineteenth century, with the introduction of modern technology, was catastrophic for Daoism. It is only since 1980 that Daoism has once again been practised openly in China, but many of its ideas have been taken around the world by Chinese immigrants.

Legalism

So far we have examined the two great philosophies that emerged during the period of the Warring States – Confucianism and Daoism. A radically different philosophical approach was that of 'Legalism' (*fajia*). The term *fa* refers to ways in which state power can be exercised by the use of laws and punishments. As the conflicts between the Warring States became more intense, the interests of the state were put above those of the individual. War was openly advocated as a means of strengthening the power of the ruler, expanding the state and making people submissive. The old feudal divisions of power were rejected in favour of a single centralized administration headed by an absolute monarch. The state would be governed by a set of laws, violations would be punished and conformity would be rewarded. It is therefore not surprising that Legalism was a favourite with despots.

In its early form, Legalism was probably a development of a need for a more rational organization of society. This was to be accomplished by focusing the power in the hands of a single ruler and adopting a centralized government. In the seventh century BC Duke Huan of Qi appointed Guan Zhong (d. 645) as his chief minister. Guan Zhong was an excellent organizer and a skilled politician. He devised the institution called *pa* ('hegemon'), the so-called Lord Protector, which was the role that the Duke was the first to fill. By increasing the power of the ruler, the state of Qi was to become the strongest of its time. The text entitled *Guanzi* ('Master Guan') is attributed to Guan Zhong, but it is actually dated much later. Although much of it has Confucian ideas, it seeks to maintain traditional virtues by differing degrees of social control and legal enforcement. The *Guanzi* became the general model adopted in various forms by most imperial dynasties.

Legalism further derived from the teachings of Xunzi,

another of Confucius' disciples (see the previous chapter). Xunzi believed that, for the most part, people were evil and looked out for themselves first:

> Human nature is evil; its goodness derives from conscious activity. Now it is human nature to be born with a fondness for profit. Indulging this leads to contention and strife, and the sense of modesty and yielding with which one was born disappears.[14]

Consequently, the Legalists designed a series of draconian laws that would make a nation easier to control. The fundamental aim of both Confucianism and Legalism was the reunification of a then divided China, but they took different approaches. Confucianism depended on virtue and natural order; Legalism used an iron fist.

Men like Shang Yang (d. 338 BC) completely rejected the traditional virtues of rightness and humanity expounded by Confucius. Credit for the rise to power of the state of Qin is usually ascribed to the innovative methods of Shang Yang, who became known as Lord Shang. He was regarded by some as an evil genius. *The Book of Lord Shang (Shanjun Shu)* contains a variety of material representing the views of dictatorial leadership:

> Ordinary people abide by old practices, and scholars are immersed in the study of what is reported from antiquity. These two kinds of men are all right for filling offices and for maintaining the law, but they are not the kind who can take part in a discussion that goes beyond the law. The Three Dynasties have attained supremacy by different rites, and the five Lord Protectors have attained their protectorship by different laws. Therefore, a wise man creates laws, but a foolish man is controlled by them; a man of talent reforms rites, but a worthless man is enslaved by them.[15]

Households were made responsible for their members' behaviour. All subjects were supposed to work for the benefit of the state, and everyone was ranked in seventeen grades accordingly. However, it was Han Feizi, writing in the third century BC, who argued that all books not written by Legalists should be destroyed.

Legalism resulted in the suppression of dissent by the burning of books and the burying alive of dissidents. Maltreatment of the opposition is nothing new in China. Because the system starts with the idea that the Emperor is the Son of Heaven and has the Mandate of Heaven to rule, there is no such thing as legitimate dissent and thus no concept of 'loyal opposition'. Legalism advocated techniques such as maintaining an active secret police, encouraging neighbours to inform on each other, and the creation of a general atmosphere of terror.

*   *   *

The period of the Eastern Zhou from 771 to 221 BC was a time of social and political turmoil in China. Yet, as has been shown in these last two chapters, the questions raised resulted in a variety of different social theories and philosophies. Although Confucian and Daoist philosophies were to have a continuing influence, Legalism and Moism were also to contribute to the rich mixture of ideas that were to form the spirit of China.

Further reading

Hoff, Benjamin, *The Tao of Pooh and the Te of Piglet*, London: Egmont, 2002. An amusing read that draws out many concepts of Daoism in an easy format.

Kohn, Livia, *Daoism and Chinese Culture*, Cambridge: Three Pines Press, 2004. An excellent text by one of the leading scholars of Daoism.

Miller, J., *Daoism: A Short Introduction*, Oxford: Oneworld, 2003. A straightforward introduction.

Waley, A., *Three Ways of Thought in Ancient China*, Stanford: Stanford University Press, 1982.

Websites

Daode Jing. The GNL attempts to distil several popular English translations into a readable poem. It is a paraphrase rather than a translation. Compare with the translation by Legge. http://www.chinapage.com/gnl.htm

Tao Te Ching **translation by J. Legge.** http://www.sacred-texts.com/tao/taote.htm

Chuang Tzu. This translation by Burton Watson is one of the best renderings of the complex text. http://www.publicappeal.org/library/unicorn/chuang-tzu/index.htm

Chapter 4

RELIGION IN THE QIN AND HAN DYNASTIES

221 BC–AD 220

In 221 BC, the period of the Warring States came to an abrupt end when the kingdom of Qin finally defeated all the competing kingdoms, and formed a unified empire. Our knowledge of this period comes mostly from the *Chan Guo Ce* ('Intrigues of the Warring States') and the historian Sima Qian's *Shi Ji* ('Records of the Historian'),[1] which contains the earliest biographies. During this period wars became larger and more devastating, as iron and even steel were used in weapons, and millions of peasants were enrolled as infantry. The powerful crossbow cocked with the feet became the weapon of choice in the fifth century BC, and in the next century cavalry replaced chariots. Iron also enhanced industry and agriculture, and large irrigation projects resulted in an increased population and the building of great cities. Ministers enhanced their power and influence by recommending and winning wars with other states.

Qin, the Legalist state

The Qin kingdom emerged in the west of the region that had been formerly occupied by the Zhou dynasty before it moved its capital to Luoyang in the east. However, Qin did not rise above its rivals until Prime Minister Shang Yang came to power in 359 BC. He exercised a firm grip on the finances of the state that enabled the development of a stronger fighting force than any other. He registered people into groups of five and ten households who bore mutual responsibility should anyone in the group commit a crime. Once a man reached 16 or 17 years of age and was 5 feet (1.5 metres) tall, he was obliged to perform military service, fulfil his labour obligations and pay taxes. This meant that in order to monitor this system, for the first time the state had to keep a careful record of its subjects. This register led many people to think that the gods must keep a similar register of each person's allotted life-span.

Another major innovation of the Qin was that a man gained promotion in the army depending upon his achievements rather than hereditary privilege. Promotion for a solider depended upon the number of severed heads he was able to submit to his superior. This change in administrative strategy resulted in the increasing efficiency of the Qin army and the conquest of all competitors. The Qin state divided its population into twenty different ranks, each with its own requirements concerning dress and lifestyle.

Zheng, the future First Emperor, was born in 259 BC in a time of almost continual war, as the seven feudal states struggled for supremacy. His father was King Zhuang Xiang of Qin, and his mother was a former concubine of Lu Buwei, the king's wealthy merchant supporter. Later, critics were to claim that the First Emperor was actually the son of Lu Buwei, but what is in no doubt is that his determined character was that of previous Qin rulers. The King died in 246 BC when Zheng was only thirteen, so his mother, assisted by Lu Buwei, acted as regent. Following a court scandal concerning his mother, Zheng took complete control in 238 BC.

He was clearly ambitious, determined and visionary. He became influenced by a radical young scholar named Li Si, who was an ardent Legalist. His ideas provided Zheng with a strategy to fulfil his ambitions, and with Li Si as his Prime Minister, he introduced sweeping land reforms that created a sound agricultural base for feeding the troops. He turned the army into an elite fighting force the like of which had never been seen before. They no longer took prisoners, but slaughtered them, and so became the dread of their opponents. Between 230 and 221 BC, through a mixture of cunning and strategy, Zheng systematically annihilated all states competing with the Qin. In 221 BC, the last of the states was subdued and for the first time China was united under one supreme ruler.

In order to acknowledge his supreme status, Zheng decided that he needed a new title. The rulers of the Warring States had used the title *wang* ('king'), which was the title used by the Zhou. Zheng assumed the title *Shi Huangdi* ('First August Emperor'), *Huang* meaning 'Emperor' and *di* deriving from Shang ideas of 'highest deity'. The First Emperor would be followed by his son as the Second Emperor, and so forth. The Emperor sat at the head of the vast empire and enforced his absolute will by physical force.

Shi Huangdi began to implement a series of major reforms. He toured his empire five times between 220 and 210 BC, both to show himself to his people and to make offerings to the gods in the various regions. Not only did he recognize the importance of a strong army, he also realized the importance of farming for the economy, as had Shang Yang. Shi Huangdi instituted a radical policy that unified all measures and imposed a standard currency throughout his empire. A standard circular coin with a square hole in the middle replaced the variety of shapes and sizes used by the states of the previous period. This new currency was especially convenient because it could be threaded on strings to make a length that would be a larger unit. Standard units of length and volume were also introduced. Vehicles were built with a standard size of axle so that they could run more easily on the new roads that were being built throughout the empire.

One of the most significant standardizations was that of the written script. In the Warring States period scribes had used a so-called 'Large Seal Script' to write, and over the years many regional variants of the same characters had emerged. The Qin introduced a simpler script called 'Small Seal Script', and they forbade the use of any different variants. This ruling ensured a linguistic unity throughout the vast region, which was unchanged until simpler characters were introduced after 1949. The result was that China has a common written text, even though it still has many different dialects.

The First Emperor also instituted massive building projects. Within the first ten years of his reign 6,800 kilometres (4,000 miles) of road were built, which rivals the Romans' road-building of the same period. Irrigation canals were constructed, and new walls were built that connected the existing border walls to produce what was to become the Great Wall.

The Emperor had a tower built on Mount Langya and a stone inscription set up to praise the power of Qin and make clear his will. The inscription read:

A new age is inaugurated by the Emperor;
Rules and measures are rectified,
The myriad things set in order,
Human affairs are made clear
And there is harmony between fathers and sons.
The Emperor in his sagacity, benevolence and justice
Has made all laws and principles manifest.
He set forth to pacify the east,
To inspect officers and men;
This great task accomplished
He visited the coast.
Great are the Emperor's achievements,
Men attend diligently to basic tasks,
Farming is encouraged, secondary pursuits discouraged,
All the common people prosper;

All men under the sky
Toil with a single purpose;
Tools and measures are made uniform,
The written script is standardized;
Wherever the sun and moon shine.[2]

One of the largest building projects of Shi Huangdi was the construction of his own tomb. The historian Sima Qian says that the massive scale of the construction involved more than 700,000 conscripts. The location of the tomb is some 15 miles (24 kilometres) north-east of the modern city of Xian, formerly called Chang'an. It was here that the terracotta army was discovered by a group of peasants in 1974. These life-size figures make up an army of some 7,200 warriors. These were believed to provide protection for the great Emperor from his many enemies as he entered the afterlife. The actual tomb of Shi Huangdi has not yet been excavated but the ancient texts tell that his body is in a bronze casket surrounded by a great map of his empire with the rivers and lakes made of liquid mercury.

Despite these accomplishments, Qin was viewed as a tyrant. His many conquests and building projects diverted the people from agriculture and resulted in famines. Following two failed assassination attempts, he became increasingly paranoid about death. He used to sleep in different rooms in his palace almost every night and disclosure of his whereabouts was punishable by death. This paranoia was probably exacerbated by the increasing quantities of mercury salts that he was consuming, which were believed to prolong life. At the end of his reign he was obsessed with gaining immortality, and shamans and fortune-tellers became frequent visitors to his palace.

The First Emperor seemed to become increasingly mentally unstable and confused. As famine swept through the land, Shi Huangdi went on a journey to the eastern shore to seek the mythical island of Pengali. As he was returning in high summer in 210 BC, he contracted a fever and died. The astute Prime Minister Li Si concealed his death and conveyed the corpse of the Emperor back to his capital. The smell of the decaying body was disguised under a cartload of dead fish.

Li Si managed to pass a decree requiring the Emperor's first son to commit suicide, and placed the second son Hu Hai on the throne. Court intrigues continued and the young Emperor came under the influence of the eunuch Zho Gao, who encouraged him to purge the court officials. In 209 BC the eunuch ordered Li Si to be put to death and took over himself as Prime Minister. When in the following year a series of rebellions broke out throughout the country, Zho Gao forced the second son to commit suicide. A young boy was installed as Emperor, but after only forty-six days he surrendered to rebel forces under the leadership of general Liu Bang.

Most books regard Shi Huangdi as a megalomaniac and tyrant, but he is nevertheless a towering figure in the history of the Chinese people. Today he is mostly known for the construction of the immense terracotta army and the Great Wall. However, his major contribution was to instil into the people a sense of unity that was never to depart. The sudden and dramatic collapse of the Qin had a profound effect upon the thinking of the Chinese. It proved that terror and strength alone could never rule the world.

The emergence of the Han dynasty

Amidst the confusion of the period, Liu Bang emerged to defeat all his rivals and establish the dynasty he called Han. Liu Bang was born a peasant, but turned bandit. He gained much popular support by denouncing the Qin dynasty for its brutal laws, and he soon became head of the main anti-Qin army. His forces finally defeated the Qin and captured the capital, Xiangyu. However, there were conflicts between the rival groups, and Liu Bang had to fight against the other anti-Qin forces before he could establish himself as Emperor. He took the throne name of Emperor Gaodi and he reigned from 206 until 195 BC.

Gaodi undertook to abolish the Qin laws, but in practice he retained most of them and merely made them less draconian. Strong laws were essential to rule such a great area and population. The Qin had abolished the aristocracy and emphasized instead individual ability. The new Emperor realized that to govern such a vast region, he needed a ruling aristocracy, and so he appointed nine of his brothers and nephews as kings over various areas while he personally ruled over only one third of the land. Qin Legalism was slowly replaced by Han Confucianism, based on the belief that good government depended on the consent of the people, not force. Later Chinese historians saw Gaodi's rise to power as another illustration of the general teaching of the 'Mandate of Heaven'. Bad rulers would be replaced by those who were more moral.

Gaodi never lost his peasant accent, and his manners shocked the upper classes. However, he was a good judge of people and was endowed with a good measure of common sense. The first years of the Han dynasty were difficult, as he had to suppress rebellion in various parts of the Empire. The Xiongnu people also invaded from the north and were only bought off with gifts, and a peace treaty was signed. In 195 BC Emperor Gaodi was killed by an arrow while fighting in battle, but he had appointed his docile teenage son Huide (reigned 195–188 BC) to succeed him, knowing that his wife Empress Lu would guide him as a regent. Huide died in 188, and Empress Lu ruled until her death in 180, when her son Wendi took the throne and the Han dynasty became finally established.

The Han dynasty was the first great imperial dynasty and lasted for 400 years, with only a short interruption in the middle. The Han period is therefore divided into two parts: 206 BC to AD 9 and AD 23–220. To this day the term 'Han' is synonymous in many ways with 'Chinese'. The history of the Han dynasty includes many notable emperors, but their detailed history is outside the scope of this book, which focuses on religious thought. Readers are therefore pointed to the many excellent histories of the period.

During the Han period many elements of religious thought merged into a complex body of thought. The intellectual history of early China has often been distorted by rigidly classifying Confucianism, Moism, Daoism and Legalism into narrow categories. Such neat categories oversimplify the situation, in which teachers had much in common. After a period at the beginning of the Han dynasty when Daoist teaching seemed to predominate, in the second century BC Confucianism became the state religion.

Han Confucianism

Confucians suffered greatly during the short-lived Qin dynasty, but with the advent of the Han dynasty they were faced with new opportunities. Classical Confucianism had to adapt to the new situation in order to meet the social and spiritual needs of the people. Most Confucians took on the challenge with seriousness and ridiculed those who failed to adapt as 'despicable Confucians' (bi ru).

One reason for the success of the Confucians was that they preserved and reintroduced religious rituals and court ceremonies. These were highly valued by the new rulers, and the Confucians were encouraged to arrange well-ordered court ceremonial in the manner of the Zhou kings. Another reason for the rise of Confucianism was the scholars' skill in state administration. Although Emperor Gaodi was not personally in favour of Confucian teaching, he was impressed by the advice that he received from these scholars.

When the young Emperor Wudi (r. 141–87 BC) took control of the state, he asked for advice on good governance and how to remedy the problems facing the country. The Confucian scholar Dong Zhongshu submitted a treatise advocating first, the establishment of a Grand Academy to train scholars for official positions, and these officials were to be selected on the basis of their talents and moral virtues. Second, the Emperor himself should practise the ideals contained in the Confucian classics, since, Dong Zhongshu claimed, these demonstrated the principles of Heaven and Earth. These recommendations impressed the Emperor and resulted in Confucianism becoming the religion of the state. Dong himself became the leading scholar of the period and continued in the tradition of Confucius–Mengzi–Xunzi. He favoured the ancient texts and went on to write a comprehensive philosophy based upon the unity of heaven, earth and human beings that would form the basis of peace and harmony. Heaven was perceived as a transcendental reality and the source of human life, and human beings must faithfully fulfil Heaven's mandate.

Dong went on to give three pieces of advice for a good ruler:

> A real ruler sincerely listens to heaven and follows its decree. He educates the people to complete their nature and upholds the law to maintain the social order and check the desires... Having carried out these three measures, the ruler will have a solid foundation for his empire.   (From *Hanshu*)[3]

Different versions of the Confucian classics led to different understandings and ultimately different schools. Of these, the best known are the Old Text School and the New Text School. As Dong Zhongshu had pioneered the New Text School, it became the orthodox position and its adherents the official scholars. The New Text School explored the philosophical meaning contained in the texts, while the Old Text School read the classics from a historical perspective.

As a result, the two schools portrayed Confucius in different ways. The New Text School presented him as a saviour of the world without whom human beings would have remained in darkness. To the Old Text School, Confucius was merely an ancient teacher who transmitted the wisdom of the past.

In 51 BC and AD 79, two conferences were sponsored by the imperial court to examine the true meaning of the classics and to moderate the differences between the two schools. The controversies were partially resolved through a number of leading scholars of the period, especially Zheng Xuan (AD 127–200), whose commentaries were to remain the standard for many years to come. However, by the end of the Han period Confucian learning had become so scholastic and irrelevant to the contemporary situation that the influence of Confucianism declined. Young creative thinkers were impatient with the established scholarship and turned to Daoism.

Popular religion during the Han dynasty

Although the Han court had adopted Confucianism as the official religion and had implemented many court rituals, this did not influence the ordinary people. The issues that faced the Han were probably little different from those that faced other cultures at the time. They were concerned with the nature of spiritual powers and whether they could be contacted and worshipped. The Chinese were especially anxious to determine the destiny of human beings after death, and sought to avert the worst effects of evil influences.

Gods and spirits

During the Han period the people recognized a supreme deity, *Di* or *Shang Di*, that was seen as the moral ruler of the universe. *Shang Di* had come to prominence during the period of Zhou, and remained an important part of Han cosmology. As was mentioned in Chapter 1, the Zhou believed that their emperors ruled under the 'Mandate of Heaven'. During the period of the Warring States, with rival kings, none could claim such a mandate, but with the consolidation of the state under the Qin and Han dynasties, such a claim to supreme authority once more became viable. It was probably from 31 BC onwards that *Di* became the focus of one of the major rituals observed by the Emperor and his court. 'Heaven', through the 'Mandate of Heaven', thus became an integral part of the claim of Chinese Emperors to rule.

In addition, there were a variety of local spirits (*shen*) attached to particular localities that were associated with the forces of nature and presided over occupational skills. Knowledge of the *shen* comes from the first five chapters of the *Classic of the Mountains and the Lakes (Shan Hai Jing)*, which drew heavily upon pre-Han traditions and listed the sites inhabited by these gods.[4] These gods are described as being of hybrid form, possessing, for example, human heads and the bodies of oxen, sheep, snakes or birds. They were believed to be ranked in a hierarchical system of command, with Heaven at the top and various gods below. For example, the gods of the five sacred mountains would outrank those of the lesser peaks. These nature gods could have a great impact on human life in that they determined the fertility of the land, the amount of rain, sunshine, and natural disasters.

These nature gods had to be propitiated through regular seasonal sacrifices offered at special altars, and performed by various individuals from the King down to the common peasant. Heaven and Earth should be worshipped particularly by the Emperor, while the various gods of the mountains, fields and waterways had to be attended by the local people.

In addition to these nature gods, during the period of the Han new figures were added to the cosmology. Most important were the Five Emperors (*wudi*) as representatives of the cosmic powers of the five phases, each worshipped in their respective season and with their matching colour. The central deity was Taiyi, who ranked slightly above the others.

The human soul and the afterlife

Richard Von Glahn concisely describes the changes in thought about the afterlife during the Han period:

> During the four centuries of Han rule, Chinese conceptions of death and the afterlife underwent a profound transformation brought about not only by new ideas about the divine, but also by changes in the relationship between the living and their ancestors. Han Chinese expressed deep anxieties about the fate of the dead. The spirits of the dead were believed to endure as vital beings in the tomb yet at the same time were subject to divine judgment and punishment. The emerging pantheon of celestial and terrestrial deities was complemented by a vision of a vast underworld bureaucracy conceived in the image of the Han imperial state and its organs of justice. The infernal gods meted out severe punishments to mortals who led a sinful life, penalties that might also bring harm to their descendants. Given the grim fate awaiting the dead in the afterlife, the spirits of the ancestors, always feared, now were pitied as well. No longer seen as gods with the power to confer or withhold blessings, the ancestors instead were regarded as abject ghouls wracked by deprivation and suffering. The purposes and forms of ancestor worship shifted accordingly. Dread of postmortem punishment also spawned numerous religious sects devoted to the expiation of sin through faith healing and austere living. Promise of salvation from mortal misery as well as infernal punishment kindled popular allegiance to these upstart sects and prepared the ground for the transplanting of Buddhism to Chinese soil in the centuries after the fall of the Han dynasty in 220 CE.[5]

Originally graves had been dug in pits, but during the Han period the custom arose of building shrines surmounted by a mound of soil to make a hillock. Our information concerning the afterlife is gained from the art that adorned the tombs of the rich. These were spacious chambers, often divided into two or more separate rooms laid out horizontally, with brick walls, arched doorways and gabled ceilings. These multi-chambered brick tombs replicated the world of the living, their scale and amenities graded according to the deceased's rank in mortal society, which as time wore on was determined more by the individual's own achievements in public life than by the hereditary status of his or her family. Of the tens of thousands of tombs that have been excavated since 1949, one of the most remarkable was that of Countess Dai, which dates from 168 BC. The tomb contains the well-preserved corpse of the Countess, the wife of Li Cang, the chancellor of the regional king. Her family took elaborate care to embalm the corpse and encase it within multiple heavy-timbered coffins sealed in lacquer; in other cases, the body of the deceased was wrapped in suits of jade joined with gold filigree. Like the tomb of the Qin Emperor, this tomb provided what amounted to a home for her soul after death.

The human soul was considered to consist of two elements known as the *hun* and the *po*, which correspond to *yin* and *yang*. This multiple nature of the soul is common in many traditional societies.[6] The *hun* corresponds to the yang element, and is the bright, light, intelligent, spiritual element of the person. The *po* relates to the *yin* and is the dark, heavy, sensual, physical element. At death the *hun* and *po* separate. The *hun* rises to heaven and becomes a spirit (*shen*) or ancestor. The *po* stays with the body in the physical world and becomes a ghost (*gui*). Ideally a person should die at a good age with members of the family in attendance. The body is buried with proper respect and rituals; the *hun* will embark on its somewhat perilous journey to the heavenly realm. For this purpose different types of talisman were provided by way of decoration within the tomb.

One of the best paintings found on the top of the inner-most coffins shows a symbolic representation of the journey that the *hun* would take to reach the Blessed Isles of the East. There the soul will receive the necessary suste-nance to prepare it for the next stage, whereby it will be led to the gates of paradise. It will remain a contented member of the family and may bestow benefits on the living.

Different measures were taken by the Han to provide comfort for the *po* that stays with the body in the grave. The *po* had to be supplied with a legal contract to the land of the grave as well as with goods. Miniature houses, granaries, boats and items of a more personal nature were placed in the tomb. Some tombs included basins for washing and incense-burners and lampstands. These items were designed to discourage the *po* from leaving the body and returning to its former home to bother the living. Countess Dai's tomb contained a variety of meat dishes, cups of beer and forty-eight suitcases for her journey. For the First Emperor, the soldiers of his army were full sized, but in the Han period the images were usually of a smaller scale and are now on display in many Chinese museums. Ancestors were believed to be conscious and knowledgeable of their descendants' affairs. They required regular supplies of food, wine and incantations, and they in turn would send good fortune and provide protection. The relationship was strictly reciprocal, and disasters and illnesses were attrib-uted to neglect of ancestral duties. Today, in Hong Kong and Taiwan, grave goods are mostly paper replicas of desir-able items.

Another category of spirit beings was ghosts. When people died violently, it was believed their ghosts would come back for vengeance. Other ghosts were those who had been neglected by their families and were hungry, and so came in search of sustenance. To deal with these, people took precautions such as hanging demon-dispelling branches or talismans over their doors and uttering spells when entering an unknown area. Once a ghost or demon made itself known, a slipper might be thrown at it or a mirror held out to show the spirit its hideous shape. It would then quickly vanish.

There were four ill-defined ideas concerning life after death. One approach to the afterlife was by way of the Blessed Isles of the East. A second way was explained in terms of the whole structure that underlies the universe. A third idea, which is parallel to the paradise of the Eastern Isles, was the magical realm of the West, ruled by the Queen Mother of the West. Finally there was a somewhat vague notion of the 'Yellow Springs', a shadowy world not unlike the Old Testament notion of *Sheol*.

Myths of the Eastern Isles were known in the fourth century BC, and it has already been mentioned that the First Qin Emperor may well have sought to find these isles. Different traditions give these as three, four or five islands. It was believed that the elixir of long life could be tasted on these isles, and this was a route to the world of *di*.

The paradise of the Queen Mother of the West occurred in a number of myths and cults. She was supposed to live in a 'mountain of jade' in a magical realm where the sun sets. The iconography portraying her as a regal figure presiding over a mountain-top kingdom of feathered immortals and fabulous creatures developed only in the last two centuries of the Han dynasty. She fills the role of partner of the kings of the earth, and later she has her own consort who is the King Father of the East. Her meeting with these partners is associated with the seasons. She is regarded as timeless, none knowing her beginning or end, and she is the donor of the elixir of life. The strength of these beliefs, especially in royal circles, is shown by the fact that in 102 BC an expedition was sent to Central Asia. One of its aims was to acquire the heavenly steed that would convey the king to the land of the immortals.

Yin and yang

The most significant development of Han cosmology was *yin* and *yang*. The literal meanings of these terms are the shady and sunny sides of a hill, or simply darkness and light. *Yin* and *yang* are not things or substances but modes of the psycho-physical substance known as *qi*. *Yin* is *qi* in its dark, dense, earthly mode, and *yang* denotes the bright, light, heavenly mode.

The body contains *qi* that, although being one, comes in two forms: a basic primordial *qi* that connects it to the cosmos and *Dao* in general, and an earthly *qi* that is replenished by breathing and food, and enables the body to survive in everyday life. Both forms of *qi* are necessary and interact continually with each other. Once a person is born, they begin to loose their primordial *qi*, especially through interaction with the world by expression of passions and desires and by sensory exchanges. Once people have lost a certain amount of *qi* they get sick. Healing, then, is the replenishing of *qi* by the use of drugs and acupuncture. Longevity is attained through a basic state of good health achieved by increasing the primordial *qi*. To do this one must follow specific diets and undertake breathing exercises, massages, meditations and sexual practices. This is still practised today under the name of *Qigong*, which claims to increase life expectancy and vigour in old age.

The fluctuation of *qi* was also mapped out according to a system of Five Phases. The Chinese love of classification and hierarchy extended this system in various ways:

Yang	Rising growth	Wood	Jupiter	East
	Maturity	Fire	Mars	South
Equilibrium	Tranquillity	Earth	Saturn	Central
	Rising growth	Metal	Venus	West
Yin	Maturity	Water	Mercury	North

The Five-Phase System involves the correlation of things of the same category and the transformation of one category into another. The static correlation can be illustrated in Chinese medicine. Healing involves the use of medicines in the same categories. For example, since the lungs and beans are both classified as 'fire', if a person has a health problem with the lungs, they would be encouraged to eat beans.

Table of Correspondence for the Five-Phase System					
Agent	Wood	Fire	Earth	Metal	Water
Seasons	Spring	Summer		Autumn	Winter
Divine rulers	Tai Hao	Yan Di	Yellow Emperor	Shao Hao	Zhuan Xu
Sacrifices	Inner door	Hearth	Inner court	Outer court	Well
Animals	Sheep	Fowl	Ox	Dog	Pig
Grains	Wheat	Beans	Panicled millet	Hemp	Millet
Organs	Spleen	Lungs	Heart	Liver	Kidneys
Numbers	Eight	Seven	Five	Nine	Six
Colours	Green	Red	Yellow	White	Black
Directions	East	South	Centre	West	North
Planets	Jupiter	Mars	Saturn	Venus	Mercury

The belief in immortality and its attainment is at the root of many later Daoist ideas and practices. To attain it, a person has to transform all their *qi* into primordial *qi* and proceed to increasingly refine it to ever subtler levels. This finer *qi* will eventually turn into pure spirit, with the person becoming increasingly identified with spirit-people and transcendants. This requires intensive meditation, radical forms of diet and bodily disciplines. The result is that death is bypassed, magical powers are attained and residence in paradise is achieved.

The belief in immortality and its attainment resulted in many later Daoist ideas and practices. It gave a new perception of the human body as a replica of the greater universe. The *Huaninanzi Honglie* ('Great Words from Huanian') describes it as follows:

> The roundness of the head is an image of heaven, the square-ness of the feet matches the pattern of earth. Heaven has four seasons, five phases, nine directions, and 360 days. Human beings have accordingly four limbs, five inner organs, nine ori-fices, and 360 joints. Heaven has wind, rain, cold, and heat. Human beings have accordingly the actions of giving, taking, joy and anger. The gall bladder corresponds to the clouds, the lungs to the breath, the liver to the wind, the kidneys to the rain, and the spleen to the thunder.[7]

This integrated understanding of the human body applied to the newly emerging technique of acupuncture. Here the body was divided into five key storage centres of *qi*. These are the *yin*-organs: the liver, heart, spleen, lungs and kid-neys. These were assisted by six *yang*-organs that would process rather than store *qi*: the gall bladder, small intes-tine, stomach, large intestine, bladder and 'triple heater' (an organ with no match in Western medicine). Each of these was then associated with a specific energy channel or meridian that directed *qi* through the body. Along these one could access the *qi* by use of needles and massage.

The so-called 'conquest' series illustrates the dynamic application of the theory of *yin–yang* to human history. A natural cycle of wood–fire–earth–metal–water was consid-ered to exist. When wood is burnt it produces fire; fire produces ash; earth produces metal ore; metal, when heated, becomes liquid; water makes vegetation grow. The conquest cycle was the dominant court ideology of the Qin and early Han dynasties.

The *yin–yang* theory was an attempt to provide structure to ancient ideas, and to provide a holistic model that would govern nature and culture, empirical and spiritual, and the individual and society. It sets a middle ground between monism and dualism. Monism is a system of thought in which there is only one ultimate reality and all distinctions are illusory. This is best illustrated by the Hindu theory of *Advaita Vedanta*. Dualism is the Western philosophical distinction between body and mind. The theory of *yin–yang* recognizes that differences are real, but are in a complementary relationship as aspects of a more fundamental unity (the *dao*). During the Han period these ideas were incorporated into both Daoism and Confucianism.

Divination

As was shown in previous chapters, divination had been important in China from the earliest times. Two principal methods of divination had been practised: the use of shells and bones, and the use of stalks. During the Han dynasty the principal method of divination was the formation of a linear pattern of six lines, by casting and manipulating the stalks of the yarrow plant. The yarrow plant was associated with longevity because the plant itself only grows slowly.

Although there is no evidence for how the yarrow method of divination was practised in the Han period, it seems likely that it was similar to the way it is practised today. Forty-nine out of an original fifty stalks were cast. The way the stalks fell determined whether the line that emerged was complete or split, and whether it was fixed in that form or on the point of changing into the other. Thus each line of a hexagram is either solid (*yang*) or broken (*yin*), and, because a hexagram has six lines, there are only sixty-four possible hexagrams. The answers one finds in the *Yijing* give the relations between people, within a family, or in a state.

As in many other societies, so in Han China there was a strong belief that certain times and localities possessed inherent qualities that made them auspicious or inauspicious. Certain days were considered to be particularly fortuitous for certain activities. Certain places were considered to be particularly auspicious due to their location. It was this principle that was eventually to lead to the practice of geomancy (*Feng Shui*).

Religious movements in the latter Han era

During the later part of the Han dynasty a number of new religious movements emerged. One of the most significant was the major transformation of Daoist beliefs that occurred in the second century AD. Some Daoists began to believe that Laozi was in fact a deity and could appear to his followers and bring them salvation.

Emperor Huan is said to have founded a temple to Laozi about AD 147, and he made offerings to the deity Laozi. There is also one source that says that the Emperor also prayed to the Buddha, a foreign deity from India who was often associated with Laozi during this period. The next chapter will more fully discuss the coming of Buddhism to China. The worship of Laozi provided an alternative to Confucian teaching, which stressed filial piety and veneration of the ancestors.

The Celestial Masters

Many peasant leaders claimed to have had visions of Laozi, who foretold the beginning of a new utopian era. This resulted in a series of uprisings against the Emperor. These movements were known by two names – either the 'Celestial Masters' or 'Five Pecks of Rice'. The later name results from the offerings that were asked of their followers. The movement started in AD 142, when Zhang Daoling (originally called Zang Ling) had a vision of the deified Laozi, who appointed Zhang to be his earthly representative. Zhang grew up in Jiangsu where he studied the traditional Daoist arts of making potions to seek immortality. It was when he moved to Sichuan Province that he received his revelation. Sichuan is a region that even today has many non-Chinese minorities, and one of these could have been the source of his mystic experience.

Zhang's teaching differed greatly from early Daoist teaching. The Five Peck Daoists worshipped the *Dao* in the person of the deified Laozi. Early practitioners had taught only selected disciples the breathing exercises, sexual techniques and medical potions that were considered to enhance an individual's ability to attain immortality. Zhang taught that immortality was open to all people and not just a select few. He established a formal hierarchy, with the initiated presiding as a priesthood over the laity. The laity made offerings to the priests and promised to confess their wrongdoings and give up the worship of unclean gods who required meat offerings. In return the laity were promised good health. These Daoists therefore associated illness with violation of their teachings, and so priests were required to hear people's confessions before they could recover. Members also recited *The Way and Integrity Classic* as a means of curing illness.

The movement adopted a military-style organization, and Zhang came to control a large area in the south-west of China. After about thirty years of consolidation, the area was attacked by the warlord Cao Cao in AD 215. Zhang submitted to him, and was criticized by many of his followers, who left him in large numbers. They migrated to various parts of the empire, thus spreading their Daoist ideas further afield.

The Yellow Turbans

Another Daoist movement was the 'Yellow Turbans', who were active at the same time in the area between the Yellow and Huani rivers on the eastern coast of China. The Yellow Turbans shared many of the practices of the Five Peck Daoists, especially the association of illness with wrongdoing, and they too encouraged confession of sins. The Yellow

Turbans gave the sick holy water as a cure, and if the person did not recover, it was believed that their sins were too great to be absolved. They also established their own religious hierarchy with a leader, a second tier of thirty-six senior adepts and then a further tier of adepts.

The beginning of a new century or period has often been seen by religious movements as the beginning of a new spiritual epoch, and because of this such movements have often been called millenarian movements. This is the belief that the world is coming to an end and that a newer and better one will take its place. The new world will be one of peace and prosperity. Within the Christian tradition, such movements believed that the first phase of the new era would last for 1,000 years – hence the name 'millenarian'. Often, the millennium is ushered in by the coming of a saviour who will lead his chosen people into the new age. These movements usually occur in periods of economic and social crisis. As we will see, such movements have been common throughout the history of China.

The year 184 AD was the first year of the sixty-year cycle in the Chinese calendar. This was an auspicious year, which the Yellow Turbans prophesied was to mark the beginning of a new age. This was probably reinforced by a series of epidemics that had broken out in the years leading up to 184, which would also account for the Daoists' stress on healing. They called this the 'Era of Great Peace' (*taiping*), a name that would be used by another religious movement in the nineteenth century (1,700 years later).

The Yellow Turbans gained support at different social levels, from peasant farmers to palace eunuchs. They planned to begin a rebellion in the third month of 184, but the government officials discovered the plot and arrested some of the leaders. The rebellion therefore began ahead of schedule and some 360,000 insurgents from eight provinces joined it. The central government quickly dispatched its own imperial troops and recruited the armies of several independent generals. The Yellow Turban rebels were no match for such a combined force, who killed or captured the leaders and scattered the rebels. The Yellow Turbans disappeared as quickly as they had emerged, leaving the Five Pecks as the only surviving Daoist movement.

Possible Christian contact

As will be noted later, it is generally considered that Christianity was first taken to China by the Syrian missionary Alopen in AD 635, the ninth year of the reign of Zhenguan of the Tang dynasty. However, recently Wei Fan Wang, a retired Professor from Nanjing Theological Seminary, pointed out archives stored in the Museum of Xuzhou, Jiangsu Province.[8] They were stone carvings from the Eastern Han dynasty (AD 25–220). These funeral objects resemble the artistic style of early Christianity in the Middle East, while also having characteristics of Han China.

The carvings are said to include the symbol of the fish, which was widely used by early Christians. Another carving seems to describe the creation story with, at the top, the sun and moon, a big fish and birds. On the right are wild animals and to the left, domestic animals. Professor Wang proposes that this could be illustrating creation. News of this explanation even found its way into the *China Daily*, but the evidence is far from conclusive.

The end of the Han dynasty

There are still many uncertainties about the fall of the Han dynasty. A common explanation is that the empire experienced a massive shortfall of funds at the end of the second century after famines and epidemics. The elite continued to live in an affluent lifestyle, maintaining enormous households and extensive harems. The revolt of the Yellow

Turbans shows something of the growing unrest, especially among the peasants.

The Han dynasty was eventually to collapse in AD 220, and three centuries of disunity were to ensue. However, the 400 years of the Qin and Han dynasties were to leave an indelible imprint of a unified state on the minds of the people. They now used the same standard of measures, wrote with the same characters, used the same money and recognized a common emperor. In the years following the fall of the Han dynasty, leaders tried to reconquer the territory of the empire, which was eventually to happen for most of its forthcoming history.

This can be compared with the Greek and Roman empires of Europe. The Roman empire collapsed not only due to internal weakness, but through invasion by peoples from outside the empire. These peoples carved out their own states and used their own languages and customs. Although Charlemagne sought to unite Europe under the Holy Roman Empire, Europe remained divided even though it was in the main Christian.

The 400 years of Qin and Han rule formed the cultural contours of Chinese society until the twentieth century. A powerful, educated class owned the land and supported the imperial role. The market economy of the Han and the role of the government continued. One element that would change was that of religion. The religious world of the Han that was dominated by Confucian and Daoist teaching would change as missionaries came from the West.

Further reading

Loewe, Michael, *Everyday Life in Early Imperial China*, London: Transworld Publishers, 1973.

Von Glahn, R., *The Sinister Way: The Divine and the Demonic in Chinese Religious Culture*, Berkeley: University of California Press, 2004.

Video: *The First Emperor*, Channel 4 Productions, 2006.

Film: *Hero*. A classic film set at the time when the Qin state was seeking to conquer Zhou. The unveiling theme is 'all under heaven'. Whatever the cost, it is best that all of the states be united under *Tian*, as only then will there be peace.

Websites

The Emperor's Terracotta Army. This is an excellent site about the excavations, but it can be slow to connect. http://www.bmy.com.cn/index_eng.htm

Maps of China. This site has a variety of interesting timelines and historic and geographic maps. http://www.chinapage.com/timemap.html

Yijing. To see an online version of *Yijing*, look at this site, but there are many others. http://sundialler.com/yi_jing/

Chapter 5

BUDDHISM COMES TO THE MIDDLE KINGDOM

From the Han dynasty to the Sui dynasty
(AD 50–600)

There is a legend that one night the Emperor Mingdi (reigned AD 57–75) had a dream in which he saw a golden figure flying in front of his palace. On asking his courtiers for an interpretation, one of them, Fu Yi, said that he had heard that far away in India there was a sage whose body was of a golden hue and who had attained liberation. This man, he said, was called the Buddha. The Emperor accepted his explanation and immediately sent a delegation to India to enquire after this wise man. The delegation returned with the *Sutra of the Forty-Two Sections*, which was received by the Emperor and deposited in the temple outside the wall of the capital, Luoyang. The question that is left unaddressed is how Fu Yi knew of the Buddha and his teaching, if Buddhists had not already arrived in China. Many scholars think that this story was developed to give authority to the presence of Buddhist monks in Luoyang by placing the initiative of inviting the monks upon the Han monarch. There could well have been Buddhist communities in China that antedated the Luoyang group.[1]

As was mentioned in the previous chapter, the Han dynasty came to an end in AD 220, throwing the region once again into a period of rival states, each contending for hegemony over its neighbours. Even so, this period of the three kingdoms of Wei, Shu and Wu is often remembered in Chinese literature as a golden age of chivalry and

romance. The exploits of the founders of these three kingdoms were immortalized in the novel, *Romance of the Three
Kingdoms*. Each ruler tried to re-establish unity and
claimed a legitimate right to the Mandate of Heaven, but
none were able to restore control.

Then, in 311 the unthinkable occurred when the
Xiongnu people from the north conquered the former Han
capital of Luoyang. Like the fall of Rome in 410, the capture of Luoyang was a shock to the Chinese people, who
continued to see Luoyang as the centre of civilization. The
Xiongnu were nomads who roamed the long region of the
steppe stretching from the Liao River in Manchuria to the
Gansu corridor in the west. From 316 to 589 China was
divided between traditional Han Chinese in the south and
the Xiongnu rulers over the Chinese in the north.

In 589, the Turkic-Chinese general, Sui Wendi, founded
a new dynasty over a restored empire that was to be one of
the high points of Chinese civilization. He was born into a
Buddhist family, and although he accepted Confucian rituals, he realized that Buddhism, with its offer of salvation to
all, regardless of nationality and rank, was a powerful force
for reunification, and he actively sponsored its propaga-
tion. During the four centuries of political disunity following the end of the Han dynasty, China exhibited a steady
conversion to Buddhism, which is the subject of this chapter.

The first Buddhists (AD c. 50–311)

The earliest known Buddhists in China were the foreign
merchants from Central Asia and possibly India. They
arrived in the Chinese capital near the beginning of the first
century AD and established small, isolated communities in
the major cities. They came along the trade route that ran
across Central Asia from the Middle East to China. It was
the German scholar Ferdinand von Richtoven who, in the
1870s, coined the term 'Silk Route' for this caravan route.

Contrary to the common imagination, there was no single 'Silk Route' that stretched all the way from Rome to China. The most frequented routes actually led to what is now Pakistan and India. It was unlikely that an individual trader would go all the way from beginning to end. There were major trading centres along the route, and traders probably traded between these centres, making up a chain of transportation. Silk was indeed initially traded along the routes because the Chinese discovered how to manufacture the material. By the fourth century, silk was being manufactured in Persia, India and Byzantium.

The earliest mention of Buddha is in a Chinese biography of Prince Ying, half-brother of Emperor Mingdi and prince of a northern kingdom. In AD 65 the Emperor issued an edict allowing those who had been condemned to death to ransom themselves by payment of a certain number of rolls of silk. The prince seems to have had a guilty conscience and so took advantage of the pardon, and sent thirty rolls of silk to the Emperor to express repentance. The Emperor did not consider Ying to be guilty of any crime and refused to accept them. Ying used the money from the ransom to prepare a sumptuous feast for the pious laymen and monks living in his kingdom. It is likely that Ying himself was a convert to Buddhism, and the official who wrote the edict certainly knew some specialist Buddhist terminology. This implies that a Buddhist community existed in China prior to AD 65.

It was during the reign of Emperor Huan that the Buddhist missionary An Sigao (An Shih-kao) arrived in the capital Luoyang from Parthia, south-east of the Caspian Sea. He was a member of the Parthian royal family, and it is generally believed that he arrived in China in 148 and stayed for twenty years. It is notable that he was Parthian and not an Indian, which shows how far Buddhism had spread by that time. In Luoyang An Sigao began translating the Sanskrit texts into Chinese, and many of these

translations survive today. The language of these early translations tends to be simple, with a limited vocabulary. The
sutras translated by An Sigao were primarily concerned
with concentration and meditation. Later, in the second half
of the century, there were half a dozen known foreign monks
working in Luoyang on such translations, but it seems there
were no Chinese monks until the fourth century. This was
because the Han emperors only allowed foreigners to build
Buddhist monasteries and enter the new religion.

The official histories mentioning Buddhism are biased
towards to the literate city dwellers. Recent archaeological
evidence suggests that Buddhism permeated quietly
through many areas of the country, where most people considered Buddha to be a powerful foreign god. The Chinese
were particularly concerned to gain knowledge of the elixirs
and practices that contributed to longevity and superhuman powers. As with many Indian religions, Buddhism had
much to say about methods to enhance the intuitive
faculties through meditation. Thus, the early Buddhist
missionaries found that the scriptures containing these
methods appealed to the Chinese.

Opposition

An interesting text that illustrates some of the issues facing
the Buddhist missionaries is the *Mouzi: Disposing of Error*.
The book is in a conversational style with an exchange
between Mouzi and a Chinese scholar criticizing Buddhist
ideas and practices. The issues they cover include:

- Why is Buddhism not mentioned in the Chinese
  Classics?
- Why do Buddhist monks do injury to their bodies? The
  Confucians held that the body is a gift from one's
  parents and that to harm it is to be disrespectful
  towards them. Reference is made particularly to the
  way Buddhist monks shaved their heads once a month.

104 THE SPIRIT OF CHINA

- Why do monks not marry? Clerical celibacy was the greatest obstacle to Buddhism in China because of the importance of having descendants.
- The Chinese veneration of ancestors was based on the belief that if the soul of the departed was not fed, it would suffer.
- Why should a Chinese allow himself to be influenced by Indian ways?
- Does Buddhism not have a recipe for immortality?[2] This shows the continuing Daoist quest for longevity.

Keyi *translations*

Religious concepts are always difficult to translate into another language, and, as we have shown, the process of translating Buddhist ideas into Chinese was especially difficult. The Buddha had done much of his teaching in Magadha, the everyday language of the state in North India where he lived. His teaching was written down only some centuries later, when it was transcribed into Pali in Sri Lanka, and into the linguistically similar language of Sanskrit in North India. Sanskrit and Chinese belong to two totally different language groups: Chinese is one of the Sino-Tibetan languages while Sanskrit is Indo-European. Sanskrit has closer associations with English than Chinese.

To assist in the process of translation into Chinese, the early translators used Daoist equivalents for unfamiliar concepts. This process was known as *Keyi* ('concept-matching'), and this meant that in early times Buddhism was seen as a sect of Daoism. There were indeed many similarities between Buddhism and Daoism. For example:

- Buddhists, like many Daoists, did not offer animal sacrifices.
- Both had an emphasis upon meditation.
- Both abstained from certain foods.
- Both were concerned about immortality.

However, there were also difficulties with this process. A word like *Dao*, for example, was used to translate *magga* ('path'). This automatically carried with it many Daoist overtones unintended in the original Sanskrit scriptures of India.

Another fundamental concept that was difficult to translate was *karma*, which in early Buddhism related to the idea that each individual was in a continual state of flux resulting from one's own actions. As one is in a daily process of change, at death an individual also changes. This is the doctrine of non-self, which is different from the Brahminical notion of the eternal nature of the soul. During the early days of Buddhism in China, it appears as though the people had difficulty in understanding the idea of repeated rebirths without some abiding entity. Thus the monks taught that a human being consists of a material body and a spiritual soul. The body comes into being at birth and disintegrates at death, while the soul is eternal and indestructible. Due to the effects of *karma*, the soul is forever linked to the cycle of rebirths. This idea that the soul is eternal fitted in with the prevailing Daoist belief that on death the soul can continue to exist as a ghost.

Depending upon one's previous existences, a person could be reborn as an animal or even a demon. This notion of the soul was totally different from that of traditional Chinese thought, and although early Buddhist missionaries tried to teach the subtle nature of *karma*, the Chinese Buddhists clung to their traditional view of the underworld.

When Buddhism first came to China, the people knew nothing of the philosophical debates that had divided Buddhism into various schools during the previous 400 years. The Chinese received each Buddhist scholar as bringing the authoritative text of the teaching of the Buddha. However, during the previous centuries Buddhism had divided into two main streams with many different teachings. The two main streams were Theravada (disparagingly called Hinayana, 'lesser vehicle') and Mahayana ('great vehicle'). Theravada were more conservative and claimed to keep closer to the original teaching of the Buddha, while the Mahayana were more embracing in their views and were more speculative in their writings. The Theravada tradition was stronger in Sir Lanka, while Mahayana was influential in the north of India and especially in the region of the current state of Afghanistan. It was therefore the Mahayana Buddhists who were more directly located on the ancient 'Silk Route'.

Initially the Chinese had no choice about which text was to be translated, as this was more a matter of the discretion of the foreign missionary. As the translations became available and were read, then it was likely that some texts proved more popular than others. The Mahayana texts seemed to be more appealing to the Chinese, particularly as they spoke of the compassionate *Bodhisattva* who refrains from entering *nirvana* in order to help more people. There was also the teaching of the universal accessibility of Buddhahood, which was especially developed in the *Lotus Sutra*.

Foreign rulers

It was Shi Le (AD 274–333) who led the Xiongnu in their conquest of Luoyang in 311. He was born to a Xiongnu chief, but was kidnapped around the age of twenty-five and sold as a slave to the Chinese. He escaped and joined a gang of robbers in northern China. The success of the gang soon resulted in it growing into an army powerful enough to conquer Luoyang. The story is told that prior to the capture of Luoyang, one of his generals introduced him to the Buddhist missionary Fotudeng (d. 349). The illiterate Shi Le was more interested in miracles than the teaching of Buddhism. The monk thereupon took his bowl, filled it with water, burned incense and said a mantra over it. The story tells of how, to the amazement of the onlookers, beautiful blue lotus flowers suddenly sprang up. Shi Le was impressed and later granted the Buddhists the right to build monasteries throughout the area he controlled. This gave Buddhists an important foothold in the north of China. Fotudeng's biographer tells that he was able to cause rain to fall on command and use Indian medicine to heal the sick. News of such miracles attracted many of the ordinary people to Buddhism. The non-Chinese like Shi Le were especially drawn to Buddhism because it provided an alternative to Confucianism, which empowered literate Chinese officials. In other words, they were attracted to Buddhism because it did not originate in China.

Translating the teaching

The conquest of the north from 316 onwards resulted in a division of Buddhism between the north and the south. Fotudeng essentially founded the Sangha in the north, and was instrumental in converting many of the Chinese people. The Chinese looked to Fotudeng to protect them from the barbarian rulers, who, being Buddhists, honoured him as a great teacher. The rulers adopted the ideal that kings supported *dharma* in a similar way to the Indian king Asoka. This was seen as the two wheels of *dharma*: Buddha and king.

Kumarajiva

The monumental task of translating the vast number of Buddhist texts was tackled on a massive scale by the famous scholar Kumarajiva (344–413). He was born to a high-ranking minister in India, who had migrated to Kucha in Central Asia where he could study Buddhism full time. Although Kucha is now part of modern China's Xinjiang Autonomous Region, in the fourth century it was an independent kingdom. The importance of Buddhism for Kucha can be seen in the fact that there were some 10,000 monks in a town of 100,000 people. Just outside Kucha, at Kizil, are important caves that have some of the most significant paintings by Indian artists, showing that this was an important centre for Buddhist art and scholarship. The relationship between merchants and Buddhism is illustrated by one of the paintings in the caves. It depicts a scene in which the Buddha uses his hands as torches to light the way for a merchant who stands beside him, his ox laden with trade goods.

Kumarajiva's fame as a scholar and translator reached the court of the northern rulers, and plans were made to kidnap him and bring him to Chang'an. He arrived in 402 where he was welcomed with great honour, surrounded by many monks and scholars. His task was to retranslate the most influential Mahayana scriptures, and to produce a definitive edition. During the following years Kumarajiva and his assistants produced a stream of new translations, including the popular *Amitabha Sutra* and *Lotus Sutra*.

Although Kumarajiva was apparently not able to read or write Chinese, he had immense learning and understanding of the Buddhist teaching. Seng-jui's introduction to the translation of the *Larger Perfection of Wisdom Sutra* states: 'The master would take the foreign text in his hand and would expound it orally in the language of China. In addition, he transcribed the foreign sounds and from time to time explained the meaning of the text.'[3] As mentioned previously, early translations had made use of Daoist concepts with the so-called *Keyi* method. This did not permit an accurate rendering of the original text, and it was this that Kumarajiva sought to achieve.

His reputation as a genius was such that the rulers thought that it was a waste for him not to have children. He was therefore provided with concubines, whom he accepted, and for which he was criticized by other monks, but it is not known whether he fathered any children.

Chinese pilgrims

The quest for religious texts resulted in the scholar Faxian (Fa-Hsien) leaving China in AD 399 on a remarkable journey to India. He travelled for thirteen years on an established trade route to the place where the Buddha had first taught. After a considerable search, Faxian found documents in Paliputra (now called Patna), where he stayed for three years, paying scribes to record the lectures of Buddhist teachers. He then returned home via Sri Lanka, where he visited the jade Buddha. The sea journey back was hit by storms, and we read that he prayed fervently to a *bodhisattva* named Avalokistevara. By the time he returned, and unknown to him, the entire *Vinaya* had already been translated by someone else.

A later Chinese pilgrim was Xuanzang who left China without official permission in AD 627. However, when he returned in 643 he was given a warm welcome by the Emperor, but had to decline high office. His adventures on the long journey to India eventually inspired the novel *Journey to the West*, in which he is given as companions a monkey, representing wisdom and loyalty, and a pig, representing sensuality. The monkey becomes the hero in the novel, assisting the monk, Tripikata, out of many difficulties. The Japanese television series entitled *Monkey Magic* has become something of a cult classic.

Pilgrims not only returned with hundreds of texts; they also came back with relics. In India these had become the focus of devotion in the many *stupas* that were erected during and following the time of King Asoka. It was believed that as powerful objects, relics were capable of producing miracles, and for this reason they became highly desired artefacts in China. There are even accounts of relics being stolen by people from another region of the country.

Buddhism's appeal to women

The Buddhist missionary Fotudeng, mentioned earlier, found that it was not only men who were attracted to his teaching. The biographical text, *Lives of the Nuns*, gives information about sixty-five women who became nuns in the fourth to sixth centuries AD. Most were from higher levels in society and could read and write. One woman who met Fotudeng was An Lingshou, who wanted to become a nun. This shocked her father, who saw no other role for a woman than to be a wife and mother. She explained that she wanted to work exclusively for religious purposes, and even so, she argued, why should she submit thrice to father, husband and son before being respected? An Lingshou's argument did not persuade her father, so the story continues that Fotudeng spread sesame oil and safflower onto her father's palm. There he saw a woman in monastic robes preaching the *Dharma*. Fotudeng explained that this was his daughter in a previous life, and so her father finally gave his consent. An Lingshou went on to bring about the conversion of more than 200 women and establish five or six monasteries.

This story shows how, for Chinese women, to join a nunnery provided a unique alternative to family life within the Confucian system. This tension between the religious quest and obligations to family was something reflected through the lives of all the nuns. Some resisted marriage while others married and had children before joining the nunnery. Some cared for ageing parents and mourned for three years after their deaths. All seemed to have difficulties with the additional rules governing women until, in the 370s, a group of Sri Lankan nuns taught the Chinese nuns the accepted vows.

The Northern Wei dynasty (AD 386–534)

In the fourth century AD, the Tabgach people gradually moved from what is now Inner Mongolia to northern Shanxi Province. They derived more of their income from taxing Chinese farmers, and they adopted Chinese laws. In 386 a new ruler named Tuoba Gui took power, and this is the traditional date for the founding of the Northern Wei dynasty. In 396, Tuoba Gui assumed the Chinese title of Emperor and soon afterwards began to build his capital at Pingcheng in Shanxi. He forcibly resettled some 300,000 Chinese of various skills to create a new city.

The Tabgach rulers continued to worship their own gods of the steppe while recognizing the teachers of Buddhism. Little is known about their indigenous gods except that they were local deities that presided over rivers, mountains and various geographical sites. The Buddhists were controlled by a distinct department of the central government that specifically supervised the monasteries. Sometimes Buddhism was more favoured than at other times, and sometimes major building projects were undertaken, like the huge caves that were dug at Yungang just outside the city of Datone in Shanxi Province.

Emperor Xiaowen (reigned 471–99) began to implement a series of reform measures under the term *Hanhua*, which literally means 'becoming like the Han'. This is usually understood as an attempt to make the empire more Chinese in character. The first thing was to move the capital from Pingcheng to Luoyang, which had lain in ruins since the attack of 311. During the ten years it took to build the new capital, the royal family dropped their family name and adopted the Chinese name of Yuan. They ordered court officials to do likewise, and both to speak Chinese and wear Chinese clothes at court. The arrival of the Northern Wei court at Luoyang in 494 unleashed a great burst of creative activity. High officials were commissioned to lay out palace precincts and city wards, design palatial buildings, parks and ponds, and create the courtly attire, accessories and musical instruments employed in rituals of state. The process of Sinization was one that was to be followed by many foreign invaders who came to control significant portions of the region of China.

In 499 the Emperor suddenly died, leaving his thirteen-year-old son with a regent. The military leaders sought to dispose of the regent, and the Northern Wei entered into thirty years of unrest, until they in turn were conquered by another northern people, the Erzhu.

Even during this difficult time, Buddhism continued to grow. Many Buddhist monasteries were built around AD 500, and these consisted of three types.[4] The 47 largest were those built and supported by the state, and these housed officially ordained monks who conducted all the Buddhist observances for the Emperor. The second category was those built by the families of high officials, who built as many as 839 monasteries. Finally, there were many smaller temples and monasteries scattered throughout the country that numbered some 30,000. In Luoyang alone there were some 100 Buddhist establishments in AD 476.[5] No wonder one prince complained, 'Today there is no place that does not have a Buddhist sanctuary.' Although the total number of monks did not exceed 1 per cent of the population, they did control a sizeable share of the economy.

In AD 520, there was a court-sponsored public debate in Luoyang between Buddhists and Daoists over the *huahu* theory concerning the relationship between Laozi and Buddha. Did Laozi leave China and reappear in India as the Buddha, or did the Buddha will his own rebirth in China as Laozi? The debate resulted from the old Han notion that Buddha and Laozi were equal sages, and that both Buddhism and Daoism wanted to absorb the other. In the process of the debate, both Buddhists and Daoists pushed the dates of their respective founders further and further back. The Buddhists were finally considered to have won the debate.

Religion in southern China

Although modern Chinese think of the River Yangze as Central China, during the fifth and sixth centuries, the Han regarded it as the south. At that time, the cultural and political centre of China was around the Yellow River. The south was regarded as an uncivilized place with a hotter and wetter climate that resulted in malaria and other sicknesses. However, following the conquest of Luoyang in 311, many descendants of the Han aristocracy moved south and established Nanjing as their capital. There were some non-Chinese communities in the same area, but little is known about them. Although the climate was hotter, it was ideal for growing rice, and over the following centuries a vast irrigation system was constructed in the region.

In the south of China, Daoist teachers were more active than Buddhist monks, and many of the northern migrants continued to study Daoism. Although Buddhists and Daoists attacked each other, they also borrowed much from each other and so both traditions changed. Both Buddhism and Daoism also incorporated many of the local deities and built monasteries for their monks.

Emperor Wu of the Laing dynasty (reigned 502–49) was particularly interested in religion, and as a young man he studied under a great Daoist teacher, Tao Hongjing (456–536). Hongjing was concerned about a series of revelations recorded by his wife's ancestors more than a century before. Because he studied these texts on Mao Shan mountain, the new Daoist school took that name.

Mao Shan (Shangqing)

Just as the 'Five Pecks' movement, mentioned in the previous chapter, developed from the revelation of the divine

Laozi, the Mao Shan Daoists claimed that their teaching came from Yang Xi and his encounter with immortals between 364 and 370. Yang Xi was a member of the local aristocracy, and the revelations were initially limited to this group. As the revelation was from the 'Heaven of Highest Clarity' (*Shangqing*), it is also called by this name.

The Mao Shan followers retained some of the 'Five Pecks' teaching, but avoided the practices that had formerly been criticized. Their most distinctive teaching was their belief in a totally new cosmic order consisting of seven levels accommodating both immortals and spirits of the dead. The lowest level was where the souls of the dead went to await judgment. This replicated the traditional Chinese view of the afterlife, where they would most likely remain for ever. The Mao Shan Daoists claimed that they had authority to intervene with the officials of the underworld courts. They could therefore offer their disciples a way of escaping this grim underworld by ascending to higher levels through a series of revelations from secret texts. The Mao Shan teachers charged their disciples considerable sums for these texts, and stressed that the transmission could only be made through a certified teacher. The disciple had to make an oath of secrecy every time they received a new revelation or text from their teacher. The movement was essentially a secret brotherhood.

The Mao Shan texts included instructions on alchemy and the production of elixirs. They also give guidance on advanced meditation practices and visualizations designed to enable the individual to purify his or her *qi* in order to become aware of the divinities that dwell within the human body. *The Scriptures of the Three Primordial Realized Ones* talks of the visualization of the 'Three Ones', who are the deities of the three primordial energies in the human body. When they are in place, the twenty-four energies of the body can be extended and the body can be developed to a cosmic stage:

The Upper One is the Celestial Emperor;
He resides in the body centre [in the head].
The Middle One is the Cinnabar Sovereign;
He resides in the Crimson Palace [in the heart].
The Lower One is the Primordial King;
He resides in the Yellow Court [in the abdomen].[6]

The emphasis of Mao Shan on individual spiritual practice meant that it tended to appeal to the elite rather than the peasants.

The Numinous Treasure school

Another Daoist movement at this time was the Numinous Treasure school (*Lingbao*), which drew much of its inspiration from Mahayana Buddhism. At the end of the fourth century, Ge Chaofu, a member of the Ge family, published a text called *Lingbao* which he claimed came as a revelation from one of his ancestors, Ge Xuan. In this revelation, creation is presented as proceeding through long periods of rise and fall, and this depends on the power of special talismans. These talismans are charts on which are drawn heavenly symbols that represent the original power of the *Dao* in graphic form. They are not only responsible for the creation and continuity of the cosmos, but they bestow the bearer with magical powers and the divine right to rule. Famous talismans are the *Hetu* (River Chart) and the *Wuyue Zhenxing Du* (Chart of the True Shape of the Five Sacred Mountains). These two were believed to convey absolute power over all under heaven.

Later followers integrated Buddhist doctrine and terms into the original teaching to make texts that are therefore a syncretistic mixture of Mahayana and Daoism. They include Daoist rituals and confessions with Buddhist ideas of *karma* and rebirth. Like the teachers of Mahayana, the Numinous Treasure movement offered salvation to everyone through the person of a *bodhisattva*:

Once he ('the Healer to Deliverance') was sitting under a withered mulberry tree, deep, deep in meditation for a hundred years. The Heavenly Venerable of Primordial Beginnings descended into his presence. He transmitted to the Lord of Tao the true law of the Great Vehicle of Numinous Treasure. The Lord thus received the wondrous sacred scriptures in ten sections.

Thus the Heavenly Venerable came to reside in the country at this time. He spread joy to all its dwellings. He gave his teaching freely to the people of the time. Many were those who through him received the True Law that opens the gates of heaven.[7]

This movement also established a monastic system with vows similar to those found in Buddhism. Nevertheless, Numinous Treasure remained distinctly Daoist in that it promised immortality. By this they meant that when the body died, the soul would travel to a place of purgatory where it would be purified. In 1445, the *Lingbao* scriptures were compiled into the wider Daoist Canon.[8]

Buddhism in the south

Even with the emergence of these Daoist movements, Buddhism continued to make steady progress in the south. Emperor Wu, mentioned earlier as the monarch who studied the Mao Shan scriptures, converted to Buddhism and in 504 urged all his court to do likewise. In 517, he ordered the destruction of Daoist temples while actively supporting the Buddhist monasteries in the south.

In 527, Emperor Wu proclaimed that he wanted to become a monk, and even went as far as offering his sacrifices to the monastery. However, the court officials paid the monastery a large fee to redeem the Emperor so that he could return to the throne. Two years later, a devastating plague afflicted the region, and the Emperor repeated his commitment to the monastery. Again he was redeemed by the court officials, and this time the monks and laity were offered a huge banquet. These incidents give insights into the commitment of the Emperor to Buddhism.

By the middle of the sixth century Buddhism had established an enormous influence in China, where there were thousands of monasteries and as many as 2 million monks and nuns. This placed a great financial burden upon the Chinese economy. For example, monks did not serve in the army, and as they did not work in the fields they were seen as a drain on the national resources. The extravagance of the wealthy in building monasteries and supporting the Sangha resulted in appalling misery for the peasants, many of whom starved or sold their children.

During this period, the teaching of both Buddhism and Daoism was understood only by the elite. Most people were concerned about the practical problems of coping in a dangerous world and preparing for what would befall them after death. Peasants were looking for holy men and women who could cure their sicknesses, perform miracles and bring them salvation.

* * *

Although China was divided during much of the period from AD 200 to AD 600, both north and south saw the increasing influence of Buddhism. Initially Buddhism was a religion of foreign monks residing in China, with their Chinese disciples following one of the various Indian schools. By the fifth century various Chinese schools of Buddhism began to emerge including, as we shall see in the next chapter, those of Pure Land, Tiantai, Huayan and Chan. L. G. Thompson succinctly summarizes the introduction of Buddhism into China in the following words:

> The transplantation of Buddhist thought to China is one of the great intercultural movements of history. Among the many lessons we may draw from that movement is that accommoda-

tion of a foreign culture is only accomplished as a result of many modifications and reinterpretations that make it comprehensible and even naturalise it. In the case of Buddhism, one must recognise that first there was Indian Buddhism; then there was Indian Buddhism in China; and finally, after many centuries of adjustment, there was Chinese Buddhism.[9]

Further reading

Chen, K., *Buddhism in China: A Historical Survey*, Princeton: Princeton University Press, 1964.

Kieschnick, J., *The Impact of Buddhism on Chinese Material Culture*, Princeton: Princeton University Press, 2003.

Websites

The Silk-road Foundation. A fascinating website with everything you could possibly want to know about the Silk Road/Route. Includes information on travellers, the history of silk, folklore, sports and games, food – and much, much more. www.silk-road.com/toc/index.html

The Silk Road: Trade, travel, war and faith. A British Library/British Museum site that includes a viewing of the Diamond Sutra, found at Dunhuang in 1907, which is the earliest printed book with a date (11 May 868). www.bl.uk/whatson/exhibitions/silkroad/main.html

The Romance of the Three Kingdoms. The translation by C. W. Brewitt-Taylor is published free on this site along with a map and a popular game. http://www.threekingdoms.com/

Chapter 6

RELIGION DURING THE TANG DYNASTY

The Tang dynasty (AD 589–960)

The Han dynasty (206 BC–AD 9 and AD 23–220) was the first great imperial period and it lasted 400 years. After the fall of the Han, as we have seen, the region was divided into a number of kingdoms, with those in the north coming under the rule of non-Chinese. Then, in 589, the Sui dynasty reunified China, and although this dynasty was to last for only thirty-six years, it prepared the way for the Tang, which was to last for nearly three centuries and was to be one of the peaks of Chinese civilization. As the empire flourished, the people became more confident and more open and enthusiastic about foreign ideas than they would ever be until perhaps the end of the twentieth century. This was a time of cultural and artistic achievement with an expansion of scholarship and trade. No wonder many books entitle this 'China's Golden Age'.

The Sui dynasty (AD 581–617)

The reuniting of the empire proved easier than anyone could have predicted after 250 years of disunity. Yang Jian was born into a powerful military family and until he was twelve years of age he was under the care of a nun in a Buddhist monastery. He then entered the military and became a general under one of the Northern Zhou. In 566 he married a woman of mixed Xiongnu and Chinese ancestry. Northern women tended to have a greater role in society than Chinese women, and she insisted that he would not take any concubines and would only have the children she bore. Twelve years later his eldest daughter married the mentally unstable prince of the Northern Zhou, who soon succeeded his father as king. A short time later the young king fell ill and died, and the empire passed rapidly to his six-year-old son. This gave Yang Jian the opportunity to seize power, first by claiming to be the regent of the young king and then, in 581, by founding his own dynasty known as the Sui. He took the throne name of Emperor Wendi and reigned from 581 to 604.

In 589, Emperor Wendi undertook a military campaign in the south with the aim of uniting the Chinese peoples. However, during the years of division the peoples of north and south had grown apart. Emperor Wendi was a very able administrator with a strong sense of duty. His first task was to ensure internal peace by removing the private armies that had flourished during the period of disunity. He ordered complete disarmament, and settled former soldiers on the land as peasant farmers. He appointed competent ministers and replaced the northern system with an impartial system of selection along southern lines. He carried through a major redistribution of the land and essentially doubled the taxable population. Above all, he insisted that all people be treated equally with regard to the law. He was so strict on this matter that he even punished his third son who violated the law.

The defender of Buddhism

During the closing years of the previous Northern Zhou dynasty, the court officials sought to move against the growing Buddhist and Daoist establishments. In 574 they introduced laws to restrain both communities, even though many devotees had resolved to protect the teachings of the Buddha (the *Dharma*). Many believed that they were approaching the end of an age when religious life would disappear, and it would be then that a new Buddha would come to the earth.

In 580, Emperor Wendi rescinded this ban on Buddhism and Daoism. He saw himself as a grand donor to Buddhism and began patronizing Buddhism by building a national network of monasteries, and instituted chanting during the Buddha's birthday in the new moon in May. In his capital of Luoyang he constructed 120 new Buddhist temples, one of which had the responsibility to supervise all the monasteries in China and establish the standards for the monks. In this way the Emperor drew the state and the Sangha together. His most extravagant action was for the celebration of his sixtieth birthday in 601, when he ordered the construction of *stupas* all over the empire to house relics of the Buddha. He sent monks and nuns from the capital to celebrate their opening and called a national holiday for one week. The Emperor seemed to be emulating the ancient Indian king Asoka (reigned 272–32 BC) who came to be seen as a model of a Buddhist king, especially in the Theravada tradition.

Emperor Wendi arranged for his second son Yang Guang to marry a southern woman and sent him to live in the south of the empire. There he was ordered to arrange for Buddhist scriptures to be recopied and new monasteries and libraries to be built. Yang Guang succeeded his father in 604, possibly by foul play, and took the name Emperor Yangdi. Although he was a devout Buddhist, he absorbed southern interest in Daoism and supported Confucian scholars. Although he followed his father's vision to form a great empire, he lacked the management skills to carry it through. He liked luxury and was extravagant in rebuilding the second capital at Luoyang. He continued his father's work of building canals to link the major rivers together to ease communication and transportation between north and south. By 618, 2,000 kilometres (1,250 miles) of canals linked the entire country, but this was at great cost to the nation.

The fall of the Sui and the founding of the Tang

Emperor Yangdi's downfall came as a result of his foreign adventures. In 609, be began a number of campaigns. In the south he tried to conquer what is now Vietnam; in the north-east he invaded Korea; and in the north he moved against the eastern Turks. The campaign against Korea ended in failure. Yangdi was so preoccupied with the war that he ignored the mounting unrest at home due to the high taxes and flooding of the Yellow River. Rebellions broke out in China, resulting in the Emperor being killed. Known originally as Li Shimin, a general in the Sui dynasty swept through the northern region and in 618 declared his own father, Li Yuan, as Emperor of the new dynasty.

Like Emperor Wendi, Li Yuan belonged to the aristocratic family of the northern Chinese and was of mixed Chinese and Turkic ancestry. He took the throne name of Emperor Gaozu (reigned 618–26), and he named his dynasty 'Tang' after the region where he had formerly served. Gaozu was an able ruler with a shrewd judgment of political, economic and military matters. In 626, a palace plot led to the death of his first son, and Gaozu abdicated in favour of his second son, Li Shimin. Emperor Tang Taizong (reigned 626–49) was to become one of China's most accomplished rulers. Allowing for the exaggeration of his biographers, he still stands out as a remarkable personality. Under the rule of his father he excelled as a military leader. Findling and Thackeray write:

> During the 620s, when the Turks were making threatening moves toward the Tang, Taizong twice dashed out of the gates of Chang'an on horseback and rode into the Turk encampments, where he actually challenged the Turk khans to personal combat. Overawed by his bravado and confidence, the Turks on both occasions backed off. Taizong predicted that the Turks would eventually weaken themselves through civil war, and in the late 620s his predictions came true. In 630 the

Turks decided to avoid self-destruction by submitting to the Tang, and they agreed to recognize Taizong as their 'Heavenly Khan.' With this, Taizong became without question the most powerful man in the world. He reigned as emperor over the Chinese and as Heavenly Khan over the hordes of warlike Turkic mounted warriors on China's northern frontier.[1]

He was accomplished in the Classics, a calligrapher and scholar. He had an incredible capacity for work and employed teams of secretaries. He restrained public works so that they did not become overly burdensome on his people. This reasonable approach gave the Tang a prestige which far surpassed that of the Han.

Taizong was a pragmatist and used Daoism and Buddhism to supplement Confucian teaching when it proved useful. Confucianism encouraged stability and provided good officials, and so he sponsored state academies, improved the examination system and used ancestor worship to strengthen the legitimacy of the ruling family. A legend arose that the Emperor dreamed he was summoned before Yama, the King of the Dead, before whom he was charged by his two younger brothers with a question. Why in 626 did he kill his brothers in front of the Palace and imprison his loving father? If he failed to give a satisfactory answer, he would not be able to return to the land of the living. The Emperor was terrified and could not answer. His interrogators finally answered the question for him: 'A great sage would be willing to destroy his family in order to save the kingdom.' The Emperor was allowed to return to the land of the living. Among other things, the story shows how the jurisdiction of the court of the dead extends even to the realms of the living.

Another story that demonstrated how Taizong followed Confucian principles concerned the execution of 300 men accused of crimes. As we have seen, Confucian teaching taught that people committed crimes because their rulers lacked virtue. Taizong agreed to set the criminals free to visit their families, provided they returned for the day of their execution. His trust was shown to be well founded when, to the surprise of all China, every man came back for his execution.[2]

Emperor Taizong had been aided in his coup by Buddhists monks, and so he began to patronize Buddhism and encourage the publication of Buddhist texts. At the commencement of his reign he had banned foreign travel, with the result that the monk Xuanzang (c. 596–664) left the country without permission to go to India. When he returned sixteen years later he was warmly welcomed by the Emperor. Buddhist institutions became an integral part of Chinese life. Buddhist monasteries ran schools; in remote areas they provided lodging for travellers; in towns they offered the elite a place to gather for social occasions. Monasteries owned large tracts of land and so played a major part in the nation's economy.

Chinese schools of Buddhism

As was shown in the previous chapter, when Buddhism first entered China it was essentially a world-denying religion which did not resonate with the Chinese world-affirming worldview. Gradually, Buddhism took on Chinese forms, and it was during the period of unity under the Sui and Tang dynasties that these Chinese schools of Buddhism became popular. Four schools emerged in China that had no direct precedents in India, but they were essentially Mahayana in expression. We will here focus on four of these new Chinese schools: Pure Land (*Jingtu*), Meditation (*Chan*), *Tianti* and *Huayan*.

Pure Land Buddhism (Jingtu)
Pure Land Buddhism emerged as the greatest and most influential of the Mahayana expressions in China, and was

the least philosophical. It did not develop into an institutionally distinct school, as it did in Japan, but it did come to dominate the lives of many of the common people. According to the Chinese tradition, the founder is said to be Hui Yuan. He was a zealous Daoist until about AD 380, when he converted to Buddhism and entered a life-long quest for a real understanding of the Mahayana tradition. In about 400 he took as his principal scripture the *Sukhavativyuha Sutra*, a Sanskrit text probably written in the first century AD in India, which in the Chinese translation is known as *Wu-liang-shou Ching*. In the Chinese tradition the Pure Land is attributed to the teaching of Nagarjuna and Vasubandhu, but there is little support for this designation. What it does do is provide a respectable ancestry within the Indian school of Madhyamika.

This text taught salvation by faith in Amitabha and contained vivid descriptions of the heaven over which he was said to rule. It taught that the power inherent in the name of Buddha Amitabha can remove all obstacles to salvation and the mere utterance of his name (*Amituo*) can assure rebirth in his kingdom. The legend is based chiefly on the *Sukhavativyuha* and tells the story that aeons ago, the Bodhisattva Dharmakara made forty-eight vows, among them the promise that all who call on his name shall be saved. He eventually became the Buddha Amitabha, and ten aeons ago, in accordance with his vows, he established the Pure Land that lies one million billion Buddha-lands away. The devotees honour Amitabha by multiplying copies of his statues as well as the sutras that tell of him.

As far as is known, there was little specific devotion to Amitabha before the sixth century, and the first dated image of Amitabha is at the Longmen caves outside Luoyang city, dated at AD 519. During the seventh century many images of Amitabha were erected throughout the country. These changes occurred during the collective

lifetimes of the three great Chinese patriarchs of Pure Land:
T'an-luan, Dao-ch'o (562–645) and Shan-Dao (613–81).

T'an-luan's major contribution was a commentary on the
Sukhavati Sutra. In a period of political uncertainty, T'an-
luan thought that the golden age of spiritual enlightenment
was past and there were no more great sages like the
Buddha. In Chinese Buddhism a great gap was opening
between the ultimate state of Buddhahood and the conventional realm of *samsara*, and progress from one to the other
was almost impossible. How then in this present age could
one make spiritual progress? T'an-luan adopted the
distinction between the difficult and easy path that had
been proposed by Nagarjuna, and used this to provide a
religion for the majority of people who were unable to
make progress through their own actions. Through faith in
the power of Amitabha and his great vows, one could be
reborn in *Sukhavati* (Pure or Happy Land) and there be
almost certain to attain enlightenment.

The school's appeal to the masses lies in its simplicity
and ease to follow. It also answers the philosophical and
religious problem of how it is possible through one's own
finite deeds to attain a state of unconditioned enlightenment. T'an-luan adopted five forms of practice mentioned
by Vasubandhu, but he placed particular emphasis on the
virtue of reciting the name of the Buddha Amitabha.
Continually repeating the name with a unified mind is said
to purify the mind from all its sins, and to ensure rebirth in
the Pure Land. Through the power of Amitabha even the
worst sinner can attain to the Pure Land.

T'an-luan's disciple was Dao-cho whose main contribution was his response to the critics of Pure Land thought.
He experienced the persecution of Buddhism in China, and
taught that old practices were not suitable for this new age
and people should repent of their sins and call upon
Amitabha. He did not condemn the conventional way, but
pointed out the difficulty of gaining enlightenment in the

contemporary tainted world. It was better therefore to aim at enlightenment in the Pure Land of *Sukhavati*. This was not a sensual paradise, nor a realm of desire and attachment.

The third great exponent of Pure Land was Shan-Dao (613–81) who lived in the Chinese capital, Chang'an. He taught that humans are bound in a vicious circle of sin and error through the three poisons of greed, anger and stupidity. They have little power to save themselves, but through a sincere vow of faith in Amitabha, continual filling of the mind with thoughts of him, and accepting his mercy and merit, it is guaranteed that all will gain enlightenment. Shan-Dao made little impact on the nobility of China, but attracted many followers among the ordinary people. Some of these were sufficiently enthusiastic for *Sukhavati* that they committed suicide in order to hasten their rebirth and subsequent enlightenment. There is even a legend that Shan-Dao himself eventually committed suicide.[3]

How shall a person be saved? The answer of the Pure Land Masters was faith in Amitabha. This faith consisted of three features: sincerity, devotion and desire to be reborn in *Sukhavati*. These three aspects of faith apply to all beings, but if one is missing then there will be no rebirth in the Pure Land. It is necessary for the devotee to Amitabha to engage in five forms of religious practice. The first is the continual recitation of the name of Amitabha, which is the most important activity. Second, there is chanting the sutra of Amitabha. Third, there is meditating on Amitabha. Fourth, there is worshipping him and his images, and the fifth is making offerings.

Shan-Dao is said to have told the parable of the white path, which is often used within Pure Land teaching. A man is on a journey to the West when he comes to two rivers. On his left is a river of fire, and on his right waves of water. Between the two rivers runs the white path that is only about the width of a foot, but there are a hundred steps to take from east to west. As the man stands looking at the situation, a band of thugs come towards him from one side, and wild animals from the other, causing him to be filled with terror. At that very moment he hears a voice encouraging him to go forward, as to stay would mean death. Then from the far side of the path is a voice calling him to walk forward with a fixed purpose and not to fear the fire or the water. As he sets off the thugs call him to come back, but he continues and finally reaches the west bank in safety.

In the parable the shore stands for the world of *samsara*, and the far shore for *Sukhavati*. The thugs and wild animals are our senses and consciousness. Fire is anger and water is greed and affection. The white path is the desire for the Pure Land. The voice from this shore is that of Sakyamuni Buddha who points the true way, and that from the far shore is Amitabha and his vow to save. This easily remembered story encapsulates the heart of the teaching of the Pure Land sect.

In his saving activity Amitabha is assisted by two great powers, the Bodhisattva Avalokitesvara (Guanyin), known as the Goddess of Mercy, and Manjusri (Wenshu), who represented Amitabha's omnipotence and wisdom. Guanyin was initially the Indian Avalokitesvara who was male in India and became female in China sometime after the Tang dynasty.

Chun-Fang Yu in her important study of Guanyin argues that the feminine Guanyin must be studied in the context of new cults of goddesses of that period.[4] These are the cults of the Queen of Heaven and the Goddess of Azure. These may have been in response to the overwhelmingly masculine character of the three religions. Guanyin, the 'Goddess of Mercy', offered new expressions of religiosity that provided the male children necessary for the continuity of the family. Guanyin therefore served Confucian family values, and was adopted into every home.

Tiantai

Tiantai is so called because the founder Zhiyi (538–97) lived and taught in the Tiantai (Heavenly Terrace) Mountains south-east of Hangzhou on the east coast. He found favour with the Sui rulers and eventually became a resident holy man in the capital. It is also known as the lotus school because of its use of the *Lotus Sutra*. It was an attempt to bring order and harmonization to a mass of contradictory ideas. Tiantai has for this reason been regarded as a watershed in Chinese philosophy, because all subsequent developments in Buddhism defined their position in this regard.[5]

Tiantai taught that when the Buddha became enlightened, he preached the doctrine of the *Hua Yen Sutra* (*Buddhavatamasaka-mahavaipulya* sutra) in which he presented his teaching fully and exactly. However, his disciples were unable to grasp the profound teaching, and so the Buddha preached to them the Theravada scriptures. The disciples then followed these more elementary teachings until they were led to the basic concepts of the Mahayana, and then to the more advanced concepts of *sunyata*. Finally, in old age, the Buddha revealed to a few of his closest followers the doctrines of the *Lotus Sutra*. The result was that an attitude of tolerance pervaded the whole of Chinese Buddhism, because no interpretation of the Buddha's teaching was outside the scheme.

Zhiyi claimed direct transmission from Nagarjuna, and so circumvented Indian authorities and even Kumarajiva who translated the *Lotus Sutra* into Chinese. Zhiyi taught the mutual identification of the whole and the parts. All realities in time and space criss-cross, and all can be made present to the mind at any time. Thus, all the Buddhas were present in a grain of sand, and the 'absolute mind' embraced the universe in its entirety from the highest (*nirvana*) to the lowest (hell). The eternal Buddha is represented in innumerable forms working out his purposes, that include the salvation of all suffering beings. Buddha therefore has evil as an element of his nature. It is argued that if this was not so he would be unable to manifest himself in the evil paths to help deliver sentient beings trapped in hell.

The centre of Tiantai philosophy is the 'harmony of three in one'. The Chinese were already familiar with the harmony of *yin–yang*, but in Tiantai the harmony was of three equal elements. It is essentially the Chinese counterpart of the Christian Trinity, but there are differences so it is not completely analogous. In Tiantai, this idea arises from the following verse in the *Lotus Sutra*:

> What is produced by cause and condition
> Is what I mean by the Empty.
> Known also as conditioned co-arising.
> It is also what is meant by the Middle Path.

Zhiyi interpreted this to mean that reality is (1) empty and (2) real, yet (3) neither. Everything in the universe is simultaneously empty, real and neither. Any one of the three can be taken as a starting point and will in sequence be negated, affirmed, transcended, and returned to itself. In order to make the picture complete, Zhiyi insisted that a person should always learn to look at reality from all sides: the positive, the negative and neither. As such the practitioner is given an exhilarating sense of utter freedom as every vision, every colour, and every aroma is, as such, the middle path.

Tiantai was patronized by the Sui rulers, and so when the Sui dynasty fell, it too fell into disfavour. The new Tang rulers, whose name was Li, considered themselves descendents of Laozi and gave Daoism official support. However, as mentioned earlier, during the reign of Emperor Taizong, the pilgrim Xuanzang returned from India and was much honoured. A new large-scale translation project began under his auspices. Xuanzang brought back the new Yogacara philosophy of 'consciousness only', which for a while was the rage of the capital, until it was superseded by the Huayan school supported by Empress Wu of Zhou (reigned 684–705).

Huayan

Huayan means literally 'wreath' or 'flower garland'. This was one of the most syncretistic expressions of Chinese Buddhism and based its principal teachings on the *Avatamasaka* ('Flower Garland') *sutra* ('Huayan'). Huayan insists that there is in actuality no difference between the absolute and phenomena. Ultimate reality is not some transcendental One but this very world, and phenomena are themselves the absolute. Huayan philosophy is usually condensed into the formula 'all is one; one is all'. It is sometimes called totalism because it holds that any one part of the universe is immediately the numinous whole of the universe.

According to legend, Fazang had been a member of Xuanzang's translation project but left after a disagreement with Xuanzang. With the coming of Empress Wu to the throne, Fazang suddenly had a rise in his popularity and became a favourite of the Empress because of his creativity in finding devices for vividly illustrating for her these abstract ideas that the philosophers were debating. One such illustration is the hall of mirrors. Fazang had constructed a room lined with mirrors on all sides and on the ceiling and floor. In the centre of the room he placed a candle. Not only was the candle reflected in each of the mirrors, but also each mirror reflected each other mirror, as well as itself reflected in every other mirror. The effect was as if you stood between two mirrors and saw an infinite regress of images, each contained within the other.

Another analogy was that of the golden lion. We can intellectually distinguish the lion shape from the gold, but in actuality there can be no such shape without the gold that is shaped. Similarly, gold always has a shape, whether it is a lion, a temple, or a blob. So too, the phenomenal world is the ever-shifting form of the absolute. Huayan thus offers a fully non-dualistic view of the relationship between the absolute and phenomena. A similar analogy is that of waves on the sea. This argument is that the wind of ignorance ruffles the ocean of the mind, producing the waves of phenomenal forms. Although the rising and falling of the waves may create an illusion of samsaric change, in truth the waves are water – the same essence as the ocean. In this way, the Mahayana dictum 'samsara is nirvana' is affirmed.

Fazang, like other Chinese Buddhist scholars, sought to form a way of categorizing between different Buddhist doctrines. His classification took the form of five different categories of teaching, based on their sophistication and varying accommodation to the limitations of sentient beings. His premise was that since humans differ in terms of talent for awakening, there must be different teachings to address these individual differences.

The five categories of Fazang's classification are:

1. Hinayana: in the early Buddhist tradition, it was taught that the self did not exist, but that factors of existence were real.
2. Initial Mahayana: this includes the early teachings of emptiness as found in the Prajnaparamita literature and the Madhyamika tradition, as well as the early Yogacara tradition.
3. Final Mahayana: this includes traditions and texts such as the Tathagatagarbha Sutra, the Lion's Roar of Queen Srimala, and the Mahayana Awakening of Faith, which speak of the 'womb' or 'embryo' of Buddhahood (tathagatagarbha) as the matrix from which the world arises.
4. Sudden Teaching of the One Vehicle: the term 'sudden' here indicates that this teaching makes little or no accommodation for those who lack a special talent for

awakening. Later commentators included in this category the Chan tradition, which had not yet really established itself at the time of Fazang.

5. Comprehensive Teaching of the One Vehicle: this category specifically refers to the Huayan tradition. Fazang believes that the Huayan tradition is doctrinally superior to the other schools, which are merely provisional and are incomplete.

Fazang's categorization is based on an unconvincing historical model, in which the *Huayan Sutra* was the first Sutra preached by the Buddha while still within the throes of his enlightenment. Like other schools, it disappeared as a separate school as a result of the persecution of 845.

The Chan school

Chan Buddhism is undoubtedly one of the most original products of Chinese philosophy working upon the basis of Indian thought, and developing it through the traditional ideas of Daoism and Confucianism. It was essentially a revolution in Buddhist philosophy. The Chinese character *Chan* is derived from the Sanskrit word (*dhyana*) meaning 'meditation', and so the school was designated 'the meditation school'. When it was brought to Japan in the twelfth century, the Chinese character *Chan* was pronounced *Zen*.

This school traces its lineage back to a story about the Buddha, who one day gathered his disciples together to teach them, but in fact he said nothing. He merely held up a flower. All the disciples looked puzzled except Kasyapa, who smiled with understanding. The Buddha handed him the flower and said that he was passing onto Kasyapa a teaching that was beyond words. Chan sees itself as being a 'mind-to-mind' transmission.

Later Chan traditions claim that it was the Indian monk Bodhidharma (d. 532) who brought the teaching to China towards the end of the fifth century. He then travelled north to the Shaolin monastery (legendary home of the Chinese martial arts) where he spent nine years in 'wall-gazing'. It is said his legs atrophied and fell off, and to stop himself from falling asleep he cut off his eyelids. When his eyelids fell to the ground they sprouted into tea plants, and so tea was introduced to China. Tea originated in India and was popularized in China by Buddhist monks who used it to help them stay awake during long periods of meditation. Meditation is common to most schools of Buddhism, and it seems as though Chan was reacting against the emphasis upon philosophy prevalent in some other schools.

Bodhidharma was reckoned to be the twenty-eighth patriarch from Sakyamuni Buddha and the first of the Chan school in China. The next important figure in the Chan tradition is Huineng (638–713). His story is told in one of the central texts for Chan, the *Platform Sutra of the Sixth Patriarch*, which interestingly is the only Buddhist sutra that does not claim to be the words of the Buddha. The key issue of discussion is whether enlightenment is gradual or sudden, or whether learning or practical realization is more important.

Organizationally, Chan only became an independent school during the time of Pochang Hui-hai (720–814). Until this time most Chan monks lived in monasteries of the Lu-tsung under the regulations of the Vinaya. Pochang made a new set of rules for Chan monks, which tried to revive the simplicity of living conditions and combine the teaching of the Vinaya with Confucian rules of etiquette. The monks went on their begging round each morning, but then they were expected to work. This was a totally new innovation within the life of the Sangha, but answered one of the problems that Buddhism had in addressing the Chinese way of life. This resulted in a rapid period of growth during the Tang dynasty, and there was a second period of growth during the later Sung period.

The chief tenet of Chan is that Buddhahood is achieved

through instantaneous enlightenment. The Chinese are a practical people and were not so much interested in theories as practical achievement. Chan worked for enlightenment in this very life, and denounced the misuse of piety as an end in itself. In particular they set themselves against the excessive worship paid to the scriptural tradition, and insisted that salvation could not be found by the study of books. This did not mean that they did not study any books. Their writings are full of quotations from the sutras, but these were always considered secondary to the practice of meditation and spiritual realization. In protest against the excesses of devotion, a famous Chan master in the eighth century burnt a statue of the Buddha when he was cold. Similarly, to correct the contemporary misunderstanding of the role of the Buddha, another Chan master coldly stated, 'If you meet the Buddha, you ought to kill him if he gets in your way.' Chan was intent on restoring Buddhism as a spiritual philosophy rather than devotion as within Pure Land. For Chan, enlightenment was the direct experience of realizing the Mind-essence in its fullest. The following four lines are believed to capture the essence of Chan:

No reliance on words.
Transmission outside the scriptures.
Point directly at the minds of men.
See Your (Buddha) nature and be enlightened.

Chan claimed that within their ranks numerous people attained 'enlightenment' all the time. This resulted in a new ideal figure – the *Roshis*.

According to Chan the highest principle is inexpressible, but it was not content to leave it that way. Chan tries to make the insight into a concrete experience by a technique of making apparently contradictory statements (*Gongan*, or in Japanese *koan*). In other words, 'stating it through non-statements'. For example:

In the square pool there is a turtle nosed serpent.
Ridiculous indeed when you come to think of it!
Who pulled out the serpent's head?

The *koan* is an enigmatic phrase insoluble by the intellect,
and is meant to baffle the intellect until it is realized that
the intellect is only a matter of thinking *about*. Similarly,
the *koan* exhausts the emotions until it is realized that emotion is merely feeling *about*. It is when the disciple is
brought to this intellectual and emotional impasse that the
experience becomes immanent.

Soon after the death of Huineng, the meditation hall
came to be used in Chan monasteries, and lay persons
learned the practice in their own homes. During the Tang
dynasty the Chan monasteries attained greater wealth and
influence than at any time in the history of Buddhism in
China. However, the great monasteries were economically
unproductive, and this eventually led to the great persecution of 845 when the government confiscated the property
of the monasteries and forced the monks and nuns to
return to secular work.

A multicultural society

Under Emperor Taizong, China became a world super-
power. While Europe was in the midst of the Dark Ages,
Chinese troops swept through Central Asia and brought the
Tarim Basin under Chinese administration. Military expansion brought trade as the way to the West was now wide
open. It was a time of confidence, vitality and openness to
new ideas.

During the Tang dynasty, the capital Chang'an (now
Xian, Shaanxi Province) grew to be the largest and most
cosmopolitan city in the world, with a population of 1 million. Chang'an was a rectangle of 9 by 8 kilometres (5.5 by
5 miles) and covered nearly 80 square kilometres (30 square

miles). The walls were 5 metres (16 feet) high and made of pounded earth. Nine large thoroughfares linked the 12 gates. The city was subdivided into over 112 smaller areas separated by walls that were closed and opened according to curfew. Chang'an is one of the few Chinese cities to retain its original layout, and the present-day city walls were rebuilt in the Ming dynasty.

It has been estimated that one third of the city's total population were non-Chinese. They lived in the quarters in the western part of the city. They not only brought their religions with them, but built religious centres. The Persian-speaking merchants sacrificed live animals at fire altars and sang hymns in the Zoroastrian temple, and traders from Syria continued to practise the Nestorian form of Christianity.

Nestorian Christianity

In 635, at the time St Aidan began to preach the gospel in Northumbria, a group of Nestorian monks completed the 3,000-mile journey over mountains and deserts to the imperial city of Chang'an.

> Two dozen monks clad in white robes and carrying icons and crosses formed an odd procession as they entered through the city gate, a massive entryway rising six stories above them. They wore beards and shaved the crowns of their heads. Their leader was a bishop named Aleben.[6]

They were welcomed by Emperor Taizong, and as they had brought books telling of a saviour who would free humanity, they were set to work in the imperial library to translate the Scriptures. The Emperor took religious tolerance for granted, and he studied the new faith. He even provided a name for the new religion – 'The Luminous Religion' – and the manuscripts themselves are simply referred to as the 'Jesus Sutras'.

In about 1625, workmen digging a grave some 50 miles south of Xian found a carved stone slab buried in the earth. It weighed about two tons, and its front was carved with 900 Chinese characters. The stele dated from 781 and told the events and teaching of this early mission. Today this stele is in the museum in Xian and its story has been told by Martin Palmer:

> The Way does not have a common name and the sacred does not have a common form. Proclaim the teaching everywhere for the salvation of the people. Aluoben, the man of great virtue from the Da Qin Empire, came from a far land and arrived in the capital to present teachings and images of religion. His message is mysterious and wonderful beyond our understanding. The teachings tell us about the origin of things and how they were created and nourished. The message is lucid and clear; the teachings will benefit all; and they shall be practiced throughout the land.   (3:8–13)[7]

In 1908, the French scholar Paul Pellit arrived at Dunhuang at the site of some recently discovered caves. He found thousands of ancient documents including the 'Jesus Sutras'. Many of these were sent back to the Louvre museum in Paris. In 1961, the Chinese government declared the region of Dunhuang a national monument, and today the town is a major tourist site. The International Dunhuang Project was founded in 1994 at the British Library to gather all the manuscripts together in digital form. The Jesus Sutras show a mixing of Christian teaching with Daoist maxims and Eastern meditation. The story of Jesus is told with simplicity, as the following section illustrates:

> After the Messiah had accepted death, his enemies seized the Messiah and took him to a secluded spot, washed his hair and climbed to 'the place of the skulls', which was called Golgotha. They bound him to a pole and placed two highway robbers to the right and left of him. They bound him at dawn and when

the sun set in the west the sky became black in all four directions, the earth quaked and the hills trembled. Tombs all over
the world opened and the dead came to life. What person can
see such a thing and not have faith in the teaching of the scriptures? To give one's life like the Messiah is a mark of great
faith.[8]

Within a few decades, the Nestorian faith gained thousands
of converts in several major cities, though its greatest
growth may have been among foreigners trading in China.
Aleben was careful to point out that Christianity contained
nothing subversive to China's ancient traditions. He also
pointed out that loyalty to the state and filial piety to one's
parents was not contrary to Christian teaching. He ensured
that a portrait of the Emperor was painted on the wall of
the Nestorian church.

As Samuel Moffett comments, the missionary expansion
of Nestorian Christianity in China was quite remarkable:

> The pattern of expansion was a complete reversal of that of the
> missionary conquest of Europe. There the gospel moved cen-
> trifugally out from a fading Roman centre to win the barbar-
> ians on the fringes of the empire. In East Asia the faith came
> centripetally from the barbarian outerland to reach the heart
> of civilization, China.[9]

With the fall of the Tang Dynasty, there was a rapid decline
of Nestorianism in China. With Muslim control of the Silk
Route, the Nestorian church was cut off from the mother
church. In 986 a monk from Najran who had been sent by
the Nestorian Patriarch to China in 982 was reported to
have said: 'Christianity is extinct in China; the native
Christians have perished in one way or another; the church
which they had has been destroyed and there is only one
Christian left in the land.'

The later Tang

Following the death of Emperor Taizong in 649, it was his son Tang Gaozong who took over the throne. It seems that one of Taizong's concubines schemed her way to get rid of any rivals and married the new Emperor. Her husband suffered from ill health such that Empress Wu became the *de facto* ruler of China in 660. She was in fact to be the only Empress of China.

The Empress Wu

The previous emperors of the Sui and Tang had patronized Buddhism, and Empress Wu also sought support from the Buddhists because, unlike the Confucians, they recognized the greater role of women. In 673 she commissioned and contributed to the construction of a monumental statue of Maitreya at Longmen. The features of the statue are said to have been based on the Empress herself.

It appears that the Empress became infatuated with a cosmetic merchant in the late 680s, and she appointed him abbot of the White Horse monastery outside Luoyang. This monk wrote a commentary on a minor Buddhist text called *The Great Cloud Sutra*. This told of a female *bodhisattva* who retained her female form, rather than transforming herself into a man, so that she could better help all living beings. The sutra prophesied that 700 years after the Buddha's death she would be reborn as a princess in a small kingdom in south India, where she would be loved by her people for her great beauty. Empress Wu used this story to justify her accession to the throne.

In 690, she proclaimed herself empress of a new dynasty, the Zhou. She later proclaimed herself to be the Buddha Maitreya come as a female monarch, under whom the entire world would be free of illness, worry and disaster. Empress Wu is the only woman in Chinese history who took the title of monarch. Her hold on the government was so strong that she was not deposed until 705, when she was more than 80 years old and ailing. After seven years of palace in-fighting, the Tang dynasty was re-established and Emperor Xuanzong took office.

Tantric Buddhism

Tantra was initiated in India and is based upon the idea that there is a cosmic force, perceived as being female and known as *shakti*. This pervades everything and must be aroused to allow liberation to be attained. To activate this force one has to undergo specific initiatory rites that include learning secret spells, rituals and visualization of cosmic diagrams (*mandala*). This teaching emerged around the sixth century, and was soon transmitted to Tibet. There it merged with the indigenous Bon religion and eventually became the national religion, as will be discussed in Chapter 8.

In 706, three Buddhist missionaries arrived in China from India, bringing with them the esoteric teachings of Tantric Buddhism. Subhakarasimha (637–735) transcribed the scriptures into Chinese. These missionaries taught that although people are sunk in ignorance, they have the Buddha-nature within them. The Buddha-nature can only be realized and full salvation attained by putting into practice certain esoteric teachings that borrowed heavily from Hindu mythology. The cosmos is conceived as a great being, the gods and goddesses being symbols of its function, energy and will. Magic formulae are used to invoke the gods, with the use of *mantras* (mystic sounds), *mundras* (signs) and *mandalas* (diagrams).

The form of Tantra taught was that of the 'Right Hand', derived from the *Mahavaiocana Sutra (P'i-lu-chenua Ching)*. Ultimate reality was represented as a body divided into two complementary elements, one active and one passive. The parallels with the Daoist concept of *yin* and *yang* were immediately obvious to the Chinese. Daoists thought of *qi* as being an underlying cosmic force, and had their own spells and talismans to exorcise demons and give good fortune. The arrival of the Tantric texts was incorporated into Daoist practices, and new diagrams emerged that looked like *mandalas* and sacred diagrams that used a representation of Sanskrit text.

The mixture of magic and promise of Buddha-nature caused the teaching to have great popular appeal in China. It became known as the 'School of Mysteries' (*Mi Tsung*). The Mi Tsung School emerged in China about the same time as Nestorian Christianity.

The first coming of Islam to China

The first Muslims to arrive in China came by way of the Silk Route and were known as *Dashi* (Arabs) as early as 638. They became politically significant in 756 when Caliph Al Mansur lent some of his troops to Emperor Suzong (756–62). As these early Muslims were from 'the West' (*xi yu*), places usually identified as Arabia (*Dashi*) and Persia (*Bosi*), they were strikingly different from the Chinese in culture, language and physiognomy. Like other foreigners in China during the seventh to the ninth centuries, these Muslim traders were known as 'foreign sojourners' (*fan ke*). The term for Islam was 'the religion of the Hui' (*Huijiao*), which means 'return towards religion'. To call oneself a 'Hui person' was to state a religious affiliation.

Today there are fifty-five official minorities (*minzu*) in China, including ten that are Muslim. The Hui are the most populous, but unlike other Muslim minorities, they are a highly complex and mixed group. To promote and disseminate its classification of the Hui (and the other non-Chinese 'races'), the PRC government funded scholars to write 'concise histories' and other texts that established the 'facts' about the Hui race. These texts discuss racial 'origins', characterize the Hui nationality's essential traits, and illustrate where the Hui fall in the universal progression of history and the nation's developmental hierarchy.

Further reading
Benn, C. *Daily Life in Traditional China: The Tang Dynasty*, Greenwood Press, 2002.

Gillette, M. B., *Between Mecca and Beijing: Modernization and Consumption among Urban Chinese Muslims*, Stanford University Press, 2000.

Hickley, D., *The First Christians in China*, London: China Study Project, 1980.

McRae, J., *The Northern School and the Formation of Early Chan Buddhism*, Honolulu: University of Hawaii Press, 1986.

Palmer, M., *The Jesus Sutras*, London: Piatkus, 2001.

Reigert, R. and Moore, T., *The Lost Sutras of Jesus*, London: Sovereign Press, 2003.

Weinstein, S., *Buddhism under the T'ang*, Cambridge: CUP, 1987.

Websites
International Dunhuang Project. An interesting project directed by the British Library, exploring issues related to the Silk Route. http://idp.bl.uk/

Chapter 7

NEO-CONFUCIANISM AND NEW RELIGIOUS MOVEMENTS

The Song dynasty (AD 960–1279)

Although the Tang dynasty reached great heights of civilization, it suffered internal strife in governing such a large
geographical area. Gradually the dynasty saw power at the
centre move into the hands of the eunuchs, and in the
provinces, to military governors. It was inevitable that the
dynasty would finally collapse, resulting in another period
of unrest, before a new and more vigorous dynasty
emerged. This was to be the Song dynasty founded in 960.
The Tang had generally patronized Buddhism, but the Song
ushered in a period of reform in politics, education and the
economy. This led, among other things, to a revival of
Confucianism, to produce what is known in the West as
'Neo-Confucianism', following the designation given by the
Jesuit missionaries. Neo-Confucianism was especially
attractive to intellectuals. Daoism and Buddhism, however,
did not disappear, but in various ways they took on new
expressions. Significant developments also occurred within
popular religion, with the emergence of new gods and
deities.

The end of the Tang dynasty

Emperor Xuanzong (reigned 713–55) is credited with
restoring the Tang dynasty after the rule of Empress Wu,
and for forty years he ruled over a strong and prosperous
empire. Then, sometime in the 740s, when the Emperor

was nearly sixty, he fell in love with the wife of one of his sons. She decided to leave her husband and went into a Daoist nunnery. Her husband finally divorced her and remarried. The young woman then moved into the palace and was given the title Precious Consort Yang. Although the Emperor and his consort were very close, she also had relations with a non-Chinese general named An Lushan. Palace intrigues worsened until in 755 An Lushan led a rebellion against the ageing Emperor. Advancing from his base in the north-east of the country, he soon captured the eastern capital, Luoyang, and moved on Chang'an. The Emperor and his court fled from the capital just before the disastrous defeat of his army.

The Emperor took Precious Consort Yang with him as he fled south to Sichuan. Most of the court blamed the Precious Consort for their problems, and the troops finally mutinied and refused to go any further unless the Emperor killed his concubine. He eventually gave in to the soldiers' wishes and ordered his chief eunuch to strangle her. Over the years this tragic love story has caught the imagination of many Chinese artists. One of the most popular poems in Chinese is that by Bai Juyi (772–846) entitled 'A Song of Unending Sorrow', which was written some fifty years after the event.

The poem tells of the Emperor's love for the young woman that eventually led to her death. The poem is not altogether correct in its historical detail, but it captures something of the feelings found in Chinese literature.

It was early spring. They bathed her in the Flower Pure Pool,
Which warmed and smoothed the creamy-tinted crystal of
     her skin,
And, because of her languor, a maid was lifting her
When first the Emperor noticed her and chose her for his
     bride.

> The cloud of her hair, petal of her cheek, gold ripples of her
>   crown when she moved,
> Were sheltered on spring evenings by warm hibiscus
>   curtains;
> But nights of spring were short and the sun arose too soon,
> And the Emperor, from that time forth, forsook his early
>   hearings
> And lavished all his time on her with feasts and revelry,
> His mistress of the spring, his despot of the night.[1]

Emperor Xuanzong ruled for only a few months after the death of his consort. One of his sons deposed him and was only able to regain Chang'an with the help of mercenaries. The rebellion finally ended in 763, but the Tang dynasty was seriously weakened. Tibetan troops raided the capital, an activity that was to become common every autumn. The Emperor's weakened authority allowed the eunuchs to gradually gain control of the Emperor's personal army. The stage was set for the end of the dynasty.

Criticism of Buddhist establishments

During this period the Buddhist establishment came under growing criticism. This was particularly seen in one Buddhist ritual that occurred at the Dharma Gate monastery and involved the procession of a relic of the Buddha from the monastery to the capital. The proponents claimed that the celebration went back to the time of the Indian King Asoka who, in the third century BC, distributed relics of the Buddha all over the world. The first reliable date for the festival in Chang'an is in the sixth century. It was, however, in 629 that Taizong, the founder of the Tang dynasty, sponsored an elaborate procession to carry the finger-bone of the Buddha from the monastery to the capital and back, a distance of some 240 kilometres (150 miles) in total. The procession occurred every 30 years. In 819, the

Confucian scholar Han Yu (768–824) was shocked by the hysteria that occurred along the route. Devotees were burning the crowns of their heads and roasting their fingers. He was concerned that some would go so far as severing a whole arm.

Han Yu also began to argue that the tax-exempt status of the Buddhist establishment was draining the resources of the state. Throughout the ninth century the state had struggled with the problem of diminishing tax returns, and the An Lushan rebellion of 755–63 had only worsened the situation. There was a shortage of currency because of the high content of copper that the coins contained. In contrast, the Buddhist monasteries were in control of vast wealth, as recorded by the Japanese monk Enin, who in 840 was living in Chang'an when Emperor Wuzong (reigned 840–46) issued a series of imperial edicts designed to reduce the wealth of the Buddhist monasteries.

It was said that in 830 some 700,000 men and women declared themselves to be monks or nuns.[2] They constituted 2 per cent of the total population of 60 million. This was a significant section of the population who were educated, exempt from tax and dependent on donations from the community. In 842, the Emperor posted an edict requiring all Buddhist monks and nuns less than fifty years of age to return to lay life. Three years later he ordered all tax-exempt Buddhist monasteries to close. He only allowed a limited number of monasteries to remain open with a reduced number of monks in residence. This short-lived attempt to suppress Buddhism did little to solve the central government's main problem of a shortage of money, as it was now struggling with attacks from the Uyghurs from the north. Although the Buddhist establishment survived the persecution, it never recovered the political and economic position that it had under the Tang dynasty.

Emperor Wuzong was a convinced Daoist and was fascinated by the notion of immortality potions, and he drank many of these potentially lethal cocktails that eventually affected his sanity. He died aged only thirty-three. As his sons were too young to rule, in 846 the thirteenth son of Xianzong was made Emperor. He reversed the anti-Buddhist measures, revived Buddhist festivals and allowed some rebuilding. He, however, was also a convinced Daoist and became the fourth Emperor in four decades to die from such elixirs.

A series of uprisings began in 874. A failed examination candidate named Huang Chao (died 884) emerged as the leader of the rebels, and in 880 he conquered Chang'an and declared himself founder of a new dynasty. However, the rebels were unable to establish a stable regime and withdrew from the ravaged city. After 885, the Emperor was essentially a puppet of the eunuchs and military governors. Between 907 and 960 a succession of regional kingdoms existed, making this into a period that historians call the 'Five Dynasties'.

Out of this period of disunity there once again emerged a strong general who was able to reunite the Chinese people. Zhao Kuangin (reigned 960–76) had the throne thrust upon him by some of his officers. He became ruler of the kingdom of Zhou, with his capital at Kaifeng. He then proceeded to conquer Yangzi in 963, Sichuan in 965, Guangdong in 971, Anhui, Jiangxi and Hunan in 975. The Emperor's policy combined strength with leniency, and this enabled him to reorganize the army and reimpose central authority. After his death in 976, his younger brother Taizong (reigned 976–97) succeeded him and managed to conquer much of the remaining territory. Taizong was a scholar, good at calligraphy and fond of writing poetry. He encouraged Confucian studies and the publication of the classical texts.

The Song dynasty (960–1279) was a period of active reform in politics, education and the economy. Many new technological innovations were made during this period, including the printing of books, paper money and gunpowder. Public education increased, partly due to the invention of printing, and the civil service examination became a more important avenue of social mobility.

Neo-Confucianism

As we have seen, Buddhism had steadily grown in influence until it was essentially the state religion under the Tang. In so doing, it had sidelined the Confucian scholars, but during the late Tang period a new movement began to coalesce around a group of scholars who sought to revitalize Confucian teaching. Members of this group began referring to their teaching as *Daoxue*, meaning 'Learning of the Way'. The implication of this title was that neither Buddhism, which spoke of the Eightfold Path (*Babudao*) nor Daoism (*Daojiao*) taught the true Way. These scholars considered that China's social and moral fabric had been spoiled by Buddhism and Daoism, and that it was this that had contributed to its political weakness. This new movement was therefore an attempt to revitalize Chinese civilization by returning to the Confucian classics as a basis for contemporary life. However, as Chang has written, 'Without the introduction of Buddhism into China there would have been no Neo-Confucianism'.[3]

During the period of the Northern Song (960–1127) there were a number of exponents of *Daoxue*, but during the Southern Song period (1127–1279) the scholars Cheng Yi (1033–1107) and Zhu Xi (1130–1200) were prominent. The Cheng-Zhu school, as it came to be known, became officially sanctioned as the orthodox interpretation of Confucian teaching. For almost 600 years, until the fall of the Qing dynasty in 1905, this system was the basis of the civil service examination. Thus, it had a great influence upon Chinese intellectuals even though they may not have agreed with the system itself. 'Neo-Confucianism' provided a comprehensive world-view based upon the 'ultimate transformation', which was that of becoming a sage.

The social goals of the movement were especially prominent during the Northern Song period, when most
Neo-Confucians were actively involved in government and
political reform. Fan Zhongyan (989–1052) was prime
minister and introduced a series of reforms aimed at
rationalizing the government bureaucracy and bringing the
civil service examination more in line with the skills that
were needed by the contemporary state.

One of the most original thinkers was Wang Anshi
(1021–86), who also served as prime minister. He was
concerned with the financial problems of the Song administration caused by the continued military expenditure, and
thought that this could best be met by increasing the productive capacity of poor peasants and traders. Wang
reduced land taxes by 50 per cent, introduced cheap credit
for peasants and small traders, and undertook water-con-
trol measures. Welfare measures included the provision of
reserve granaries and peasant education. He also encouraged the establishment of orphanages, hospitals and public
cemeteries. Many of these functions had been performed by
Buddhist monasteries, so he essentially brought these back
under state control. These reforms were bitterly attacked by
the large landowners and money-lenders whose interests
were affected. His rival, Sima Guang (1019–86) overturned
many of the policies that Wang had tried to introduce.

The loss of the north to the Jurchen invaders resulted
not only in the focus shifting to the south, but most Neo-
Confucians turning away from social reform to self-cultivation. In this regard they adopted the teaching of Mencius as
the authoritative interpretation of Confucian teaching. As
was mentioned in Chapter 2, Mencius took the goodness of
human nature as a premise, and so the Neo-Confucians
devoted much of their attention to outlining practical methods of self-cultivation. This was a subject about which
Mencius had been rather vague.

The school of Zhu Xi

Zhu Xi (1130–1200) is perhaps the most important scholar in the Confucian tradition after Confucius and Mencius. Zhu Xi has been duly recognized as 'the supreme synthetic mind in all Chinese history, comparable to such Western thinkers as Aristotle, Aquinas, Leibniz, and Herbert Spencer.'[4] He was born into a family of scholar-officials in Hunan Province. When he was in his early teens his father died and he was adopted by his uncle, through whom he obtained his first government post. During his lifetime Zhu was not an influential figure in Song politics or intellectual society, but he is particularly known for the warmth of his personality and his penetrating insights.

Zhu made a number of significant contributions to Confucian teaching. First, he proposed that the four core texts of Confucian education are the *Analects*, the *Mencius*, the *Great Learning (Daxue)* and the *Centrality and Commonality (Zhongyong)*. The latter two were originally chapters in the *Record of Rituals (Liji)*. In addition, the *Yijing (Classics of Change)* became a major source of inspiration for the Neo-Confucian scholars.

Second, from the *Great Learning* he expounded a continuum of Confucian learning extending from the state to the individual:

Those in antiquity who wished to illuminate luminous virtue throughout the world would first govern their states; wishing to govern their states, they would bring order to their families; wishing to bring order to their families, they would first cultivate their own persons; wishing to cultivate their own persons, they would first rectify their minds; wishing to rectify their minds, they would first make their thoughts sincere; wishing to make their thoughts sincere, they would first extend their knowledge. The extension of knowledge lies in the investigation of things...

> From the Son of heaven to ordinary people, all, without exception, should regard cultivating the person as the root.[5]

In other words, a person's understanding of the moral order must be consistent with the objectively verifiable understanding of the natural order.

Third, Zhu developed an elegant conception of the unity of all things in their shared psycho-physical substance of *qi*. This is expounded in a concise form in the celebrated essay *Western Inscription*, so named because it was inscribed on the west wall of his study:

> Heaven is my father and Earth is my mother, and even such a small creature as I finds an intimate place in their midst.
>
> Therefore that which extends throughout the universe I regard as my body and that which directs the universe I consider as my nature.
>
> All people are my brothers and sisters, and all things are my companions.[6]

There are two key phrases in this passage that are the two most important concepts in Neo-Confucian metaphysics. The phrase 'that which extends throughout the universe' refers to *qi*, and 'that which directs the universe' refers to *li*, meaning order. This led to a complex metaphysics, the investigation of which is beyond the scope of this volume.

Fourth, Zhu Xi appreciated the difficulty of this process of self-transformation and sought to provide a structured curriculum and guidance for his students. His main dictum was that learning should be for the sake of the self. He insisted that the ordinary person required assistance from the sages to help them in their progress.

The school of Lu Xiangshan

Lu Xiangshan (1139–93), whose personal name was Lu Jiuyuan, was a contemporary of Zhu, but differed in his views. Zhu argued that the functioning of the human mind (*xin*), and not the fundamental moral nature (*xing*) is identical with the principle *li*, and stressed the need for study and inquiry. Lu, however, placed the emphasis on honouring the moral nature. Of greater concern to Lu was the question of how one can become good. The recognition of the problem of evil by the Song philosophers was due in part to the influence of Buddhist metaphysics. For, according to Buddhism, life is evil, and this is caused by human craving for pleasure and rebirth. However, the Song moralists were too realistic to accept the pessimistic Buddhist teaching and instead of aiming at otherworldliness, they unanimously believed that, although evil exists in the world, human beings were endowed by heaven with a good, spontaneous nature, which, even if temporarily lost, could be regained and restored to its original state of goodness. Lu emphatically stressed this optimistic belief. For him highest knowledge of *dao* came from constant inner reflection and self-examination. In this way one develops, or rediscovers, the fundamental goodness of human nature.[7]

The Neo-Confucian teaching on self-cultivation is similar to the realization of Buddhahood in Mahayana and the idea of immortality in Daoism. As with the figure of the *bodhisattva*, the Confucian superior person breaks the habits of thinking for personal interests and seeks primarily the interests of others. Similarly, the Daoists aspired to the 'perfect person' (*zhenren*), while the Neo-Confucians understood self-cultivation to involve the transformation of the whole person, including the non-physical nature.

The Neo-Confucians managed to keep three key elements together, which was to produce a rigorous worldview. First, they maintained Confucius' emphasis on learning. Second, they recognized the importance of Mencius' teaching on realizing one's innate moral nature. Third, they produced a well-thought-out cosmology and metaphysics.

Neo-Confucianism turned Confucian learning from

being an exegetical study of the classics prominent in the Han and Tang Dynasties to the study of philosophy. The concepts of *li* (principle), *qi* (material force), *xin* (heart/mind) and *taiji* (ultimate), with their practical application in meditation, popularized Neo-Confucianism. The teaching spread from China to some of the surrounding Asian countries. Although Confucian ideas had reached Korea and Japan in earlier centuries, it was with the new tradition that it became a major influence in these countries.

Developments in Daoism

Although it was the Neo-Confucians who seemed to dominate intellectual life during the Song dynasty, there were also significant developments within Daoism. Daoist texts were collected and an attempt was made to establish an authoritative Daoist canon. There were also developments of spiritual techniques to purify the *qi*, and this resulted in the growth of a number of new schools.

Chapter 3 discussed the basic ideas and practices of early Daoism. By far the most important innovation in the Daoism of the Song period, however, was the development of 'interior alchemy' and the so-called 'three cinnabar fields of the body':

> The body, on the pattern of the universe, is divided into three parts; each of these has a center (called the 'cinnabar field') where the hypostases of the primordial One come to settle. Thus, in the lower belly, two or three inches below the navel, is the lower cinnabar field, which goes by many names, among them Gate of Fate (*ming*, 'fate,' is also used for the vital force). In the thorax, the middle cinnabar field lies in the heart, or Scarlet Palace. The upper cinnabar field, in the head, occupies a 'palace' called the *niwan*. In these three cinnabar fields live the 'three worms,' the chthonic powers who bring destruction and death. Thus, these cinnabar fields are three special places, home simultaneously of health and death, Heavenly Originals, and worldly demons.[8]

The *jing* is the vital essence associated with the lower field; *qi* is vital breath associated with the central field; and *shen* is spirit associated with the upper field. The underlying concept was to refine as much *qi* as possible into *shen*, and avoid the transformation of one's *qi* into *jing*. The following are some of the techniques that were expounded.

First was the nourishing of the spirit (*shen*), which generally involved meditation and visualization. The word *shen* had an earlier meaning of 'gods' (see Chapter 1), but in these techniques they are considered to mean the most highly purified form of *qi* that circulates in the body and accounts for sensory and intellectual knowledge. The *hun* and *po* souls are considered to be forms of *shen*. Although popular belief holds that each person has one of each, some Daoists believe that every person has three *hun* and seven *po* and one can synthesize more spirits from one's own *qi*. These synthesized spirits act as personal guardians who can lead one to the realms of heaven.

A second technique was the nourishing of the vital breath (*qi*) itself. One method called *taixi*, 'embryonic breathing', is based on the idea that the *qi* we are born with gradually dissipates as we get older. *Taixi* is a way of reversing the process by clearing up the blockages to the flow of *qi* through the body. Through a combination of breathing exercises and visualizations of the *qi*, a person is able to refine the *qi* into *shen*, which is conceived as a spiritual 'embryo' that can then leave the physical body.

There are many Daoist stories of immortals who have ascended to heaven by this means. An additional teaching is the means of transcending the physical body called *shijie* (deliverance from the corpse). In this case the person appears to die, but afterwards the corpse in the coffin is found to have changed to some object like a staff. This indicates that the body has been transformed into purified *qi* and ascended to heaven. In both these cases the physical body is not left behind but transformed into a purified version of its true essence.

A third approach was that of nourishing the 'vital essence' (*jing*). 'Vital essence' is primarily the sexual fluids that are considered to be condensed forms of *qi*. The *jing* can therefore be nourished by interrupting sexual intercourse before orgasm and directing the *jing* through visualization. A man should direct this to the highest cinnabar field, while a woman should suppress menstruation. Another means was the combining of the male and female essences in sexual rituals, which resulted in the manifestation of a deity called the Peach Child. These rituals were described in detail in the *Celestial Master Text*, and were considered at the time to be scandalous.

Among the many new Daoist schools that emerged during the Song period, the two major ones were *Zhengyi* (Orthodox One) and *Quanzhen* (Complete Perfection), otherwise known as the 'Golden Flower Movement', both of which continue today.

In AD 142, Laozi appeared to Zhang Daoling, a small landowner who had withdrawn into the mountains of Sichuan. Laozi, as we have seen, had been venerated among the people as a great holy man and was deified a little later, in 165, under the title Taishang Laojun ('the very high Lord Lao'). Laozi is said to have brought to Zhang Daoling a new law, the 'Orthodox One' (*Zhengyi*), that was to propagate the rule of the 'Three Heavens', deliver the world from the decadence caused by the 'Evil Six Heavens', and re-establish a perfect state among the chosen people. The god Laojun had effectively removed the 'Mandate of Heaven' from the Emperor and given the 'Celestial Master' the responsibility of ruling the chosen people.

By the third century AD, the movement had moved from the lower class and peasant circles, where it first developed, up to the aristocracy. Despite the appearance of divisions at various times, the original organization has survived to modern times, led by a line of hereditary Celestial Masters, the descendants of Zhang Lu, who continue to maintain their ascendancy and preside over this movement. *Zhengyi* specialized in the performance of rituals of healing and renewal of local communities. It was and remains popular in southern China and in Taiwan.

Quanzhen was founded in northern China by Wang Zhe, and focused on inner alchemy. Wang Zhe promoted a syncretism uniting the Three Teachings (Confucianism, Daoism and Buddhism). He was strongly opposed to wine, sexual intercourse, anger, and the love of wealth, and he integrated into his system both Confucian virtues and Buddhist methods, extolling the reading of both the Confucian classics (especially the *Classic of Filial Piety*) and the Buddhist sutras (especially the *Heart Sutra*). He preached poverty and asceticism, in direct contrast to the views current among the Daoists of his time. *Quanzhen* does not have a hereditary priesthood like *Zhengyi*, but its priests are trained in monasteries. Today, the headquarters of the Daoist Association of China is at White Cloud Monastery in Beijing, which is a *Quanzhen* monastery.

Buddhist schools

It was during the Tang dynasty that Buddhism was most influential, and it was at this time that new Chinese schools of Buddhism emerged. However, it was during the Song period that Buddhism really infiltrated Chinese culture. Chan Buddhism fared particularly well under the Song because the government decided that it would be easier to control one school rather than several, so they chose Chan. In this way institutional Buddhism became predominantly Chan. During this time the Chan scholars compiled the teachings of the great Tang masters that have been passed down through the tradition.

Chan

Two lineages of Chan became more distinct during the Song period: Linji and Caodong. The most important Linji figure was Dahui Zonggao (1089–1163) who popularized *gongan* meditation, which is known as *koan* in Japanese. *Gongan* means a legal case, and is used in Chan for a short question or anecdote that has no logical answer. A well-known example in the West is: 'What is the sound of one hand clapping?' A teacher assigns a *gongan* to a student who uses it as a focus of meditation until he or she makes a response that demonstrates to the teacher that the student has reached a new level of enlightenment.

During the Song period the most important Caodong teacher was Hongshi Zhengjue (1091–1157), who developed the technique of 'silent illumination'. This was an advanced form of meditation that rejected the common Buddhist practice of contemplation upon a single sensory or mental phenomenon such as breathing. Caodong teaches objectless meditation that aims at a radical non-dualism beyond the normal mental categories. It was during the Song period that chanting was introduced into Chan from the Pure Land tradition. Chanting was reinterpreted as another form of meditation, which focused the mind on Amitabha.

The teachings of the Chan masters were recorded and became important texts in Chinese Buddhism. These writings included collections of gongan such as the *Wumen Guan* ('Gateless Barrier') and the *Biyanlu* ('Blue Cliff Record'). The Chan masters spoke of instantaneous enlightenment in this lifetime, which was a radical reworking of the early Indian Buddhist teachings that involved thousands of lifetimes before achieving *nirvana*.

The Maitreya Society

Although the Chan masters tried to teach the laity in terms that they could understand, it was Pure Land Buddhism that remained popular. The illiterate peasants were drawn to the teaching of a personal saviour such as Maitreya Buddha. Following the fall of the Northern Song, many people migrated south. It appeared to them that the end of the age was about to come.

According to Mahayana, Maitreya is now living in the Tushita heaven, awaiting a favourable opportunity to be reborn on earth as the next Buddha. During the interval between the passing of Sakyamuni Buddha and the coming of Maitreya, the pure *Dharma* would progressively deteriorate, so the end of the age would be one of misery and decay. It would be at that time that Maitreya would descend to restore the pure *Dharma*, and bring peace and prosperity to the realm. During the period of his presence on earth a just and virtuous ruler would sit on the throne and rule the people.

To prepare for the coming of Maitreya and to keep alive the hope of the utopian future, the Maitreya Society was formed. Under the Tang and Song dynasties, ambitious rebel leaders capitalized on the popularity of the cult by claiming that they were the incarnation of Maitreya himself or the virtuous ruler come to bring peace and tranquillity to the people. It is easy to see how attractive such claims would be to the poor masses when experiencing periods of unrest and rampant corruption in the government.

The most serious of the revolts against the Northern Song was led by Wang Tse, who was a minor army officer who started a rebellion in Hopei. The story is told that as a young man he left home to join the army, and his concerned mother tattooed on his back the character *fu*, meaning 'blessedness', hoping that this word would protect him and bring him back home safely.[9] However, members of the Maitreya Society considered the word as a supernatural omen, and proclaimed him their leader. He managed to combine all the Maitreya groups in the area into one, and commenced the rebellion in 1047 by occupying Peichou in

Hopei. He not only captured a considerable amount of military hardware, but conscripted all males aged twelve to seventy into his army. To prevent people escaping, he organized a mutual guarantee system, in which each member of a group would stand guarantor for the others. If one of the group escaped, the rest would be executed. The Song troops besieged the city. First they tried to scale the walls, but were repulsed. They then tunnelled underneath the walls and when the project was completed, they surprised Wang and suppressed the revolt.

With the suppression of this revolt the Song authorities banned the Maitreya Societies, and required local officials to keep close scrutiny on members of such societies if they should reappear. Although the movement was suppressed, this was not to stop similar movements developing, of which the most significant was the White Lotus Society that will be considered in the next chapter. As will be shown, throughout the following centuries such millenarian movements were going to have a major impact on Chinese society. The continual emergence of such movements explains the recent concern of the Chinese authorities with groups like Falun Gong which they have classed as 'dangerous cults'.

Popular religion

Popular religion in most areas of the world tends to relate to local deities and, as Hansen has shown, during the Song period the popularity of many local deities broke out of their limited territories to spread across the country.[10] As traders began to travel further to buy and sell their goods, they took their gods with them for protection and good fortune. Hansen categorizes the various types of deities popular at this time:

1. Traditional and commoner gods who had been historical people and had a temple near their place of birth.
2. Buddhist, Daoist and Confucian gods who had no home temple because they were considered to be more cosmic in nature.
3. Generic and bureaucratic gods including local earth gods and city gods who usually had personal names, but were referred to by their offices.
4. Animal and nature gods, such as rivers and mountains. These had been more important in past ages, but were dying out by the Song.
5. Regional gods, such as Zitong, originally from Sichuan, who helped aspiring officials pass the civil service examination.

Female deities

Two female deities who would come into the second of Hansen's categories were the Bodhisattva Guanyin and the goddess Mazu. Guanyin was the name given to the *bodhisattva* in Sanskrit called Avalokitesvara who in India was perceived as male. Somehow in the transmission of the deity to China it had become transformed into a female figure. This was probably because Guanyin was the Bodhisattva of Compassion, and was pictured as wearing a long flowing robe and hair tied up. The popular *Lotus Sutra* contains a chapter devoted to Guanyin who is said to grant immediate salvation to anyone in suffering who calls on her name. Guanyin became one of the most popular deities throughout East Asia and was incorporated into Chinese popular religion, where her identity was often merged with other goddesses. Today Guanyin is once again a popular figure in China, with images of her being restored in all areas of the country.

An interesting example of the emergence of a divinity is illustrated by Mazu. She was a young woman, surnamed

Lin, who was born in the first year of the Song dynasty. She lived on the coast of Fujian Province and was considered to have demonstrated special spiritual powers through her devotion to Guanyin. She was said to have been able to help fishermen to survive storms at sea.

> One day she went into a trance and dreamt that there would be a storm and that it would destroy all the boats in the fleet. Running down to the beach she pointedly fixed at their father's boat which, when the storm suddenly blew up, was the only one to be saved.[11]

She died unmarried when only twenty-seven years of age. After her death the local fishermen used to call upon her help when in storms, and many reported her intervention. As her fame grew, so apparently did her powers, until she could aid anyone in distress.

In 1123 an imperial emissary to Korea claimed that he had seen Mazu during a storm. He petitioned the Emperor to grant her a title, meaning she would be recognized as a member of the official pantheon. She was granted the title of 'Numinous Compassionate Lady'. A little later a temple to her was built near her home village. Her fame and power continued to grow and in 1192 she was promoted to 'Numinous Compassionate Imperial Consort'. In the following century, the Mongol Emperor Kublai Khan named her 'Celestial Consort'. In 1737, she was named Tian Hou, 'Empress of Heaven', and this is the title by which she is known today in Hong Kong and Taiwan.

There are about sixty temples dedicated to her in Hong Kong alone, most built in the early Qing dynasty. The oldest is Fat Tong Mun which was constructed in the Song dynasty, about 1266. Her birthday is celebrated by fishermen on the twenty-third day of the third lunar month.[12]

Alongside the temples to gods were shrines to worthy men, often located in schools or Confucian academies.

Unlike the gods in the temples, the images were not considered to have spiritual powers. Most of them were notable officials, generals or scholars who had done something of renown. They were local people whose memory the community wanted to keep alive. On set occasions the students and teachers in the schools would prostrate themselves and offer incense and food offerings as an expression of respect for the honoured dead.

Following the fall of the north, some of the shrines of the worthy men were moved outside their original locality. Although they were neither born in nor had served in the area, shrines were constructed to them. Three men in particular came to have shrines built to them all over the south: Zhou Dunyi (1017–73), Cheng Yi (1033–1107) and Cheng Hao (1032–85). Inscriptions credited these three men with correctly understanding the Way of Confucius and his disciple Mencius.

Spirit-possession

One dramatic expression of folk belief during this period was that of spirit possession and what Chinese writers of the Song period denoted by the term *pingfu*. As Davis writes: 'Spirit-possession was both a role assumed in public and a shared and universally recognized idiom that allowed an individual person to convert emotions into culture, and symptoms into symbols.'[13]

The *Records of the Listener* by Hong Mai (1123–1202) is a massive compilation of strange reports and includes 200 descriptions of spirit possession. Davis has placed them into three groups. First, village spirit-mediums who become possessed by earth spirits or some local deity. These spirits were believed to possess women, who, if not exorcised, would in time become mediums. Second, exorcisms by Daoist priests or Buddhist monks working through one or more boys who would become possessed by the spirit afflicting the patient. Third, rites for the dead in which relatives of the dead would become possessed by the ghost of the deceased, and would be able to converse with the living.

There had long been tension between the Daoist priests and the local medium, but during the Song period a role of 'Ritual Master' (*fashi*) emerged. The Ritual Master officiated between the Daoist priesthood and the village medium. They directed the trances of the spirit-mediums, some of whom were only children. The Daoist text *Rite of Summoning for Investigation* shows that the spirit afflicting a person was encouraged to possess either the patient himself or herself, or a young male acting as medium. The spirit would then speak through the person, identifying the cause of the affliction, that could then be dealt with appropriately.

*   *   *

In 1127, the nomadic Jurchen conquered the Song capital Kaifeng, abducting the Emperor. The rest of the court fled south and established a new capital in Hangzhou, while the Jurchen founded their own dynasty in the north of China. This marks another period of division between the north and the south of China, and is used by historians to distinguish between the period of the Northern Song (960–1127) and the Southern Song (1127–1279). In 1234, the Jurchen were in turn conquered by the Mongols whose dynasty is known as the Yuan. The Mongols then moved to conquer the Song in the south, which they accomplished in 1279.

Further reading
Davis, E., *Society and the Supernatural in Song China*, Honolulu: University of Hawaii Press, 2001.
McRae, J. R., *Seeing through Zen: Encounter, Transformation and Genealogy in Chinese Chan Buddhism*, University of California Press, 2003.

Robinet, I. (translation by Brooks, P.), *Taoism: Growth of a Religion*, Stanford University Press, 1997.

Siu-Chi Huang, *Essentials of Neo-Confucianism: Eight Major Philosophers of the Song and Ming Periods*, Greenwood Press, 1999.

Websites

Song of Unending Sorrow. This page contains some of the best known of the poems by Bai Juyi. http://www.lingshidao.net/hanshi/baijuyi.htm

Poems by Bai Juyi. This site also contains links to the many poems by Bai Juyi. http://dmoz.org/Arts/Literature/Authors/B/Bai_Juyi/

Temple of Maitreya. This site is dedicated to Maitreya, the coming Buddha. It contains photographs of paintings and statues of the *bodhisattva*. http://sangha.net/messengers/maitreya.htm

The Lotus Sutra, translated by Burton Watson. This is one of the most readable English translations of the *Lotus Sutra*. Here it is made available by SGI-USA (Soka Gakkai International – USA). http://www.sgi-usa.org/buddhism/library/Buddhism/LotusSutra/index.html

Chapter 8

THE TIBETANS AND MONGOLIANS

From the emergence of the Tibetan empire to the end of the Yuan dynasty (AD 605–1368)

Central Asia is a vast area of mountains, steppe and desert, and from early centuries successive waves of conquering tribes would explode onto the world scene, invading the neighbouring lands. The Tibetan empire emerged in the first decades of the seventh century when some of the competing kingdoms became united under the hegemony of Namri Lontsen, but it was during the reign of his son Songtsen Gampo (c. 605–50) that imperial conquest began in earnest. The documents of the Tang dynasty refer to their first contact with Songtsen's expanding empire in 634, and the first Tibetan military attack in 638. Although their particular expression of Buddhism was to be influential, they were never to have such an impact upon China as the Mongols in later centuries.

The coming of Buddhism to Tibet

The introduction of Buddhism into Tibet is usually divided into two distinct stages. The first took place during the era of the so-called Three Great Religious Kings: Songtse Gampo (c. 609–49), Trisong Detsen (704–97) and Ralpachen (805–38). By this time Buddhism had been flourishing for almost a millennium, and had been transmitted throughout South-east Asia, and northwards, by-passing Tibet, to China, Korea and Japan. Buddhism in Tibet is called *choas*, meaning 'law'.

166

The first transmission

The first transmission occurred in the seventh century when the diverse clans of the Tibetan highlands were united under a central king and they began to harass the western borders of China. When a new young king, Songtse Gampo, came to the throne, the Chinese Emperor Taitsung of the Tang Dynasty was eager to gain his favour, so in 641 the young king married the Princess Wencheng of the Chinese imperial house. Two years previously Songtse Gampo had married Bhrikuti, a daughter of the King of Nepal. Tradition tells that both these women were ardent Buddhists and influenced the young king, who brought Buddhist teachers, monks and books into Tibet from their respective homelands.

Tibetan history presents Songtse Gampo as one of the greatest kings of Tibet, who introduced literacy and formal education to the country. It tells of how he established Buddhism as the state religion of the country, displacing the previous priests, the *bon-po*, who exerted great influence among the nobility. King Songtse is also credited with sending one of his ministers to India, where he developed a system of writing for the Tibetan language, following the Sanskrit form. Songtse Gampo later became regarded as an incarnation of the Bodhisattva Avalokitesvara ('the Looking-down-Lord'), and his two wives became known as the incarnations of Tara ('the Saviouress'). The fact that they bore him no children has come to be regarded as evidence of their divine nature. The Chinese princess Wencheng was deified as 'The White Tara', while the Nepalese princess was said to be 'The Green Tara'. The significance of these figures will be returned to in the following chapter.

In contrast, Chinese history suggests that Songtse Gampo was, for much of his life, involved in various wars and did little to promote Buddhism beyond building a few temples and translating a few texts into Tibetan. After his death in about 650, Buddhism made little advance against the prevailing Bon beliefs for at least a century. Then, one of his descendants, Trisong Detsen, inherited the throne when he was only thirteen years old. Early in his reign King Trisong Detsen invited an Indian master named Shantarakshita to Tibet, and he advised him to invite his brother-in-law, Guru Padma-sambhava, a popular leader of the tantric Yogacara School. The guru promptly responded to the invitation and returned with the messengers in 747. According to legend, on arriving in Tibet he quickly vanquished all the evil deities in the land, sparing them only if they consented to become defenders of Buddhism. In return he guaranteed that they would be duly worshipped and fed, and as a result, some of the pre-Lamaist deities are recognized in the Tibetan pantheon as 'dharma protectors'.[1] In Tibet these deities are generally regarded as 'of this world', and able to grant only worldly blessings, as opposed to the great bodhisattvas who are 'beyond this world'.

Under the patronage of King Detsen, Padma-sambhava built the first Tibetan monastery at Samye in 749, and instituted the first monastic order using the Tibetan word La-ma, meaning 'Superior One'. The term was restricted to the head of the monastery and today applies strictly to the highest monks of the order. The first Lama is said to be Palbans, who succeeded the Indian Shantarakshita. Thereafter, the first Tibetans, traditionally referred to as the 'Seven Elected Ones', received ordination as Buddhist monks.

During King Detsen's reign an important debate took place under the patronage of the King, between the Chinese Mahayana School and the more conservative Indian Mahayana expression. The Chinese monks appear to have been members of the so-called 'meditation school', associated with Chan (mentioned in Chapter 6). In contrast, the Indian monks advocated the view that final liberation only came about through the continual practice of the *bodhisattva* perfections over countless lives. According to the Tibetan accounts, the debate lasted two years and the verdict finally went in favour of the Indian party, and the Chinese monks were banished from Tibet. From then on Tibet took its Buddhism exclusively from India, and there was a continual flow of ideas and literature between Indian and Tibetan Buddhists.

Ralpachen was the last of the pious kings, but he was not a strong ruler. He was eventually killed in a court intrigue and his brother Langdarma ascended to the throne. Langdarma instigated a vicious repression of the *Dharma* and effectively terminated its first transmission. He did not reign long, and was soon killed by a vengeful Buddhist monk who disguised himself as a devil-dancer and shot the King at close quarters.[2] Centralized power disintegrated, and Tibet once more divided into warring communities, and little is known of this period. The controlling influence of the Buddhists was completely lost, and the country went through 150 years of confusion. The Sangha did not entirely die out, and a few monks continued to exist among isolated communities.

The second transmission

According to tradition, it was in the remote areas of western Tibet that the 'second transmission of the Doctrine' got under way. Here emerged prosperous independent kingdoms, who received a fresh influx of teachers from India. Among these were Richen Zangpo (958–1055), a great Tibetan translator, and the Indian master Atisha (982–1054), who was persuaded to bring the *Dharma* to the kingdom. Tradition tells of Atisha being heaped with gold by a grateful people. In the east of Tibet, a Nepalese master named Smrt introduced tantric practices.

New schools of Buddhism developed with their own particular style and teaching. Once again Tibetan Buddhism was influenced by India, but with the Muslim advance into India,

Buddhism came to an end in that country, and the doorways to Tibet were closed. As Snellgrove writes: 'Tibet became a time capsule in which the Mahayana Buddhism of medieval India was reverently preserved by diligent guardians.'[3]

The Kadam School was founded in the eleventh century by the Indian scholar Atisha and his Tibetan disciple Dromton (1005–64). This school is particularly known for its great emphasis on practical application of the ideals of a *Bodhisattva* within the practitioner's daily life. The name Kadam means 'bound by command', which highlights the laws of abstinence from marriage, intoxicants, travel and possession of money. It accepts 'four deities' (Sakyamuni, Avalokitesvara, Tara and Acaia) and 'three texts' (the *Tripitaka*).

The Kadam School later evolved into three sub-divisions – Lamrimpa, Shungpawa and Mengapa – each founded by one of three brothers whose names were Potowa, Chekawa and Phuljungwa. Although there is no existing school of Tibetan Buddhism now explicitly known as Kadam, the teachings in this school are highly respected by all the four major traditions, and in particular by the Gelug school.

The Kagyu tradition also began in the eleventh century, and it traces its lineage back to the Indian master Mahasiddha Tilopa (988–1069). He was the teacher of Nalopa (1016–1100) who became the abbot of Nalanda Monastery, which was the most exalted monastery in India at that time. He was, in turn, the teacher of the first Tibetan exponent of the tradition of Marpa (1012–97). Marpa had a notable student named Milarepa (1040–1123) whose biography is one of the best-known pieces of Tibetan literature. The teachings of this school have been transmitted through an unbroken lineage of awakened teachers until the present time.

Although the Kagyu tradition was particularly known for its great non-monastic teachers, it also developed a monastic tradition beginning with Milarepa's student

Gampopa (1079–1153). The particular feature of the Kagyu lineage is that the teacher, after having mastered the teachings, clears away from the mind of the disciple defects relating to intellectual understanding, meditational experience and the various levels of realization. Upon completion of the process, the teacher is able to introduce the text of the *mahamudra* ('great seal') to the disciple.

The Sakya tradition began in the eleventh century, but was mixed with earlier eighth-century teaching. It gained the name 'grey earth' because of the colour of the soil on which the monastery was built at Sakya. Khon Lui Wangpo Sungwa became a disciple of Guru Rinpoche in the eighth century. Through the next thirteen generations, the *Dharma* continued to be propagated through the Khon family. In 1073, Sakya Monastery, built by Khon Konchok Gyelpo, established the Sakya Tradition in Tibet. He studied under Drokmi the Translator (992–1072) and became a master of many deep teachings.

Following Konchok Gyelpo, there were a series of masters who added to the teaching of the tradition. The first was his own son, the 'Great Sakyapa' Gunga Nyingpo (1092–1158) who categorized the Sakya teachings. He was considered an incarnation of Manjushri, the Buddha of Wisdom. The teachings were received directly, some of them when he was still a boy. Another important Sakya scholar was Gunga Gyeltsen Bel Sangpo (1182–1251). As an infant he would write Sanskrit characters in the dirt and then avoid crawling over them. His contribution to the Sakya School was his ability to understand knowledge from both Buddhist and non-Buddhist origins. Widely recognized as a great debater, he answered the challenge of a Vedanta philosopher and succeeded in winning the debate, causing the philosopher to convert to Buddhism.

Tibetan Buddhism has been tantric from the beginning, but the emphasis was made even stronger in the twelfth century, when the masters of tantric Buddhism fled from

India before invading Muslim armies. The Muslims especially attacked the tantric Buddhists with their many images and icons, and burned down the great centre of tantric learning at Nalanda. The library was so large that it burned for months. Many refugees took their manuscripts on horseback and fled northward towards Nepal, Bhutan and Tibet. There they established new monastic centres. In the following generations, the Sanskrit manuscripts were translated into Tibetan, Chinese and Nepalese, and the tradition was preserved.

Once the second transmission began, the various individuals and groups who remained devoted to the teaching of the first transmission formed into the Nyingma. As the new schools began to organize themselves, the Nyingma began to regard themselves as a distinct order and built their own monasteries and ordained monks. They also began to codify their teaching that they claimed had been hidden during the oppression. Nyingma consider their founder to be Padma-sambhava who was the leading teacher during the first transmission. Their teaching distinguishes nine *yana* ('vehicles') to Enlightenment, the first three being based on the sutras and the remaining six on the tantras.

Despite attempts to organize the Nyingma the *lamas* remained individualistic and followed different practices. For example, some of these *lamas* would marry; many supported themselves by exorcism, rain-making, divination and shamanistic healing. Those *lamas* who gained a reputation gathered a few disciples around themselves, but they were never a match for the new schools that emerged at the time.

A further development was brought about by Tsongkhapa (also known as Je Rinpoche (1357–1419) who is today identified as a manifestation of the *Bodhisattva* of wisdom, Manjushri. He is said to have come from the region of the great Kokonor Lake in north-east Tibet. After travelling and studying widely he established his first monastery in 1409 in the hills east of Lhasa. He founded two other great monasteries: in Drepung 1416 and in Sera in 1419. Because of their scholarly orientation and their division into colleges, these are often described as Buddhist Universities.

Although he is characterized as a self-appointed reformer of Tibetan Buddhism, Tsongkhapa did not consciously set out to found a school of his own. He was strongly scholastic in orientation, and affirmed the monastic virtues and the need to establish a firm basis in the *sutra* teachings before graduating to the *tantras*. He expounded the path to enlightenment in terms of graduated stages expounded as the *Lam-rim Chenmo* ('stages of enlightenment').

On his death, his body was embalmed and enshrined in a *stupa* at Ganden where it was venerated as a holy place. Stories have come out of Tibet that recently the *stupa* was opened by Chinese soldiers, who were shocked to find the body perfectly preserved with hair and fingernails still growing.[4] Tsongkhapa is also credited with the initiation of the 'Great Prayer' Festival (*Monlam Chenmo*) that is held in Lhasa after the New Year festival. The annual festival of *Ngacho Chenmo* commemorates Tsongkhapa's death, and is a time when thousands of butter-lamps are lit.

After his death Tsongkhapa's disciples developed his ideas into a distinctive school separate from the Kadam to which Tsongkhapa had originally belonged. This school is nicknamed 'yellow hats' which distinguishes them from the 'red hats' of earlier traditions. From these disciples came the line of the *Dalai Lamas*. The word *Dalai* is of Mongolian origin and means 'ocean', implying a vast repository of wisdom. The title of the first *Dalai Lama* was bestowed posthumously upon Gendun-drup (1391–1474), the disciple and nephew of Tsongkhapa.

It was the Gelukpa School that came to enjoy the favour

of a new generation of Mongol Khans. In 1642, Gusri Khana installed Ngawang Lobsang Gyatso (1617–82), the fifth *Dalai Lama* as the ruler of Tibet under the overall Mongol protection. The fifth *Dalai Lama* proved to be an effective and tolerant ruler. Although other schools were recognized, they were stripped of their wealth and power. Over the ensuing centuries, the regime of the *Dalai Lamas* consolidated their temporal power over the whole country.

Despite popular images of the Dalai Lama as a 'God King', Tibetan governments were mostly weak and limited. They had little control over the daily lives of the population most of whom were either peasant cultivators living in isolated and scattered communities or nomads. Consequently, Buddhism was also decentralized and survived by catering to local needs. While the ideology of the religion was towards the achievement of enlightenment, and the liberation of *samsara*, the everyday activities of the *lamas* and monks were taken up with the performance of rituals for the practical needs of the lay community. There was a large monastic community, a reasonable estimate being about 10 to 12 per cent of the male population in the main agricultural areas. There were relatively few *lamas* (a word corresponding to the Sanskrit *guru*), who were teachers and leaders of monastic communities. They were often recognized as reincarnations of past *lamas*, sometimes members of *lama* families, and were expected to be competent in the magical rituals. *Lamas* were not necessarily celibate monks or nuns, although in recent centuries most of them were.

The Mongols

The steppes of Central Asia had for centuries been the home of many different nomadic peoples, but some time around 1200 they formed, for the one and only time, into a fighting confederation that was to shake both China and Europe. The reason for this development is still a matter of debate, but one thing is clear: the disunited tribes of the Mongols became united through the personality and military skill of one charismatic leader – who in Western history has come to be known as Genghis Khan (c. 1167–1227). A more accurate rendering of his name would be Chinggis Khan (Genghis is the Persian rendering of his name), and his personal name was Temujin.

The Mongols did not have a written language and the main source of their origins comes from *The Secret History of the Mongols*, which uses Chinese characters to record Mongolian sounds.[5] The account commences with the legend of the descent of the Mongols from a blue doe deer. It goes on to give a brief history of Chinggis Khan who was born into the family of a chief in the forests of what is now the People's Republic of Mongolia. His father died when he was only nine years old and along with his mother, brothers and sisters, he was abandoned. Through the hardship of these times he learned many lessons for survival. As a young man he gathered a force of men around him, and this battle group grew into an army. One significant innovation he introduced was that he divided his army into groups of tens, hundreds and thousands, each with their own commander.[6] Loyalty was a key principle and each commander had responsibility for his own men on pain of death.

In 1206, a shaman gave him the title of Chinggis Khan which literally means 'Ruler of the Ocean' – the ruler of the world. Chinggis managed to defeat his rivals and establish himself as leader of all nomadic peoples of the steppe. By 1215, the Mongols had defeated the Jurchens in north China. After taking the northern plains of China the Mongols turned away from the warmer river valleys of southern China to conquer the European steppe, which was terrain more familiar to them. They swept through Russia in 1219, and by 1222 had reached northern India. The death of Chinggis at this time gave Europe some respite before his son Ogodei resumed the campaign of conquest.

Persia, Georgia and Armenia were conquered in 1231 and Hungary in 1236. When Ogodei died in 1241, the Mongols were plunged into a succession dispute that was only resolved in 1264 with the division of the empire into four areas, one for each of the descendants of Chinggis's four sons.

The Mongols' conquest was at breathtaking speed. This was mainly due to their creative use of horses as a fast-moving cavalry. Every solider had several horses, so they could ride for days on end without tiring the mounts. Atop the riderless mounts sat a dummy soldier who helped give the appearance of a much larger force. The Mongols were also excellent archers and could shoot the enemy on the gallop. They were also quick to see the military uses of new technology. They followed the Chinese example and tipped their arrows with iron, and they made use of Chinese gunpowder to make fire-bombs.

Cavalry was, however, not effective against walled cities where it was often necessary to lay siege. The Mongols implemented an alternative strategy – the use of terror. In 1221, the city of Herat in Afghanistan was laid waste and everyone killed except 400 craftsmen who were sent to the Mongolian capital. The Mongols piled the severed heads of men, women and children into separate piles. They did everything they could to encourage their reputation for senseless violence. This reputation spread out before them, such that when they came to a given city the residents would surrender without a fight. In these instances, the Mongols did not kill the inhabitants and only took the plunder and moved on. The people were left to govern themselves and were allowed to continue following the same religious practices.

The Song in southern China provided a different challenge to the Mongols. The Song had both larger armies and a navy. However, the Chinese did not have sufficient horses to match the Mongols and neither were the sedentary

Chinese able at mobile warfare. Although the Mongols had no experience at naval warfare, within ten years they had built up a navy to match the Song. This was mainly through the use of non-Mongols who also sailed the fleet. The Song were finally defeated by the Mongols.

There are different dates for the founding of the Mongol dynasty. The earliest is 1260 when Kublai Khan took control of Mongolia and north China. Ten years later he established the Yuan (meaning 'origin') dynasty, and in 1279 the last Song Emperor died. Only after the conquest of the south did the Mongols once again tackle the matter of governing China.

The Mongols were skilled in warfare, but had no experience in governing conquered territory. The Mongols were distrustful of the Chinese and preferred to deal with the Turkic peoples of Central Asia who could speak both Mongolian and Chinese. These included the Khitans, the Tangus and the Uyghurs, all of whom the Mongols called *semu*. For example, Yelu was a Khitan who was placed in charge of taxation by Chinggis's son Ogodei. He was a follower of the Complete Self-realization school of Daoism mentioned in the previous chapter. The Mongols were used to collecting booty once a city had surrendered, and the Chinese practice of an annual low-level tax was new to them. Even so, Yelu tried to establish fixed rates of land tax and poll tax, with people in the cities and countryside paying different rates. When Yelu lost influence at court in 1235, these attempts to govern in the Chinese style ended.

Kublai Khan was born in 1215, the year his grandfather Chinggis Khan captured Beijing. His father, Tolui, was one of Chinggis' younger sons and was in charge of northern China. As he was frequently away on military campaigns, Kublai and his brothers were brought up by his mother, the remarkable Songhagtani Beki. Persian historians write of her as being very intelligent and well educated. She ensured that her children were taught to read and write as well as being given military training. She showed Kublai that the traditional Mongol occupational policy would be inadequate for China.

The cultural gap between Mongols and Chinese made coexistence difficult. Kublai and his advisors followed a policy of dual government of what they considered the separate societies of Chinese and non-Chinese under Mongol rule. The population was divided into four groups: the Mongols themselves; people of various groups, mostly Central Asian; the northern Chinese (already accustomed to Mongol rule); and the southern Chinese. The Mongols always maintained a homeland beyond their borders.

They then assigned individual households into different occupational categories. Most Chinese were classed as agricultural workers, but some had specific tasks of serving the Emperor. Because there was suspicion of the Chinese, the Mongols forbade intermarriage between the Chinese and themselves. The Mongols suspended the civil service examinations, which for the Chinese was the primary route to office. Thus, many Chinese families had to seek new occupations such as teachers and healers.

Songhagtani Beki was a Nestorian Christian, and she encouraged Kublai to allow religious freedom. Mongol shamanism was exclusively concerned with material needs, which allowed other religions to address the issues of gods and the afterlife. Kublai himself expressed an interest in Christianity and Nestorian Christians were known to serve at court. He allowed Muslim communities to build mosques, and he patronized both Buddhists and Daoists. Kublai became more interested in the Tibetan form of Buddhism, which with its sorcery had greater appeal, and this stance was encouraged by his favourite wife, Chabi.

One interesting episode during the reign of Kublai related to a Buddhist–Daoist controversy. Before the Mongols became acquainted with Chinese Buddhism they had established good relations with a Daoist master of the

THE TIBETANS AND MONGOLIANS

Chuan-chen school. He was invited to go on a campaign into Central Asia with Chinggis from 1220 to 1224. Upon his return he was made supreme head of the Daoist institution. He was also entrusted with the general supervision over all who had entered a monastic life, which, of course, included the Buddhists, who did not like the arrangement.

The Daoists took advantage of this position and began to take over some of the neglected Buddhist monasteries and transformed them into Daoist temples. The Daoists also began distributing the *Illustrations of the Eighty-one Conversions*, which described the eighty-one incarnations that Laozi was supposed to have undergone in the past. Most of this text consisted of borrowings from Buddhist sutras. This work infuriated the Buddhists and the matter was brought to the attention of Kublai in 1255 who convened a grand assembly. This was attended by 300 Buddhists, 200 Daoists and 200 Confucians. Under sharp questioning by the Buddhists, the Daoists finally admitted that the only work left by Laozi was the *Daode Jing*, and it contained no reference to Laozi converting foreigners. Kublai declared the Daoists to be the losers and required the destruction of the disputed text.

Legend also tells a story of how Kublai invited members of several major religions to his court including Lamaist monks, Muslims, Confucians and Christians. He is said to have demanded from the Christian missionaries, who had been sent to him by the Pope, the performance of a miracle as a proof to him of the superiority of the Christian religion. If they failed and the *Lamas* succeeded in showing him a miracle, then he would adopt Buddhism. In the presence of the missionaries, who were unable to comply with Kublai's demand, the *Lamas* caused the Emperor's wine-cup to rise miraculously to his lips, whereupon the Emperor adopted Buddhism, and the discomfited missionaries declared that the cup had been lifted by the devil himself, into whose clutches the Emperor had now returned.[7]

It has been shown in previous chapters that alien peoples who conquered Chinese territories soon realized they could not embrace Confucianism or Daoism as they were indigenous religions. Buddhism, however was founded by a non-Chinese, and had been embraced by many people other than the Chinese. By adopting Buddhism the alien rulers could therefore gain the support of many Chinese already devoted to the religion, while enhancing their own culture by the superior literature and philosophy of Buddhism, without facing the danger of being submerged by Confucianism.

Kublai Khan installed the Lama of Sakya as head of Lamaist Buddhism, and conferred upon him the temporary power as tributary ruler of Tibet. Kublai actively promoted Lamaism, and built many monasteries in Mongolia and China. Under the succeeding Mongol Emperors, the political supremacy of the Sakya *lamas* was able to suppress rival sects.

The Mongols were united under the leadership of Chinggis Khan and they eventually formed what was to be one of the largest empires in history, stretching from Hungary in the west to Vietnam in the south-east. It was in the early thirteenth century that the Mongols began their raids into China, the Jurchens being the first victims. It took the Mongols some fifty years to conquer all of China and to establish what was to be called by Chinese historians the Yuan dynasty. For the first time in history a foreign people managed to conquer all of China and not just the northern part. They formed a vast area of relative peace through Central Asia that some scholars have called the 'Pax Mongolica' in a similar way that the Roman Empire formed the 'Pax Romana'.

Although travel was difficult, Mongol rule did allow communication, and it was during this time that the famous explorer Marco Polo (1254–1324) visited China. Together with his father Niccolo Polo, and his uncle, Marco

Polo made a trading expedition to Constantinople during 1253–60. As a war blocked their return, they journeyed eastward to reach Kublai Khan's eastern capital at Kaifeng in 1266. They returned to Venice in 1269. In 1271 they left again for Kublai's court (modern Beijing), which they reached in 1275. The story tells that Marco Polo became a favourite of the Khan, who employed him on business in central and north China and in the states of South-east Asia, including India. In 1292 the travellers, acting as escort for a wife of the Khan of Persia, left Kublai's realm and were back in Venice in 1295. Marco Polo soon joined the Venetian forces fighting Genoa and was taken prisoner in 1296. It was during his two-year captivity that he dictated an account of his travels to Rustichello, a fellow prisoner.[8] The prologue of the work tells of his adventures, and the remainder of the book describes places he had visited and heard of and recounts the customs of the people. Although this account has for a long time been taken as factual, though a little exaggerated, some Western scholars now regard Polo's *Travels* to be more a work of fiction based on the accumulated hearsay of various travellers who went to China.[9] Even so, this book was the main source of information about China that was available in Europe until the nineteenth century.

Christianity under the Mongols

Kublai Khan's role as founder of the Yuan dynasty was decisive in setting the way for religious policy that was to be observed by the later Khans. He displayed the religious tolerance characteristic of Mongol rule in Central Asia, even though connections with Tibetan Buddhism grew increasingly important for him and subsequent rulers. Kublai himself was a son of a Nestorian princess and remained tolerant of other religions. The establishment of the Pax Mongolica allowed commercial contacts between

East and West and the expansion of the Nestorian Church into China.

Nestorian Christians

The Nestorian communities in China were spread out in various areas from the north-east to the coastal cities of the south. Since 1275 they had been subordinate to a Nestorian metropolitan residing in Beijing. A city with a small but significant Christian minority was the southern port of Zaitun, known to the Chinese as Chuanchou. It was an important commercial city with many foreign traders, including Arabs, Jews, Armenians and even some from Genoa. Trade was conducted with South-East Asia, India and Arabia. The city gradually lost its importance when the harbour silted up. Guangzhou (Canton) then became the most important port on the south coast of China.

The presence of Nestorians in the region is not only documented by indigenous sources, but is seen in the inscriptions on tombstones. These were frequently written in Syriac script and were decorated with a cross on a lotus flower sometimes flanked by angels in flowing robes. The Nestorian community in Zaitun probably continued to thrive up to the middle of the fourteenth century when Mongol rule declined and there was a growing intolerance of foreigners.

The Nestorians also built monasteries in various parts of the country. The monastic centre at Beijing went back to earlier times, but there were also monasteries in the lower reaches of the Yangzi. The Chinese text, *The History of Chen Chiang of Chihshu Period*, gives us further information about the monasteries near Chen Chiang. Seven of these were founded by Mar Sargis, a Turkish Nestorian from Samarkand who was a high official in the service of Kublai Khan. We read that he was summoned to the task in a dream, in which he saw seven gates open in heaven and angels gave him the charge of erecting the monasteries.

These were built around 1281 and were given Chinese and Turkic names, suggesting that Turkic monks must have lived there.

The History of Chen Chiang also tells something of the form of worship. The monks worshipped towards the east where the sun and moon rise, symbolizing the creative activity of God. It tells of the significance of the cross, which is the figure for 'ten' in Chinese script. It had a dual meaning in that it was an image of the human body, and was an indicator of the four directions. *The History* also tells of how the monasteries were converted into Buddhist monasteries following the accession of Emperor Ayurbarwada (reigned 1311–20). In 1311, the walls were repainted and the Christian paintings replaced with Buddhist motifs.

Although the Nestorian Church thrived under the Yuan dynasty, it remained basically a foreign religion. Attempts were made to convert the Chinese but these had little success.

The Franciscans

A notable mission from the Western Church to Yuan China was that conducted by the Franciscans. Their writings give much information about their activities, as do the Papal decrees. Although there was tolerance and even cooperation between the Franciscans and Nestorians at the Mongol court, they were often critical of each other.

One of the most significant Franciscan missionaries in Yuan China was John of Montecorvino. He was born in southern Italy in 1247 and was known as a man of both physical and intellectual powers. A papal letter addressed to Kublai Khan and dated 15 July 1289 was sent asking the great Khan to receive John and his fellow travellers. He had to wait two years before he could proceed to East Asia. He travelled by ship to South India, and after some delay he left for China and ultimately arrived at Beijing. John was received with honour as was the case for most foreign dignitaries.

John was able to present the Papal letter to the Great Khan. In the letter, the Pope states that he had heard of the Khan's request for stronger ties with the head of the Roman Church. The Pope expressed the wish that the Khan would accept the Christian faith as well as receive John and his companions with kindness. In his first known letter, dated 8 January 1305, John tells that his plans to win the Khan had failed, but he had been received with special favour. John complained about the Nestorians seeking to discredit him as a false envoy and possibly a spy or magician. After five years of intrigues, the Khan became convinced of his innocence and sent the slanderers into exile.

John worked alone for eleven years, until a German, Arnold of Cologne, came to be with him. During this time John saw remarkable success in that he had baptized about 6,000 people in Beijing, and had trained 40 boys in the Latin Church rites. He had been allowed to build a church with a bell-tower in Beijing, and had written psalms and prayers for the converts. He also learned the 'Tartar' language and had translated the New Testament. Pope Clement V later appointed him as Archbishop of Beijing. He seemed to have enjoyed great popularity among non-Christians as well as Christians.

In 1311, the Pope sent three more Franciscan brothers with the rank of bishop to China. The writings of these brothers give us more insight into their situation. In Beijing they lived on the generosity of the Emperor, and were able to establish a church and a monastery for twenty brothers outside the city. It seems as though no Jews or Muslims were converted, and most of the Buddhists ('idolaters') who did accept the faith soon deviated from the Christian way.

The Franciscans continued to be esteemed at court and had the rank of envoys. At state festivals, they appeared before the Khan, alongside Buddhist high lamas and foreign rulers, in order to honour the Emperor. Some prominent men were converted at the court. In 1338, envoys from China appeared before the Pope bringing two letters, one of which was from the Great Khan.

With the end of Mongol rule in 1368, like the Nestorians, the Catholic Church ceased to exist in China. Some vestiges of the Christian past lingered into the fifteenth century. This shows that Christianity, as a foreign religion, was tolerated when the dynasty was of foreign origin, but when a Chinese dynasty was restored, Christianity was rejected as Chinese customs were revived.

Islam in China

Historically there are two main types of Muslim community in China. The older derives from groups of merchants and other travellers who came to China with the advent of Islam in the seventh and eighth centuries. Due to social and political pressures, and intermarriage with Chinese women, they accommodated somewhat to Chinese culture.

They became Sinified through the adoption of Chinese surnames, clothing and food habits. Gradually Chinese dialects replaced Arabic and Persian. As a result Muslims were no longer referred to as 'Arabs' or 'barbarians', but came to be known as *Hui-hui* or *Hui*. The Hui were seen as a 'national' community within China.

> The Muslims adopted the Chinese language and Chinese dress. Mosques were built in the style of pagodas, the *muezzin* making the call to prayer inside the courtyard. Knowledge of Arabic was confined to the imams or '*akhunds*', although as with other non-Arabs, the use of Arabic greetings became a Muslim shibboleth. Nevertheless, observance of ritual and dietary laws ensured that the Chinese Muslims retained a separate identity as a religious community... the Hui attitude was summed up in the phrase, 'Muslims indoors, Chinese outdoors'.[10]

The other major Muslim group consists of the Central Asian communities who came under Chinese imperial control as a result of the expansion of China in more recent times. These groups were largely concentrated in Xinjiang Province and other parts of north-west China and speak Central Asian languages. Unlike the Hui, they have maintained their ethnic and religious identities virtually intact, despite official policies which aimed to assimilate them. As will be discussed in a later chapter they have sometimes broken out in rebellion in order to establish their own autonomy.

New religious movements during the Mongol period

Many comments have already been made in previous chapters about the emergence of religious movements within Daoism and Buddhism especially. These were often lay movements that were concerned with religious practice and devotion, but some had a millenarian teaching that encouraged rebellion against the reigning dynasty. The previous chapter mentioned the Maitreya Society and how it rebelled against the Song. Similar movements occurred during the period of the Mongols. As we have seen, although they endorsed Tibetan Buddhism, the Mongols were still foreign rulers. The extravagances of the Mongol court also spurred popular discontent.

The White Cloud Society
One movement that was declared heretical and dangerous was the White Cloud Society, founded by the monk Ching Chueh (1043–1121), a native of Henan. It is said that as a youth he studied Confucianism, but became attracted to the *Lotus Sutra* and eventually converted to Buddhism. He travelled to Mount Emei in Sichuan, and then to Hang Chou, where he settled and lived at the back of the White

Cloud Monastery. In 1108, he established the Society for the purpose of opposing the prevailing Chan school. It seems that by this time Chan had become rather formalized and had lost the underlying religious experience. Ching Chueh wanted to provide something that would be easy to practise and had spiritual reality. He emphasized pure living, good works and a spirit of unity among members. He travelled widely giving teaching, and saw the Society spread and many new temples built. He also wrote several texts, but none of these survive. Our knowledge of the Society therefore comes from the writing of those opposed to them.

Branches of the Society were found mainly in the Chekiang region and each was organized under the guidance of a branch leader. Members included monks and laypeople who would meet in the mornings and evenings to recite the sutras and offer incense in the temples that had been founded. Members were strict vegetarians and were celibate. The movement included both men and women. It is not clear who the women were, but their opponents accused them of immorality. The members were very supportive of one another, and even engaged in acts of public welfare such as repairing roads.

Although there was nothing particularly unorthodox in this movement, the Chan Buddhists and Confucian writers condemned the Society as traitors to the Emperor and in league with evil spirits. As a result, Ching Chueh was banished to Kwangtung, probably in 1116. Five years later he was pardoned, but died soon after. His remains were buried at Hang Chou. The White Cloud Society continued to flourish despite the ongoing criticism, but was finally dissolved in 1320 by the Yuan government when it was accused of fraud. Some of the charges against the White Cloud Society were unfair, as they never engaged in any rebellious activity, unlike the White Lotus Society.

The White Lotus Society

The White Lotus Society was founded during the early years of the Song dynasty by Mao Tzuyuan, a disciple of the Tientai master. Following his ordination at the age of nineteen, Mao concentrated upon the practice of meditation, but like his master, he was also interested in Pure Land. He organized a society consisting of monks and lay devoted to the restraint of the passions and the encouragement of good *karma*. The group met regularly to utter invocations and sing praises to the Buddha.

The group had a number of unusual features. First, it included women and children in its membership, which raised criticism from Confucians who regarded the free mixing of men and women as immoral. Second, members were not only strict vegetarians, but also abstained from wine, onions and milk. Third, they recited a penance every morning – it was believed that this would destroy evil and remove the obstacles towards salvation. The movement was criticized as being involved with demons, and eventually Mao was banished and the movement banned. Despite the ban, the movement continued to grow.

In 1313, probably through the requests of a Korean prince, the Society was permitted to practise openly. Branches were formed in Kainsi and Fukien, with women from even noble families joining the movement. An interesting innovation of the Society was that whereas they had formerly only venerated the image of the Buddha at their meetings, now non-Buddhist deities made their appearance. The Mongol government was concerned about the growth of the movement and banned it again in 1322.

The White Lotus Society therefore became the focus of a number of rebellions against the excesses of the Mongols. In 1337, Pang Hu raised a revolt in Henan, claiming he was preparing the way for Maitreya. In 1351, Han Shan Tung stirred up a rebellion in Henan. His followers claimed that Han was the rightful descendant of the last Song Emperor.

The rebels took to wearing red neck-scarves and offered incense to Maitreya. For these reasons they were sometimes called the 'Red Kerchief Bandits' or the 'Incense Army'. For some time the rebels controlled an area of China stretching from what is now Manchuria to north-west China. In 1362, the forces of Han Shan Tung were defeated by the Mongols, but some of the members continued the rebellion and eventually managed to depose the Mongols.

* * *

The Mongolian conquest of China and the formation of the Yuan dynasty had a major impact on Chinese civilization. The Chinese eventually overthrew the Mongolian rulers and established the Ming dynasty, which was to become a summit of Chinese civilization. Today, much of Mongolia and Tibet are viewed by the Chinese authorities as historically part of greater China. However, with the opening of the new Qinghai–Tibetan railway in 2007, the influence of these people may yet have another twist, as the following news report suggests:

> LHASA, China – There's a new type of pilgrim spinning the prayer wheels at Tibet's holiest sites. Along with the Tibetans who prostrate themselves before the vacant throne of their exiled leader, the Dalai Lama, swarms of Chinese tourists rub crisp Chinese money on their foreheads and then cram the bills into collection boxes. In matching tour group hats, the Chinese visitors bow at Tibetan shrines, light candles and ring temple bells. Style-conscious young women try the Tibetan look, weaving bright strips of cloth into their black hair... It reveals 'a spiritual hunger that Chinese have to know more about Buddhism,' said Kate Saunders of the Washington-based International Campaign for Tibet. 'I think that's a sign of hope for the future'... The Chinese government deeply distrusts religion as pulling allegiance away from the ruling Communist Party.[11]

Further reading

Gillman, I. and Kilmkeit, H., *Christians in Asia Before 1500*, Richmond: Curzon Press, 1999.

Kapstein, M., *The Tibetans*, Blackwell, 2006.

Ratchnevsky, P., *Genghis Khan: His Life and Legacy*, London: Blackwell, 2002.

Turnbull, S., *Genghis Khan & the Mongol Conquests, 1190–1400*, Routledge, 2003.

Websites

Pre-modern Imperialism – The Mongols. An introductory resource for the examination of the Mongols and their empire. http://www.accd.edu/sac/history/keller/Mongols/intro.html

The Realm of the Mongols. An interesting but rather romantic portrayal of the Mongols. http://www.coldsiberia.org/

Website of the 14th Dalai Lama. This website is dedicated to raising awareness of the life and works of His Holiness Tenzin Gyatso, the 14th Dalai Lama of Tibet, and has been created under the auspices of the Office of Tibet and the Tibetan Government-in-Exile. http://www.dalailama.com/

Chapter 9

THE MING DYNASTY AND THE JESUIT MISSIONARIES

The Ming dynasty (1368–1644)

The closing years of the Mongol dynasty were marked by widespread discontent and rebellion, mainly resulting from the Chinese antagonism to alien rule. In some instances the uprisings were instigated by monks, and it was one of these rebel groups, led by Zhu Yuanzhang (1328–98), that finally managed to overthrow the Mongols in 1368 and establish what came to be called the Ming dynasty. Although his troops forced the Mongols back to Mongolia, the Chinese never succeeded in defeating them. The Chinese therefore continued to live under the fear that another Chinggis Khan would emerge and unite the Mongols and once again conquer China.

The Ming rebuilt a series of fortifications that, taken together, constitute the Great Wall as it is known today. They also forbade trade with other countries to stop possible Mongol attack from the west, but this was never very successful. It was, however, to the Manchus in the northeast that the Ming dynasty would eventually fall in 1644. However, the Ming dynasty was to be one of the peaks of Chinese civilization.

The foundation of the Ming empire

Zhu Yuanzhang was born into a poor peasant family, and he was the only child of six who was not given up for adoption or married off at an early age. During a famine in 1344 both his parents died and Zhu sought refuge as a novice in the monastery, where he learned to read and write. These early experiences left with him a conviction that the state must protect the peasants who would in turn provide the revenues.

In 1352, a terrible flood occurred when the Yellow River burst its banks, submerging vast areas of farmland and washing away whole villages. The resulting famine and epidemic caused a revolt against the Mongol rulers that spread across the whole country. Zhu became an active member of the Red Turbans and his gifts of organization quickly brought him promotion. He married the leader's daughter, and by 1359 he was in charge of the Nanjing region. His military skill and good administration gained him much popular support, and by 1368 he was established as Emperor, taking the throne name Hongwu. He named his dynasty Ming, meaning 'bright', presumably to indicate to the various millenarian groups that they had triumphed over darkness. It also implied to the Confucians the concept of 'bright' in the sense of discerning. However, he was astute enough to know that such millenarian groups were difficult to control, and one of the first things he did when he came to the throne was to issue a decree banning all such societies.

As Emperor he continued to follow many of the Mongol precedents in government. He adopted the Neo-Confucian curriculum of the Mongols, and established the role of Chancellor to rule as a kind of prime minister similar to that of the British constitution. He also retained the Mongol practice of regional government with a hierarchy of provinces, prefectures and counties. He also initiated a series of reforms that for the first time gave central government detailed information about individuals and their landholdings. In 1381, he called for a national census that recorded the name, age, birthplace, head of household, occupation, size of land, animals owned and the size of residence of every person in the empire. Because the census

Sanxingdui Museum, Sichuan Province. This giant bronze with exaggerated eyes and ears is believed to be of a deity who is able to listen and see things far away. Date: c 1200 BC.

The Great Wall is China's traditional defensive line against the people of the north. It stretches 3700 miles, and was originally built in small sections by various feudal states around the 5th century BC. It was later joined into one massive fortification by Qin Shi Huangdi, China's first emperor, at the end of the 3rd century BC. It has been renovated many times since then especially during the period of the Ming dynasty.

Xian (Chang'an) is one of the principal cities of the Wei valley in NW China. It was the capital of the Han dynasty with the splendid twelve gate city surrounded by twelve kilometers of wall.

The famous terracotta warriors, Xian, are part of the elaborate tomb complex of the First Emperor Qin Shi Huangdi. The tomb itself has not been opened, but the life size terracotta warriors that stood guard inside the outer wall have been painstakingly reassembled.

The Big Wild Goose Pagoda is one of Xian's most famous landmarks. This seven-storey tower was erected in AD 652 at the request of the pilgrim monk Xuan Zang as a fireproof storage silo for the Buddhist sutras he had brought from India. The Big Wild Goose Pagoda was the highest building in central China for over 1200 years.

A Confucian temple in the city of Wuhan that has recently been restored. Unlike Daoist or Buddhist temples, Confucian temples do not normally have images except that of Confucius.

On certain dates street parades are held, led by Daoist monks. These are lively affairs which invariably involve firecrackers and flower-covered floats broadcasting traditional music.

Young woman praying for blessing at a Daoist temple. The burning of Joss sticks and Hell Bank Notes is believed to transfer merit to the spirit world where it will be available for the departed spirit to use.

The Giant Buddha at Leshan was carved between AD 713 and 804 and overlooks the confluence of three important rivers, the Min, Qingyi and Dadu.

The Longman grottoes are situated south of Luoyang, Henan Province, along the banks of the Yi River. The construction of these Buddhist statues commenced in the fifth century A.D. and continued for over 400 years. There are more than 2300 caves and 80 pagodas.

The Buddhist caves of Dazu are found north of Chongqing. The caves are scattered over 40 different locations and contain more than 50,000 carvings dating from the Tang and Song dynasties. Many scenes depict ethical principles of both Buddhist and Confucian origin.

Entrance to the Ming Tombs. 50 kilometres northwest of Beijing City lay the Ming Tombs - the general name given to the mausoleums of 13 emperors of the Ming Dynasty (1368 - 1644).

A typical Tibetan monastery in West China. Many have been renovated in the last two decades and have active communities of monks. The colourful prayer flags usually have an image of a horse, and it is believed that as they blow in the wind they transmit blessings to the world.

The monks are an important element of the Tibetan community Here a monk of the Bon tradition teaches some of the children in the village.

Tibetan nomads live on the grasslands of the Qinghai-Tibetan plateau at an altitude of over 3,000 metres. Many are being required by the government to move to new towns. They may have new houses, but their traditional way of life is left behind and there is little new opportunity for work.

Once the winter is over it is a common sight to see Tibetans making their way on pilgrimage to major religious centres. Many travel hundreds of miles performing prostrations. The new roads recently constructed ease the journey somewhat.

High in the mountains of West Sichuan a traditional Kham Tibetan dance is performed in which the dancers take the role of warriors who will fight evil and bring peace to the community for the coming year.

The Temple of Heaven was built by the third emperor of the Ming dynasty as a setting for state rituals. The circle represents heaven and a square the earth. The circular temple is entirely made of wood supported by 28 huge wooden pillars.

During the period of the Ming and Qing dynasties, Beijing was divided into a number of walled sections, or cities. The Forbidden City was the innermost and was the residence of the Emperor and the Imperial Family, and as such was the focus of the empire. Entry was strictly forbidden to all but those on imperial business until 1911 when the last emperor was dethroned. It occupies 720,000 square metres, and there are 9,999 rooms. A moat and ten metre high wall surround the city.

The Sun Yat Sen Mausoleum was built in Nanjing after the death of the founder of the Republic of China in 1925. It has 392 granite steps that lead to the white memorial hall which is roofed with blue ceramic tiles.

The Luding Bridge was built in the 44th year (1705) of the reign of Kangxi in the Qing Dynasty. It is an iron suspension bridge over the Dadu River, and its length is 100 metres. During the Long March in 1935 soldiers of the Fourth Regiment of the Chinese Workers and Peasants' Army secured this vital river crossing. Without the bridge, the Red Army would probably have been destroyed. In the nineteenth century, the last army of the Taiping rebels was destroyed in the same area.

Tiananmen Square is a modern creation and covers an area of 98 acres. Until the mid 1970s the square was used for massive rallies and parades. In the centre is the Memorial Hall of Chairman Mao with his embalmed body on display. His picture still dominates the entrance to the Forbidden City.

Many of the traditional homes in the countryside are now only inhabited by children and grandparents as the father and mother have migrated to the city to work.

Farming in many areas remains hard work. In other areas many of the people have migrated to work in the cities with the result that fields are no longer cultivated as the old people who remain can't manage the toil involved.

The Bund, also called the Zhongshan Road, is a famous waterfront and regarded as the symbol of Shanghai for hundreds of years. It was the bustling port developed by the Western powers in the nineteenth century. Today the old colonial style buildings continue to line the river looking towards the new buildings of modern Shanghai.

Nanjing Road, Shanghai, the No 1 Commercial Street in China. Shanghai is now a city of over 18 million people and is the economic hub of China.

Hong Kong was a crown colony of the UK from 1842 until the transfer back to 'the Motherland' in 1997. It has been incorporated under the 'one country, two systems' policy. Hong Kong maintains its own legal system, police force, monetary system, and immigration policy.

Chinese New Year starts on the first day of the New Year containing a new moon and ends on the Lantern Festival fourteen days later The date is between January 21 and February 20. Spring Festival is when everyone likes to go home and spend time with their family, visiting parks and temples for funfairs and market stalls.

June 1st is Children's' Day in China and most schools have a holiday. Children are taken to the shopping centres and treated with toys and western foods.

Many temples in China have been restored and have become tourist centres and places to relax. (Qingyanggong Taoist Temple, Chengdu, Sichuan)

A pagoda style mosque in the city of Chengdu, Sichuan province. The call to prayer is made inside the courtyard, and knowledge of Arabic is confined to the imams. Nevertheless, observance of ritual and dietary laws ensure that the Chinese Muslims retain their distinct identity as a religious community.

One of the official Three Self Churches in a city location. This church was reopened in 1989 when the policy of religious freedom took effect.

did not assume any social change, the register permanently assigned families to particular occupations and localities.

Emperor Hongwu also implemented various Confucian measures designed to ensure his subjects followed traditional norms of behaviour. He often drafted texts exhorting people to follow a moral way, and even required villagers to attend readings of the codes that reminded them of their obligations. He was frustrated by the failure of his subjects to live up to the ethical standards, but abandoned the Confucian exhortations for Legalist measures designed to force people to behave. He tended to swing between periods of relative leniency and excessive violence.

As he had previously been a monk, he had a positive attitude towards Buddhism, and he sometimes convened assemblies of monks, to whom he lectured on various sutras such as the *Prajnaparamita*. The ordination of monks was encouraged. In 1372, some 57,200 Buddhist and Daoist monks and nuns were ordained, and in the following year the number reached 96,328. The numbers were increasing so quickly that measures had to be taken to limit the numbers. In 1387 ordination was forbidden to those less than twenty years of age, and examinations were introduced to assess the capability of the candidates. In 1394 monks who had wives were called to the capital to be examined on their understanding of the scriptures, and all those who failed were made laymen. In spite of these measures, the number of ordinations continued to increase so that by 1486 200,000 were ordained.

Hongwu had thirty-six sons and sixteen daughters, and so to minimize the friction in court, he appointed his sons as hereditary governors of different provinces. His sons were forbidden to return to the capital, even on the death of their father. However, the plans to avoid a war of succession failed, and after his death there were four years of conflict until Zhu Di emerged as Emperor. He was a born leader, active, intelligent and had received an excellent education in the military. He had also led a successful campaign against the Mongols, and had been given a province in the north of the country. His crack troops captured and burned Nanjing. He took the throne name of Yongle, meaning 'Perpetual Happiness', and reigned from 1403 to 1424. On accession he ruthlessly exterminated all his opponents and their families.

Yongle reaped the fruits of his father's policies, as the people were prosperous and content. This allowed him to undertake a number of ambitious policies designed to demonstrate his own greatness. One of the most outstanding was the spectacular ocean voyages that he sponsored. This has recently been brought to the attention of Western readers by Gavin Menzies in his book *1421: The Year China Discovered the World*. In 1404, under the leadership of a Muslim eunuch named Zheng He (1371–1433), an imperial fleet travelled to the west. This was the first of seven great naval expeditions that went to South-east Asia, India and Africa. Not only were these ventures seventy years before da Gama's famous discovery of the New World in 1492, but the ships were much larger than those of the Europeans. The fleet that Zheng He led in 1421 included ships 121 metres (400 feet) in length, which was five times the length of the *Santa Maria*. Although the Chinese ships were much larger and more impressive, smaller ships are often more practical for the task of exploration.

Menzies argues that the Chinese did establish small colonies as a result of their voyages, but colonization did not seem to be the aim of the venture. They brought back rare animals including a giraffe, which had similar characteristics to the legendary Chinese animal called *Qilin*. The Emperor first paraded the giraffe in Beijing in 1414, where it was perceived as an auspicious sign of his rule.

A second major undertaking of Emperor Yongle was to move his capital north to his old power base of Beijing. The Mongols were still a major threat and Beijing provided a strategic place to guard the northern approaches through the Great Wall. Although he began rebuilding there was a shortage of food in the region. It was therefore necessary to repair and extend the Grand Canal so that rice and grain could be shipped to the region. Some 335 battalions, comprising nearly a quarter of a million people, were moved to Beijing, which brought its population to over 2 million.

The fact that Beijing was a rebuilt city provides us with a dramatic illustration of the underlying cosmology of the Ming period. It allows a fascinating insight into the state religion.

The state religion

Yongle's capital was built slightly south of Khublai Kahn's city, but the parks of the Mongol rulers were retained. The new city of Beijing consisted of three sections: at the heart was the 'Forbidden City', then the imperial city where the officials and nobility dwelt, and to the south the outer city for the ordinary people. The central north–south axis runs through the heart of the Forbidden City whose three main halls are the only buildings crossing it.

The building of the Forbidden City commenced in 1406 and employed 200,000 workers. It was not fully completed until 1421, but the imperial court moved in before the outer walls and gates were finished. Even today the Forbidden City leaves visitors overawed at the size and elegance of the construction. The walls enclose an area of 250 acres consisting of many courtyards, and it has over 9,000 rooms. The defined lines and perfect proportions emphasize the grandeur of the buildings. It is an architectural complex unmatched in history.

Directly south of the Forbidden City along the meridian road is the Temple of Heaven. The complex consists of three sections: the Temple of Annual Prayers, the Temple of the Universe and the Altar of Heaven. The Temple of Annual Prayers (*Jiniandian*) is a circular structure built on a platform at three levels. The blue roof tiles symbolize heaven and the round shape reflects the belief that heaven was round, in contrast to the realm of the earth that was square. The temple has four central columns that represent the seasons, and there are twenty-four outer columns standing for the twelve months of the year and the twelve hours of the day. The Altar of Heaven (*Tiantan*) is a large, round, circular platform open at the centre. All its architectural elements have numerical significance in terms of correlating with the cosmos. The Temple of the Universe was a much smaller structure housing the tablets of heaven and the ancestors.

The sacrifice to Heaven was an elaborate ceremony that lasted two days, during which all traffic was stopped in the city. All doors and windows were closed as the Emperor proceeded from the Forbidden City to the temple. After fasting and donning special robes, he ascended the open altar to stand alone before Heaven. He would prostrate himself nine times, and offer his report before asking for help and blessings for the empire. Next the Emperor would go to the Temple of the Universe to offer sacrifices to his ancestors. He would then precede to the Altar of Heaven, where at midnight on the winter solstice he would sacrifice animals to his symbolic father *Tian* – 'Heaven'.

The significance of the winter solstice is that it was considered the point of the year when *yin* is at its height and *yang* at its lowest. This is the turning point of the year when the forces of *yang* increase and the sun increases again. The function of the Emperor at that moment was in his role as 'Son of Heaven' to facilitate the transition. A similar ritual took place during the summer solstice when the balance of *yang* began to move towards *yin*.

These state rituals illustrated that all power flows from a non-personal heaven and is transmitted through the Emperor with his 'Mandate of Heaven'. This is the same key role as played by the Shang kings in 1300 BC. These state rituals only ended with the fall of the last dynasty in 1911.

The significance of the Mandate of Heaven can be seen in an event that occurred in 1421 soon after Yongle's fleet had set sail. On the night of 9 May a violent storm broke over the Forbidden City and lightning struck the top of the newly constructed palace. Fire started in that building and spread to much of the city, burning down the Hall of Audiences and the ladies' apartments. Balls of fire appeared to travel down the Imperial Way along the very axis of the Forbidden City itself. Even the Emperor's throne was burned to cinders. The Emperor was deeply shaken by this event. Gavin Menzies writes:

> In his anguish he repaired the temple and prayed with great importunity, saying 'The God of Heaven is angry with me, and, therefore, has burned my palace; although I have done no evil act. I have neither offended my father, nor mother, nor have I acted tyrannically.'[1]

The people saw this as Heaven's disapproval of the grandiose schemes of the Emperor. Thousands of craftsmen had worked on the Forbidden City using vast numbers of trees. The renovation of the Grand Canal had put great pressure upon the people and the treasury. The fire coincided with an epidemic that killed 174,000 people in the province of Fujian alone. Yongle suffered a series of strokes, and seemed to become impotent. The Mongol leader Arughtai, perceiving China's weakness, refused to pay tribute. Yongle saw this as an opportunity to gain respect and took an army of almost a million men against the Mongols, but they just disappeared into the vast area of the steppe. On 12 August 1424, Emperor Yongle, now a broken man, died at the age of sixty-four.

Yongle's eldest son, Hongxi (1378–1425) ascended to the throne. He was a fat, sickly person who was distinctly not a military man, and one of his first acts in ascending to the throne was to issue an edict that all voyages of the treasure ships were to be stopped. When Zheng He's fleet returned home after two and a half years they were unaware of what had happened in the capital, and were probably expecting a hero's welcome. The voyage had been a great success, but the climate at home had changed. The sailors were spurned, the ships were left to rot in the docks. China turned in upon itself, concerned more with the threat from the Mongols than overseas exploration. As Menzies writes:

> One of the fascinating 'what ifs' of history is what would have happened had lightning not struck the Forbidden City on 9 May 1421, had fire not roared down the Imperial Way and turned the emperor's palace and throne to cinders... Would he [Yongle] have ordered Admiral Zheng He to continue his voyages? Would they have carried on establishing permanent colonies in Africa, America and Australia?... Would Buddhism rather than Christianity have become the religion of the New World?[2]

Buddhism during the Ming dynasty

As mentioned earlier, the number of ordained monks continually increased during the first century of the Ming dynasty. Two main schools were particularly active – the Linchi branch of Chan and Pure Land. Temples were divided into three categories: Chan devoted to meditation, Chiang concerned with instruction in the sutras, and Chiao concerned with the tantric rituals and ceremonies.

Harmonization

One of the outstanding features of Buddhism during the Ming period was the harmonization of the different traditions. It seems likely that many former Confucians accepted Buddhism, and this encouraged an interrelation between the two traditions. Yuan Hsien (1578–1657), for example, considered Buddha and Confucius to be great sages dealing with the inherent nature of humanity. Others tried to show that there was no inherent difference between their teachings. Confucius wrote that the ten thousand objects are united in oneself, while Buddhists taught that all sentient beings were related.

One of the leading figures in this process of harmonization was Chu Hung (born in 1535). He entered the monastic order when he was thirty-two years old after being married twice. He was taught by Tiantai and Chan masters. During his lifetime the Jesuit missionaries began to have an influence in China, and as will be shown later, Buddhism became their main antagonist. Chu Hung entered into the debate with the Roman Catholics, and wrote a thesis entitled *Four Chapters on the Explanation of Heaven*. He began to recognize the need for a more united Buddhist position and began to play a major part in the harmonization movement.

Chu Hung argued that in reciting and meditating on Amitabha Buddha, one should not only focus the mind on the name but also on the ultimate reality behind the name. Outside of the mind that does the meditation on Amitabha, there is no Amitabha. So, outside of the Buddha Amitabha that is meditated upon, there is no meditating mind. This comes to the Chan position that the meditating mind is the Buddha.

Chu Hung also encouraged the development of Buddhism among the laity through the practice of Pure Land. Through his writings many began to practise *nien-fo*, meditation on Amitabha, as well as following the moral principles in seeking to gain merit. As a result many people embraced Buddhism though they chose not to become monks.

Tibetan Buddhism

The Mongols had particularly supported Tibetan Buddhism, and as was shown in the previous chapter, they had installed the abbots of the Sakya monastery as having religious and political hegemony in the Tibetan region.

The Ming rulers continued the policy of the former Yuan

dynasty to support the abbots of all the great monasteries. As Kenneth Chen writes: 'The Ming Dynasty, and later the Manchu, undoubtedly patronized Lamaism out of one primary political motive – to use the high lamas of the Tibetan religion to help them maintain control over the Tibetans and Mongols.'[3] The Chinese emperors hoped that in this way they could continue to pacify the Tibetans and Mongols without the expense of military action.

Tibetan Buddhism was, however, popular in China. Emperor Zhengde (1506–21) was particularly interested in all things Tibetan, and he built a new temple in the Forbidden City to enable rituals to be performed by the *lamas*.

The Ming tombs

The Ming also revived the importance of ancestor worship at the tomb. One of Emperor Yongle's first acts in moving his capital to Beijing was to choose a site for an imperial cemetery. The site was a valley some 45 kilometres (30 miles) north-west of Beijing. This site is said to illustrate the best principles of *Feng Shui*. The tombs are set with the hills to the north and the plains to the south. They are reached by a single straight 'spirit road' that leads to the entrance of the first tomb. Stone carvings of various animals line the spirit road that has recently been renovated, and this makes an impressive entrance for modern tourists.

The tomb buildings are based on palace architecture. Emperor Yongle's tomb, one of only two that has been opened to the public, was restored in 1950. The Hall of Heavenly Favours is an exact replica of the largest hall in the Forbidden City. Sacrifices to the Emperor were held in the hall until 1924 when the ex-Emperor Pyi went into exile.

Matteo Ricci and the Jesuits

As we have seen, it was in the seventh century that Nestorian missionaries arrived in China from Persia and were received by the Tang Emperor. During the Yuan dynasty Dominican and Franciscan missionaries travelled along the Silk Route and established a presence in the north of China, but their endeavour had little impact. It was with the Portuguese seafarers that the next significant wave of Christian missionaries arrived in China. Francis Xavier led the first group of Roman Catholic missionaries to Asia, but despite his efforts he never received permission to enter China. He died on a small island near Macau within sight of the mainland. It was his successor, Matteo Ricci (1552–1610), who in 1583 received permission to live in Guangzhou, and later he was allowed to live in Beijing. Ricci was a dedicated scholar and spent many long years learning to read and write Chinese. He achieved such fluency that he was able to debate philosophy and ethics with Confucian scholars. This is all the more remarkable because this was achieved before dictionaries and linguistic training were available. He also memorized *The Four Books* of the Confucian canon, which was an accomplishment that only well-educated Chinese scholars achieved.

Matteo Ricci was born in Macerata, Italy, of a noble family. At the age of seventeen his father sent him to Rome to study law, but Ricci soon applied for admission to the Jesuit Order, into which he was received in 1571. He studied philosophy and mathematics under the well-known mathematician Christopher Klau, friend of Kepler and Galileo. He spent four years studying in India before going to China.

Ricci shared Xavier's belief that the key to success lay in the conversion of the Emperor, but it took him many years before he was invited to the capital in 1595. Ricci brought with him various European items that quickly gave him the status of a scholar among the Chinese elite. These included a glass prism, clocks and a telescope. What especially attracted the Chinese were the illuminated books that he brought. The Chinese had printed documents, but these only had austere woodblock illustrations. European books were beautifully bound with lavish illustrations. The pictures also had depth and perspective through the use of the vanishing-point. This was a technique that was unknown in China and was enthusiastically adopted by Chinese artists.

Initially Ricci and his co-worker Ruggeri dressed in the fashion of Buddhist monks with shaven heads, as they considered Buddhism to be the main religious tradition of China. However, after nine years, when he had gained a better understanding of the Chinese language, Ricci realized that the monks were not respected by the Confucian scholars. He therefore changed the manner of his dress to that of a Confucian scholar, wearing black silk robes and allowing his hair and beard to grow. He argued that Confucian teaching provided a moral foundation for Chinese society, and saw Christianity as a fulfilment of Confucianism. Gradually he adopted more and more Confucian ideas including their prejudice towards Daoist ideas. This change of role shows that his general attitude was one of accommodation to the Chinese culture. He realized that for the first time in history, Christianity was confronted with a civilization older and no less great than the Greek and Roman empires.

The name of God
Ricci also sought to explain Christianity in terms that would be accepted by the Chinese, but he was quickly faced with a problem. He realized, to his alarm, that the way he was presenting the doctrine struck some people as making Christianity appear similar to Islam and Judaism. Ricci therefore struggled with a common missionary problem of deciding how to simplify the presentation of a doctrine, without losing control of its central and definable core. He

faced a similar problem in translation as had the Buddhist missionaries centuries earlier. Does one use pre-existing Chinese words with non-Christian associations, or does one create new words? As was shown in Chapter 5, early Buddhists had adopted Daoist vocabulary in order to try to express Buddhist concepts, and only after several centuries, when Buddhist ideas had become more familiar, were they able to use loan-words from Sanskrit.

Likewise, Ricci was faced with the question of what term to use for the God of the Bible. As shown in previous chapters, the common terms used in the Confucian scriptures were *Tian* ('Heaven') and *Shang Di* ('Lord-on-high'). Ricci freely employed both these words, but if anything he had a preference for *Shang Di*. He also used the newly coined word *Tianzhu* ('Lord of Heaven') for the Christian God. In his book *The True Meaning of the Lord of Heaven* he equated God with *Shang Di*, and used the Confucian classics to prove that some of the basic concepts of Christianity were already found in the China of ancient times.[4]

The message of Jesus Christ was therefore told as follows:

> The Lord of Heaven thereupon acted with great compassion, descended to this world himself to save it, and experienced everything experienced by men. One thousand, six hundred and three years ago in the year Geng Shen, in the second year after Emperor Ai of the Han dynasty had adopted the reigning title Yuan Shou, on the third day following the winter solstice He selected a chaste woman who had never experienced sexual intercourse to be His mother, became incarnate within her and was born. His name was Jesus, the meaning of which is 'the one who saves the world'. He established His own teaching and taught for 33 years in the West. He then ascended again to heaven. These were the concrete actions of the Lord of Heaven... Unfortunately evil people, of a certain place, did not want to listen to or believe in Him. They took two sticks of wood and made a cross (the sign of the character ten); they nailed his hands and his feet and made him die on the cross.

Eventually it became evident that such an unfamiliar term as 'Lord of Heaven' caused confusion for their Chinese listeners. Other Jesuits later began to make the association that *Tian* and *Tianzhu* were identical, and that the preference for using *Tianzhu* was merely a matter of expediency because the term was less ambiguous. As Pantoja and de Ursis wrote in their *Apology* of 1616 (six years after Ricci's death):

> The Lord of Heaven (*Tianzhu*) is the Lord who has created heaven, earth and all things. The Lord of Heaven who is served in western countries is identical with (*ji*) Heaven that is worshipped in China. He is identical with the vast heaven Sovereign-on-High (*hao tian Shangdi*) to whom sacrifices are offered in China. It is only because in western languages we strive to make clear distinctions that we feel obliged to use the term *Tianzhu*. Therefore *Tian, Shangdi, Tianzhu* – they are one and the same.[5]

This association had a great impact upon Chinese scholars and many became converts. However, it is important to recognize the distinction between how the Jesuit missionaries and their Chinese converts understood the association. While the Jesuits were generally cautious in their association of *Tian* with the Christian God, for most Chinese scholars traditional connotations remained. As Zurcher writes:

> To converted literati, each and every one of whom had memorized at least the *Four Books* along with Zhu Xi's commentary, the acceptance of the Doctrine of the Lord of Heaven simply meant that *Tian* became more personalized, and that the concept of natural retribution became more concrete by the addition of some themes (all of which, incidentally, were well-known in their Buddhist forms: the judgement of the soul after death; heavenly rewards, and infernal punishment).[6]

The converts coming from a Confucian context retained much of their traditional world-view so what resulted can best be described as a 'Confucian Monotheism'.

The rites controversy

The term used for the name of God had been a subject of much debate, but one that was to become even more contentious was that of ancestor worship. This resulted from a dilemma facing any Confucian scholar who became a Christian. On the one hand, Christianity prohibited any acts of idolatry, and on the other, he had social and professional obligations to take part in a wide range of public rituals such as those to the patron deity of the city, the gods of the mountains and ancestors. Refusal to take part in these rites would bring disgrace or worse.

For the Jesuits an additional complication was the place of Confucius. In their whole approach Confucius had been seen as purely a great Chinese teacher and philosopher. The rites performed in the Confucian temple were therefore regarded as civil ceremonies that merely expressed respect and gratitude. Some aspects of the ritual certainly seemed to justify the view: the absence of overt prayers and the presence of inscribed wooden tablets rather than images. Thus, if the Christian scholar could keep in mind that he was just paying respect to the memory of a teacher, there would be no problem.

However, in some cases there was an undeniable religious character. One case was the cult of *Chenghuang*, which were a class of protective spirits who were essentially deified highly respected magistrates. In this rite the spirits of *Chenghuang* were explicitly invoked to provide protection. Some converts wanted to regard *Chenghuang* as minor deities subordinate to the Lord of Heaven, but it was feared this would lead to polytheism. A similar problem came with regard to the city gods and the gods of mountains and water. The Jesuits, in discussion with their converts during the period 1634–40, came up with an inventive approach.

The Jesuit missionary Aleni proposed that since the *Chenghuang* and city gods had to do with the protection of the city, they should be regarded as guardian angels. As the guardian angels had no authority of themselves, the believer should entrust their prayers to the *Chenghuang* with the request to transmit these to the Lord of Heaven. In order to make it clear that God is the ultimate authority, the inscription on the relevant tablet should read 'Deity who protects this city under the mandate of the Lord of Heaven'. Although attempts were made by Chinese converts to introduce Christianized *Chenghuang* rites, this was never realized.

The rites to ancestors were seen as a continuation of filial duties that were not done sufficiently when the ancestor was alive. Thus, the primary meaning of the rites to ancestors was to serve the dead as one served the living. The practice of erecting wooden tablets is an example of this. The tablet provided a focus to which people could bow, offer food or cry to express their loss. A key element of the resulting debate was whether the soul of the deceased stayed in the wooden tablet.

The rites to ancestors also had an important social function in teaching people about the harmony of the community and obedience to authority. This had essentially been the teaching of Confucius in order to bring about social stability, and as such it was encouraged to perpetuate Chinese culture and to maintain social order.

Hope for the future of Christianity

Ricci, in his study of the Confucian classics, became convinced that the Neo-Confucian teaching of Zhu Xi (described in Chapter 7) was a distortion of the original teaching of Confucius. In *The True Meaning of the Lord of Heaven*, published in 1604, Ricci sought to show that the ancient Chinese had believed in a creator God called *Shang*

Di. He criticized both the Daoist concept of *Wu* (non-being) and the Buddhist *gong* (emptiness). He argued that the Chinese term for 'heaven' is not impersonal and argues for the existence of the immortal soul separate from material creation. In this way he sought to deny the non-dualism of Chinese philosophy, while showing that Christian views are related to those of Confucius. Ricci therefore could speak of Christianity 'supplementing' the original teaching of Confucius. He also showed how self-cultivation could be achieved by the spiritual exercises taught by Ignatius Loyola, the founder of the Jesuit movement. Overall, his theology reflected the scholasticism of the later Middle Ages.

Ricci's own experience gave him eight reasons for hope with regard to Christianity in China. These he set down in a final letter to Francis Pasio:[7]

1. There had been miraculous progress in the face of immense difficulties.
2. Reason was much prized in China, and Christianity, as a reasonable religion, appealed to the intellect as well as the spiritual level.
3. The free circulation of books permitted a vast literary apostolate.
4. The Chinese, by virtue of their intelligence, were open to persuasion that not only were Western mathematics and astronomy no less than their own, but so likewise was Western theology.
5. He was convinced that from a study of their ancient beliefs they were essentially a pious people who had evolved a philosophy conforming to natural reason.
6. Peace, once established, would make Christianity more or less permanent in China.
7. By adapting themselves to Chinese psychology and etiquette, missionaries would be accepted as learned and holy men.

8. The system of Confucius provided an admirable ally against the idolatrous sects.

After writing these conclusions, Ricci began to make preparations for his own death. On the evening of 11 May 1610, Matteo Ricci closed his eyes and died.

*   *   *

Whatever the shortcomings of Ricci and his successors, one cannot but admire their attempt at an accommodation of the Christian gospel into the thinking of China.

However, not all the missionaries were so broad-minded, and the Dominican and Franciscan missionaries who returned to China after the Jesuits were shocked by this toleration. They considered the ancestor rites as genuine religious rituals that should not be practised by believing Christians. They protested to the Pope that this sort of practice should not be allowed to continue. In 1704, the Pope ruled in favour of the Dominicans and Franciscans, which, as will be explained in the next chapter, angered the Emperor of the time. In 1706 all missionaries were expelled from China apart from those who ignored the Papal decree.

The end of the Ming dynasty itself came suddenly. The last Ming Emperor, Chongzhen (reigned 1628–44), inherited a corrupt, inefficient administration, and when a severe famine occurred in 1628 the government was helpless. Bandit groups emerged all over the country, and the people revolted against the inept government. In April 1644, a powerful Manchu force advanced into the northeast of China, and the Emperor called what was to turn out to be the final council meeting of his administration. Some of the members of the council are said to have sat in helpless silence and some wept at the impending doom. When conflict finally came, the imperial troops either fled or surrendered. Chongzhen himself got drunk and ran around the palace ordering the women to kill themselves. He then went and hanged himself on a lotus tree in the grounds.

Further reading

Menzies, Gavin, *1421: The Year China Discovered the World*, London: Bantam, 2003.

Mugello, D. E. (ed.), *The Chinese Rites Controversy: Its History and Meaning*, Nettetal: Steyler Verlag, 1994.

Mungello, E. E., *The Forgotten Christians of Hangzhou*, Honolulu: University of Hawaii Press, 1994.

Criveller, G., *Preaching Christ in Late Ming China*, Taiwan: Ricci Institute, 1997.

Cronin, V., *The Wise Man From the West: Matteo Ricci and his mission to China*, Oxford: Collins, 1984. A very readable account of this great missionary.

Spence, J. D., *The Memory Palace of Matteo Ricci*, London: Faber & Faber, 1985. An examination of the way that Ricci tried to describe in print the basis of the Christian message.

DVD: *Temple of Heaven: One China, One Emperor, One God*, CBN, Inc., 2003, http://www.templeofheaven.net

Websites

Google Earth. The free Google Earth computer programme provides a fascinating perspective of the north–south axis of Beijing.

The Ricci Institute for Chinese–Western Cultural History. http://www.usfca.edu/ricci/

Ricci 21st Century Roundtable Database. A site dedicated to learning more about the history of Christianity in China, administered by the Ricci Institute, located at the University of San Francisco. http://ricci.rt.usfca.edu/

1421. A website based upon the controversial book *1421*, which gives additional evidence, maps and news of the '1421 team'. http://www.1421.tv

Chapter 10

THE RULE OF THE MANCHUS AND THE GROWING IMPACT OF THE WEST

The Qing dynasty (1644–1911)

The victorious Manchus were Jurchens from south-east Manchuria, and descendants of the Jin who had ruled northern China in the twelfth century. Unlike the Mongols, who lived on the open steppe engaging in frequent warfare, the Manchus were hunters and farmers. Although they never made up more than 2 per cent of the population in China, they managed to rule by creating a highly authoritarian and centralized empire. They did this by retaining the Ming administrative system, but putting it under tight supervision by the Manchus themselves. Once again China was ruled by alien forces, but it was to be the growing European presence along the coast that was gradually to become the dominant factor in the future of China. The Europeans would eventually bring the Manchu rule to an end. However, the period of the Manchu rule was to become another high point in Chinese civilization.

The rule of the Manchus

The dynastic name 'Qing' was chosen because of its meaning – 'pure'. The first Emperor was Shunzhi (reigned 1644–61), who came to the throne when he was only six, and his uncle Dorghon was regent. Dorghon concentrated upon consolidating the Qing occupation in the north of China, and on his death Shunzhi assumed full power. He was a conscientious young man who learned Chinese so that he could read the imperial documents himself and not be dependent on the Chinese Mandarins.

The Manchus treated the Chinese as a subject race and sought to preserve their own distinct identity. Manchus and Chinese were segregated and intermarriage was banned. They expelled all Chinese from Manchuria and it was here that the Manchus spent their summers. The Manchus continued using their own language, which effectively meant that many of their documents were not available to the Chinese. In Beijing, all Chinese people were expelled from the northern city (making it the 'Forbidden City') and were forced to live in the Chinese quarter in the south. Like the Mongols before them, the Manchus confiscated hundreds of thousands of acres of farmland in north China to support their huge armies.

The social distinction between the Manchus and the Chinese was shown in various cultural ways. In 1645, it was decreed that any man who did not cut his hair in the Manchu way and start growing a *queue* (plait) would be executed. This hairstyle became a symbol of the loyalty of the Chinese to the Manchu rule, and so for many Chinese it was a hated symbol of foreign domination. The Chinese were also required to wear Manchu clothes rather than the style used during the Ming dynasty. Foot binding was still practised by the Chinese women, but it was banned among the Manchu women. The Chinese were not trained as a military force while the Manchus cultivated an image of themselves as tough warriors.

Emperor Shungzhi was sympathetic to the Jesuits, but when he fell in love with a concubine of Mongol birth named Xiao Xian, he became more interested in Buddhism and Chinese culture. Sadly, she died when only twenty-two, and the distraught Emperor tried to follow suit, and his health deteriorated. He died of smallpox less than five months after Xiao Xian. His son Kangxi (1654–1722) was the first of three remarkable Qing rulers who were to give China over a century of peace and prosperity. All three of these Manchu rulers presented themselves as both protectors of China's cultural heritage and as Manchu military leaders.

Kangxi (reigned 1661–1722)

Kangxi came to the throne when he was only eight years of age and was to reign longer than any other Chinese Emperor. Kangxi was a gifted leader, and on reaching the age of fourteen he removed the chief regent and assumed full powers. When a major revolt broke out in 1673, the eighteen-year-old took personal control and, although it took eight years to bring the rebellion to a conclusion, he learned many important lessons.

Kangxi softened the policies of segregation that had been introduced. He prohibited the further confiscation of Chinese land and lowered taxes, thus producing a prosperous agricultural base for the empire. He reduced corruption by raising official salaries and encouraged Chinese arts and crafts. He not only became familiar with the Chinese literati culture, but also became interested in European science and technology. He was hospitable to the Jesuit missionaries at court, and appointed Jesuits to direct the imperial board of astronomy. The story is told that the Emperor became sick with malaria, and was cured by the French missionaries through the use of quinine. In 1692 he issued an edict of toleration of Christianity as long as converts continued to perform ancestral rites, the position argued for by Matteo Ricci discussed in the previous chapter. He also gave the missionaries a piece of land inside the Forbidden City, and in 1703 he gave them permission to erect a church that was completed ten years later and came to be known as Pei Tang.

During the reign of Kangxi, the Manchu continued to expand their territory. In 1683, the island of Taiwan was acquired, and over 100,000 Chinese emigrated to create a booming frontier community. In the 1690s Kangxi personally led two military campaigns to re-establish dominance in Central Asia. As we have seen, Tibet had ties with China for many centuries, and like Korea and other neighbouring states, it acquiesced to tributary status. In 1717, the Qing invaded Tibet and conquered Lhasa in 1720, but they did not interfere greatly in Tibetan affairs, allowing the local leaders to do most of the actual governing. Kangxi granted the fifth *Bainqen* the title of *Bainqen Erdini*, and afterwards it became a regulation that the titles of *Dalai Lama* and *Bainqen* must be granted by the central government. The Chinese government established a Ministry of National Affairs to deal with all matters concerning ethnic groups. Emperor Kangxi managed to consolidate China's vast territory, with its different nationalities, into a prosperous and united country.

Kangxi realized the importance of state rituals, developed under the Ming, for any ruler of China. The ceremonies at the Altars of Heaven, the Earth, the Sun and the Moon placed the Emperor within the Chinese cosmology of his predecessors. Each major ritual had its own distinctive colour: blue for offerings to Heaven, yellow for the Earth, red for the Sun and pale blue for the Moon. The Emperor also officially commenced the agricultural year by ritually ploughing furrows as part of the sacred rite at the Altar of Agriculture. These state ceremonies united the vast nation under the ancient notion of the Mandate of Heaven.

Kangxi, and subsequent Emperors, retained the shamanistic practices of their homelands and they were patrons of Tibetan Buddhism. Kangxi constructed many temples. He also showed a marked interest in the teaching of the Jesuits and in the technological and artistic skills that they brought with them to China. The Jesuits supplied the court with maps, instruments and theses on mathematics. Giuseppe Castiglione (1688–1766), whose Chinese name was Lang Shining, was an extraordinary painter who was skilled in painting in both European and Chinese styles.

Kangxi left an extraordinary personal record of his life in his palace documents, in which he comes across as a humane man with a strong sense of duty. He made a conscious effort to befriend all the faiths with which he came into contact. There have been differing interpretations of his interest in Christianity. Garnet argues that Kangxi had no basic interest in Christianity, and only saw the missionaries as being useful to him for their technical and artistic skills.[1] If Garnet is correct, it raises the question of why Kangxi become involved in the so-called Rites Controversy.

Kangxi was certainly knowledgeable of the criticism of the Jesuit position discussed in the previous chapter. He continually insisted upon Ricci's stand on ancestor worship and Confucian rites. It is also probable that he objected to the interference of the foreign Pope into affairs in his country. On 19 April 1707, Kangxi issued the following edict:

> Henceforth those who do not follow the rules of Ricci (Li Madou) [on Chinese rites] are not permitted to stay in China. If because of these practices the Pope forbids you to continue spreading your religion, simply remain in China since you have renounced the world. I would suggest that you stay even if the Pope denounces your continuation of Ricci's ways.[2]

There is some possibility that Kangxi may have been a Christian, but the evidence is small. Bishop Ting, in the twentieth century, quoted Kangxi as writing the following words:[3]

> With his task done on the cross,
> His blood forms itself into a streamlet.
> Grace flows from West Heaven in long patience:
> Trials in four courts.
> Long walks at midnight,

Thrice denied by friends before the cock crew twice,
Six-footer hanging at the same height as two thieves.
It is a suffering that moves the whole world and all ranks.
Hearing his seven words makes all souls cry.

Even so, Kangxi never became a Roman Catholic. This has led at least one Protestant to suggest that he could have become 'a true Christian believer':

The Emperor appreciated the works of the Jesuits who had come to love and admire his person and he applauded their sincerity and accorded recognition for their contributions. They won his heart and his confidence, but over time, he became increasingly disillusioned over the dividing views of the various sects of the Catholic orders and was more and more suspicious of the motives of the Papal authority. There were instances of him coming close to conversion by the Jesuits as he toggled to and fro but finally deciding against the motives of those who had sent them. At times, the Jesuits sincerely believed that he would allow himself to be converted, but although this never happened, many of his children were baptized and made public acknowledgement of their faith in the Christian God... Despite all, although he was never catechized, he was not deterred in his belief concerning the only one God of Heaven that he had learned from the ancestors which he highly respected. And he gratefully embraced the eternal salvation of Christ which he categorically declared in his poems, that he had come to receive. Emperor Kangxi was never a converted Catholic, but by evangelical Christian definition, his belief and confession made him a saved believer of Christ.[4]

This may be somewhat of an exaggeration of the situation. Whatever the facts, Kangxi granted the missionaries protection and by 1700 there were an estimated 300,000 Christians in China.

Yongzheng (reigned 1723–35)

Kangxi's later years were clouded by arguments about succession, and it was only on his deathbed that he named his fourth son Yongzheng (1678–1735) as Emperor. Yongzheng moved quickly and eliminated possible rivals, and throughout his reign he used spies to crush any hint of revolt. He held a tight control on the administration, but operated fairly and rewarded hard work and honesty. As a result he set the state on a sound footing, and banned any sort of hereditary servile status that resulted in local demeaning castes. Like his father, he took on the role of the Chinese scholar and was skilled in calligraphy, and a connoisseur of ancient bronzes, jades and porcelains. Like his grandfather, he was a devout Chen Buddhist. He died in 1735, officially of natural causes, but some rumours said he had been murdered.

Qianlong (reigned 1736–95)

The reign of Qianlong was a watershed in the Qing dynasty at which time China was the most wealthy and populous nation in the world. After a period of consolidation, he embarked on a policy of expansion. Tibet was brought fully under Chinese control in 1751 following a display of military prowess accompanied by favours to the Dalai Lama. Between 1756 and 1757 Chinese armies advanced through all of central Asia, and incorporated modern Xinjiang into the empire. Korea, Burma, Thailand, Vietnam and even the Philippines recognized the dominance of China. Within this cosmopolitan empire, official texts that were already in Chinese and Manchu were often written in Tibetan, Turkish and even Arabic.

Like his father, Qianlong was a lover of Chinese literature and arts. He was good at calligraphy and painting. He invited scholars and artists to court, and built many palaces and buildings in various architectural styles. These included a replica of the Tibetan Potala (the Dalai Lama's imposing palace in Lhasa). The Jesuits were commissioned to build a summer palace in European style. Qianlong was a strong man and a hard worker, like his grandfather.

Overall the Qing were conservative in their attitudes, introducing laws against behaviour that they considered deviant. Official injunctions were frequently issued against novels or plays, but despite this, it was a period of some of the most creative Chinese art and literature. The novel *Dream of Red Mansions*, written near the end of the eighteenth century, is one of the world's literary masterpieces.

Contact with Europeans

During the reigns of Kangxi, Yongzheng and Qianlong China advanced politically and culturally, but the world was changing. As Patricia Ebrey writes:

> The balance of world power slowly shifted in the eighteenth century without anyone in China taking much notice. Until 1700 China's material culture had been unrivalled; its standard of living was among the best in the world, and inventions flowed more commonly from east to west than vice versa. Yet by the nineteenth century, China found itself outmatched in material and technological resources by western nations.[5]

Europeans had been coming to trade at the south Chinese ports since the close of the Ming period in the sixteenth century. First it was the Spanish and Portuguese, but in the seventeenth century it was the Dutch who dominated the trade and later the British. The British allowed most trade to be handled by government-recognized monopolies such as the British East India Company, and these were staffed by young men eager to make their fortunes by trade with Asia.

In order to keep foreigners from disrupting Chinese society too much, foreigners were only allowed to trade in

Guangzhou (Canton), and were obliged to reside in a special quarter and stay only as long as business required. In Britain the demand for Chinese silk and porcelain was growing, as was the taste for tea. From the first five cases of tea imported to Britain in 1684, this rose to a weight of 400,000 pounds in 1720, and an incredible 23 million pounds by 1800. As the Chinese did not want to buy British goods, this meant that tea had to be paid for with silver. British traders were therefore eager to find a way to balance the trade deficit.

There was also a marked shift in attitude going on in Europe. The seventeenth century Jesuit missionaries had sent back reports of the wonders of Chinese society, but growing contact was painting a different picture of an out-dated feudal state. The industrial revolution was producing new inventions, and generating a growing self-confidence. The European Enlightenment had influenced philosophers like Rousseau and Hegel who emphasized social evolution. Europe began to perceive itself as the leading civilization and China was relegated to a subordinate position. The British government therefore began to make demands upon China to remove trade barriers and abandon the restrictions it placed upon traders.

In 1793 Lord George McCartney, cousin to the king and former ambassador to Chennai (Madras), was sent as an envoy to Emperor Qianlong, charged with opening British trade relations with China. He took with him 84 scientists, musicians and interpreters together with 600 cases packed with Western technological items as gifts for the Emperor. McCartney was immediately faced with the problem of getting an audience. The Emperor would not receive anyone without proper signs of respect, and Lord McCartney was not willing to 'kowtow' (a formal bow that involved kneeling and touching the forehead to the floor). McCartney was eventually given special dispensation to merely bend down on one knee. Qianlong, however, was not impressed by the gifts that the British had brought and considered that they already had all they needed. This encounter well illustrates the wide cultural gulf that separated Europe from China at this time.

The failure of McCartney's mission merely hardened British attitudes towards China, and increased the likelihood of further conflicts. The first encounter was the so-called 'Opium War' of 1840–42. The British were looking for an item that they could trade with the Chinese and so develop the market potential. Following the British conquest of most of India, opium became a potential trade item and it was shipped to China. The Chinese had traditionally used opium for medicinal purposes, but now it was used as a recreational narcotic. The Chinese authorities were well aware of the harmful effects of smoking opium, so in 1800 they banned both the importation and domestic production of opium. Even so, through Chinese smugglers, the British were still able to expand the trade to such an extent that the trade deficit was reversed.

In the 1830s the Chinese introduced further laws to ban the trade in opium, many Chinese were arrested, and additional restrictions were imposed upon British traders. Commercial interests in England were pushing for war, and in 1840 a British expeditionary force left India with sixteen warships and thirty-one other vessels. The Chinese blockaded Guangzhou, but the British merely bypassed this port and went north to Ningbo and Tianjin. The Chinese could no longer refuse to negotiate. They had to concede Hong Kong as a British colony, pay the costs of the British expedition and allow direct communications between officials of each country. The arrangements did not satisfy either country, and a second expedition was sent in 1841, this time with 10,000 soldiers. Britain managed to occupy several strategic coastal cities including Shanghai. When the foreign forces pressed forward to attack the ancient capital of Nanjing, the Chinese had no option but to sue for peace.

In Chinese eyes this is still seen as a blatant case of international bullying. The moral aspect also made it more difficult for the Chinese to appreciate that the European nations had anything of value for them. Even today in China, students are aware of this encounter, and as an Englishman I have apologized for what was done by a so-called Christian nation. On one occasion my apology was greeted with applause. I took the opportunity to express my hope that as China once again becomes a world power, it will learn the lesson. The students in the auditorium fell silent!

Trade in opium was actually legalized in 1860 and remained a major item of trade until the end of the century. It is outside the scope of this book to describe other encounters between China and Europe, but suffice it to say that each one was to the disadvantage of China.

In the European race to colonize the world, China represented the last prize in the Far East. The Opium War was designed to open China, along with its vast markets and resources, for exploitation. The war itself did physically open China, but the unequal treaty had major social and religious repercussions in China.

Protestant mission

The previous historical background is important if the reader is to appreciate the issues that were to face the early Protestant missionaries, and also the Chinese reaction to the Europeans and their religion.

Robert Morrison

The first Protestant missionary to arrive in China was Robert Morrison (1782–1834), who was sent by the London Missionary Society. The British East India Company banned missionaries from entering China, so Morrison had to travel via the USA and entered the American trading port

at Canton (Guangzhou) in 1807. He settled in the area designated for American traders and immediately began the
task of studying the language. His ability in the language
soon became evident and then the British East India
Company employed him as a translator. However, this was
a role that meant he often bore the brunt of much of the
Chinese ill will towards the Europeans. Morrison married
in 1809, but his wife Mary suffered from ill health.

Although the earlier Roman Catholic missionaries had
translated portions of the Bible, no attempt had been made
to produce a complete Bible. As Protestant missionaries
placed greater importance upon people being able to read
the Bible in their own language, Morrison started the major
task of translating the whole Bible into Chinese. He completed this in 1819, but today it is generally considered that
the quality of the translation was not good. Morrison struggled with the same issues as the Jesuits missionaries of
earlier centuries. One of the contentious issues was what
term should be used for 'God'. For the Protestants the
choice was seen as being between *Shen* (literally 'spirit')
and *Shang Di* ('High Lord'). Generally, opinions divided
along ideological and national lines: the American missionaries preferred *Shen* and the British *Shang Di*. *Shen* was
favoured by the more conservative missionaries who were
not convinced that the Chinese had any early knowledge of
a creator God. Therefore, there was no point in searching
the Confucian Classics for a term equivalent to any notion
of biblical monotheism. *Shen* appeared to be a more
neutral term like 'gods' and 'God' in English.

It will be remembered that the Jesuits had preferred
Shang Di, but this was later overruled by the Vatican in
favour of *Tian Zhu* ('Lord of Heaven'). Two editions of the
New Testament were finally published in 1850 using
different names for God. One of the few great Protestant
scholars of the period was James Legge (1815–97), who
translated many of the Chinese Classics into English

between 1861 and 1872. He advocated the term *Shang Di* for 'God', so that Chinese Protestants today call on *Shang Di*, while Roman Catholics continue to use *Tian Zhu*. However, the most widely used Bibles in China now use *Shen*.

Converts came only slowly, and by the time Morrison died in 1834 he had baptized only ten Chinese. It is interesting to explore what attracted these early converts to Protestant Christianity. They were tradesmen and farmers who had received a few years of formal literary training. They were therefore not part of the Neo-Confucian scholar-elite, nor were they among the vast, illiterate peasant majority. Their Confucian studies had given them a concern for ethical conduct, but neither Confucian self-cultivation nor the rituals common to folk beliefs satisfied their search for moral transformation. Christian monotheism and pietist teaching of being 'born again' provided them with a fulfilling answer.

Liang Fa (1789–1855) was one of the first and he was baptized by Milne, a companion of Morrison. In 1816 Liang Fa became the first ordained Chinese Protestant evangelist. He had worked with a Western printing company and so was interested in producing tracts in Chinese. He himself wrote and printed a booklet, *The Benevolent Words to Advise the World (Quan Shi Liang Yan)* that was distributed to scholars coming to Guangzhou to take the civil service examinations. The tract shows Liang's concern about the general immorality in Chinese society, disgust with the decadence of Buddhist monks and a denunciation of image worship. It also had a strong apocalyptic emphasis. This was the means by which Hong Xiuquan was introduced to Christianity in 1836. As we shall see later, Hong went on to found a religious and political movement which was to throw China into turmoil for more than a decade.

The Catholics initially cooperated with Morrison, but as more Protestant missionaries arrived after 1860 the old disagreements arose. Taoists, Buddhists and Confucians were seen to coexist, so when the Chinese saw Christians from different denominations attacking each other they were confused and perplexed. For the general population the theological differences between Catholics and the various Protestant denominations were completely incomprehensible, and they could see no more than differences in external appearances.

Catholic missionaries, as a rule, stayed in their job until the end of their days, leading a celibate life. Rome allotted the various missionary orders distinct territories, which became Vicariates when they had reached a certain degree of maturity. They saw a growing numbers of native priests. Eventually, in Jiangsu, Sichuan and Guangdong Provinces at least 10 per cent of the population were Roman Catholics, while in Hunan Province the figure was 1 per cent or less.

For the Chinese the number of Protestant mission societies was bewildering. By 1905 there were sixty-three separate organizations. Missionaries often came for limited periods and sometimes joined other mission societies. Sometimes they ceased to be missionaries in order to enter a diplomatic career, take up other jobs or just return home. Most were married and in the early years lived a comfortable life in or near the open ports. They dressed in the European style, as did other foreigners.

Hudson Taylor

A major change occurred with Hudson Taylor and the founding of the China Inland Mission. The story has been told by many writers, and in most detail in the six-volume biography of Hudson Taylor.[6] He first came to China in 1854 under the auspices of the China Evangelization Society, but was disgusted with their inefficiency and resigned. On his return to the UK he founded a new inter-denominational missionary society, which was based upon so-called 'faith' principles. He returned to China in 1866 with twenty-two recruits and a new vision of how mission should be pursued. He advocated a policy that the missionaries should seek to adapt as much as possible to Chinese culture, and so CIM missionaries wore Chinese attire, and at times even had their hair styled in the *queue*.

One notable difference with the CIM from previous missions was that their primary concern was evangelization. They therefore rejected many of the social projects that were becoming important within denominational missions. Nevertheless, they did establish some mission hospitals and schools. They also adopted the so-called 'Three-Self principle' advocated by the Anglican missionary leader Henry Venn. They considered that new churches should be self-supporting, self-governing and self-propagating. Another notable difference with his strategy was the way Hudson Taylor was willing to recruit many unmarried women as missionaries, and they were to become a major element in the later Protestant missionary movement around the world.

Issues facing the Chinese converts

The military and diplomatic battles fought between the Europeans and Chinese between 1858 and 1860 not only allowed foreign citizens the right to travel but the right for missionaries to spread Christianity. This allowed the Roman Catholic missionaries to return inland for the first time since they left in 1724. Although the Catholic Christians had tended to go underground during the period, they had fared well and in Shanxi Province alone there were an estimated 20,000 members. The Franciscans claimed ownership of properties that had been seized in the previous century. The majority of Protestant missionaries arrived a little later in the 1870s and immediately faced the devastating famine of 1876–79. Both Protestants and Catholic missions spent large amounts on relief, which was gratefully received but did not lead to many converts.

It was at this time that another issue was to emerge: should Chinese Christians pay the customary local ritual subscriptions? The French had obtained an agreement from central government that Chinese Christians need not make any payment for the temple festival. It was argued that Christians should not be expected to pay for these expenses as they did not take part in the rituals and anyway they had the expense of paying for their own buildings and leaders. However, the situation was more complex as local taxation involved the support not only of local rituals, but also public works and support of local officials. In 1862, the French minister stated his understanding of local taxation as including 'wasteful' expenses, like temple festivals and opera performances that no Christian need pay, and 'useful' ones for road works, bridge-building and welfare. He suggested that the breakdown between the two would be something like 40 per cent 'useful' and 60 per cent 'wasteful'. Although this proposal was accepted by central Government, it was often ignored at local level. Conflicts continued to emerge between Christians and non-Christians over temple tax. Catholic missionaries often claimed treaty rights for their people and involved diplomats in the disputes.

Protestant missionaries arriving later had fewer converts and took a different approach. They did not claim treaty rights for their Christian converts, but saw persecution as a trial of their faith. Speaking to CIM missionaries in 1886, Hudson Taylor argued that Christians were to patiently bear persecution and they would conquer by their example.

Another issue facing Chinese Christians was their perspective of civilization and future development. The educated Chinese looked back to a great past, but one that was becoming increasingly irrelevant. The nineteenth-century missionary saw a brighter future arising from the ashes of revolution in France and social change elsewhere. China was reliant mainly on agriculture, the West on industrialization. What was the future for China, and how could the Christian message help them in their situation?

The social status of the missionary was another problem. Could he assign to himself a rank equal, or even higher, than that of the official he happened to deal with? Extraterritoriality was a difficult problem for the Chinese, in that it allowed missionaries to enjoy many privileges. They also intervened in law cases involving their converts. Many Chinese converts were suspected as converting because of the advantage of having an influential patron.

The educated classes ceaselessly attacked Christianity. In Hunan, a book with the title *Bixie Jishi* was published in the early 1860s which listed facts and arguments against 'the evils to be beware of' in Christianity. The unknown author of the *Bixie Jishi* was certainly concerned about the fate of China. He may have wanted simply to present a solid piece of research, possibly unaware of the propaganda value of the treatise. The book shows how the West looked when seen through the eyes of a Chinese commoner. It never received a response from those it attacked. Excerpts of the book were printed and its content appeared on posters in the provincial capitals, during times of the annual examinations when it was likely to increase tensions already near boiling point.

In 1869, French missionaries had erected their cathedral on the site of an old temple. The orphanage that the sisters ran in its vicinity was under suspicion by the local people for its high walls and utter secrecy. When thirty-four of their children died in a sudden epidemic, rumours spread that the sisters had killed the children in order to make medicines from their eyes and hearts. Crowds threatened to break into the convent. When the Magistrate appeared unable to control the crowds, the Sisters called on the French Consul for help. While arguing with the Magistrate, the Consul shot and killed one of the Magistrate's men. Chaos broke out: the crowd killed the Consul, broke into the convent and murdered ten nuns. They opened the new graves and exhumed the children. Two priests also lost their lives, the cathedral was torched and four other churches were destroyed.

The Chinese government was extremely embarrassed by these events, and some of the highest officials were sent to investigate the facts. France asked for a personal apology by the Emperor. France accepted the apology and waived the sentence of capital punishment originally pronounced upon the perpetrators, and the case was closed. However, China had suffered a humiliation unprecedented in its history.

Religious rebellions

Until about 1860, the government did not consider the foreigners along the coast a major threat to the Qing dynasty. They were much more concerned about the many religious movements that were occurring throughout the vast empire.

The White Lotus sect was another millenarian movement advocating the coming Maitreya Buddha. As with previous movements, it appealed to poor peasants by promising a new world order. It was founded by Ho-shen (1750–99). It was particularly difficult for the government to quell, as the forces were entrenched in the hilly areas of Hubei, Sichuan and Shannxi provinces. Several hundred forts were constructed and the local people were organized into militia. Eventually the rebels were starved of food and supplies. In the film *Once Upon a Time in China 2*, Jet Li stars as the hero fighting against the White Lotus rebels.

In 1813, the Eight Trigrams movement arose not far from Beijing itself, seizing several cities in the north of China and even penetrating the Forbidden City. Some 70,000 people died before the rebellion was halted, but this was small compared to the Taiping Rebellion.

The Taiping Rebellion (1851–64)

The most notorious religious uprising became known as the Taiping Rebellion (*Taiping* meant 'The Heavenly Kingdom of Great Peace'). It shook the Chinese Empire to its core and effectively brought to an end the imperial history of China. The Taiping Rebellion illustrates the usual pattern of increasing social stress, an emerging prophetic figure and then a syncretistic form of religion. In this case, Chinese peasants took ideas from the Bible, and applied them to their situation to seek a new social order.

Hong Xiuquan was a Hakka born in 1814 about thirty miles from the port of Guangzhou. He came from a peasant family who worked hard so that he could study to gain academic qualifications. At sixteen he tried to pass the prefectural examinations, but he failed, as he did on two subsequent occasions. During the times of his examinations he heard a foreign evangelist preaching and received a set of nine tracts. After failing for a third time, Hong had a nervous breakdown.

The tract that Hong had been given in about 1836 was entitled 'Good Words to Admonish the Age' and it encouraged the reader to believe in God and Jesus Christ, to obey the Ten Commandments and never worship demons. Hong was attracted by the monotheism of Christianity and its moral principles. In 1843, when he failed his examination for a government job for the fourth time, Hong exploded in rage at the Manchu domination of China. He read a translation of the Bible, which told the story of how a chosen group of people rebelled against their rulers with God's help. Hong had a few months of instruction with the Protestant missionary Issachar T. Roberts in Canton in 1847.

It was during this time that Hong claimed to have had visions and in one of these he was taken into heaven where he appeared before a venerable old man with a golden beard who identified himself as the Creator. The old man complained to Hong about two things: the widespread worship of demons and the fact that Confucius had failed to teach the true doctrine. In another vision, Hong met a middle-aged man, who addressed him as younger brother. This man, whom he later claimed was Jesus Christ, instructed him on how to kill demons. God commissioned Hong as his second son, to go into the world and bring China back to the worship of the true God.

> God had a heavenly wife, and Jesus Christ, who as God's son played his part in the family, had also his own heavenly wife. When Hong was in Heaven, Jesus' wife, a kindhearted woman, was like a mother to Hong, and exerted her modifying influence on Christ when He was angry with Hong for not learning his biblical lessons well. Altogether heaven was a beautiful place with beautiful maidens and angels, with heavenly music and a heavenly wife for Hong, who was understandably reluctant to follow God's command and go back to earth for his mission, though he had eventually to obey.[7]

In 1843 he baptized his cousin Hong Jen Kan who in turn baptized him. Hong Jen Kan was to play an important part in the movement, together with his friend Feng Yun Shan. Hong removed the idols from his and his colleagues' schoolrooms, which caused him to lose his position as teacher in a village. Hong and Feng, with two others, left the village and travelled through the south of the Empire. Many famine-stricken peasants, workers, and miners were attracted to the new faith. The converts believed that God had ordered them to destroy Manchu rule and set up a new Christian brotherhood. As Hong gained more followers, he instructed them to give up opium and alcohol, end footbinding and prostitution, and destroy idols and ancestral tombs. As the number of converts increased, Hong formed a group known as *Pai Shang Di Hui* ('God Worshippers Society').

The God Worshippers were, however, attacked by local people led by the gentry, and so they organized themselves as a military force. The Taiping ranks swelled from a ragged band to several thousands, and finally to more than 1 million disciplined troops. New visions were given of the battle and the ultimate victory that would bring peace and happiness.

> Holding the three-foot sword in hand, I consolidate the
>   mountains and rivers.
> Within the four seas all are one family, all in harmonious
>   union.
> I capture all the demons and return them to the web of the
>   earth;
> Collecting the remaining evil ones, I drop them into the net
>   of heaven.
> The east, west, south, and north venerate the Sovereign
>   supreme;
> Sun, moon, stars, and constellations join in the song of
>   triumph.
> The tigers roar, the dragons sing, the world is full of light.
> With great peace and unity, what happiness there shall be.[8]

The first clash with the government forces was singularly successful, and they celebrated the victory with a public ceremony of prayer and thanksgiving. In March 1853 they conquered Nanjing, and then many other cities of the region. The movement was, however, plagued with dissent, which led to the murder of some of the army commanders. The Taiping threat to traditional Chinese thought led to loyal Chinese joining the government forces to quell the rebellion. By July 1864, the Taipings had been reduced to the control of only the city of Nanjing, which was surrounded. Hong refused to flee and on 1 June 1862 he died at the age of fifty, after a lingering illness of twenty days, possibly after taking poison. Hong's son was placed upon the throne, but he was never more than a figurehead. The fall of Nanjing led to a terrible slaughter with some 100,000 men being killed in three days.

Missionaries initially had little contact with the movement, but when they finally did, they were appalled. Charles Corwin writes:

> The rebels were resorting to violence. The Scriptures they applied were misinterpreted, distorted, taken out of context; these revolutionaries were submitting not to God but to their visible leader, Hong Xiuquan, who claimed to be a younger brother of Jesus and recipient of direct revelations from God.[9]

The movement was a curious blend of Christian and Confucian ideas.[10] It insisted upon reverence for God, while stressing filial piety. Jesus was the Son of God, but Hong was the second Son who had received a new heavenly mandate. They preached the brotherhood of all men, but also held to social hierarchy in which the ancient practices of *li* were important. They offered animal sacrifices to God, but not the traditional Chinese offerings of rice, tea or wine. They observed baptism and the Sabbath, but used flags as a symbol and not the cross. Several Daoist and Buddhist elements were incorporated into their ceremonies such as the use of drums, fire-crackers and cakes.

The distinctive Christian ideas accepted by the Taiping were respect and equality for women, and acceptance of monogamy. It was as a result of this that many women fought in the Taiping Rebellion. Another concept was a communal lifestyle, especially related to the use of land. However, Christ's teachings about forgiveness, humility and love for one another were omitted. If this had not been so, much of the violence and destruction might not have occurred.

The Taiping Rebellion lasted for 20 years, and during that time 20–30 million people died as a direct result of the conflict, and the total population of China declined by over

60 million because of the famines that occurred as a consequence of the conflict.

The reasons for the emergence of these religious movements can be briefly summarized as follows:

- The continuing anti-Manchu sentiment among the Chinese populace.
- Increasing taxation needed because the opium trade had badly affected China's balance of payments.
- There was enormous growth in population in the nineteenth century. From 1800 to 1850 the population of China increased from 300 million to 400 million, which placed great pressure upon agricultural production.
- Perhaps the most significant factor was that the introduction of Western ideologies and religions into Chinese society had caused a large number of Chinese people to abandon their traditional beliefs. Many therefore were willing to accept teaching that drew together new Western ideas with ancient Chinese patterns.

Islamic movements

At the same time, the Manchu dynasty was faced with Islamic movements in the north-west of the country. These date from the late eighteenth century, when a number of Naqshbandi *shaikhs* led a *jihad* against the Chinese Emperor from what is now called Uzbekistan, and they found support among the Muslims in Xinjiang Province. Ruthven comments:

> In response to the sinicizing policies of the Manchu emperors in the nineteenth century, the Chinese Muslims became increasingly assertive of their identity. The New Sect appeared after the return from the Hajj of Ma Ming Hsin, a *shaikh* of the Jahriya branch of the Naqshbandiya, which traces its spiritual

descent from Ali and practises the vocal *dhikr*, increasing group self-consciousness and solidarity. The New Sect and its affiliated branches appear to have been behind every Muslim rebellion in China down to the present century, including two major revolts which shook the Manchu empire. The first, led by Ma Hua Lung, lasted from 1862 to 1877 and affected most of Kansu and Shensi provinces; the second, led by Tu Wen Hsin, who took the Muslim name Sultan Suleiman, established a Muslim state which ruled half the province of Yunan. One of the leaders of the Yunan rebellion, Ma Te-hsin, was the first scholar to translate the Quran into Chinese.[11]

While these struggles were occurring, the Emperors became younger and younger, so that they had no control and little real power. In 1862, Cixi secured the throne for her son Tongzhi (reigned 1862–75), and for the next fifty years she was to rule China from behind the curtain. She was uneducated and opposed to any type of reform or modernization that might have helped China economically and politically.

From being the greatest power on earth, China was to be thrown into a period of revolt and revolution.

Further reading

Broomhall, A. J., *Hudson Taylor*, London: Hodder & Stoughton and OMF, 1981–88.

Broomhall, Marshall, *Robert Morrison: A Master-Builder*, California: WBT, 1966.

Crossley, P. K., *The Manchus*, London: Blackwell, 2002.

Krahl, R., Murck, F., Rawski, E. and Rawson, J., *China: The Three Emperors, 1662–1795*, London: Royal Academy of Arts, 2005.

Gelber, H. G., *The Dragon and the Foreign Devils*, London: Bloomsbury, 2007.

Girardot, J. N., *The Victorian Translation of China: James Legge's Oriental Pilgrimage*, Berkeley: University of California Press, 2002.

MacDonald Fraser, G., *Flashman and the Dragon*, London: Harper Collins, 2006. Although this is a work of fiction, it gives many insights into the Taiping Rebellion.

Michael, Franz, *The Taiping Rebellion: History and Documents*, Seattle: University of Washington Press, 1966.

Spence, J. D., *God's Chinese Son*, W. W. Norton & Co., 1996.

Starr, J. B., 'The Legacy of Robert Morrison', *IBMR* (1998), pp. 73–6.

Waley, A., *The Opium War Though Chinese Eyes*, Stanford: Stanford University Press, 1979.

Websites

Kangxi: True Believer of Christ. A speculative life of Kangxi, suggesting that he was a 'Christian'. http://www.patriarchy website.com/bib-patriarchy/kangxi.htm

Portraits of the Chinese Emperors. Especially look at the portraits of the three great Qing Emperors. http://www.chinapage. com/emperor.html

Chapter 11

CHINA IN REVOLT AND REVOLUTION

The end of the Qing dynasty and the formation of the Republic (1895–1949)

In the spring of 1898 gangs of young men started gathering in the villages of the northern provinces of China. The youths would form a circle and one of their members, with closed eyes and folded hands, would begin to chant. Dropping to his knees, he would begin to draw figures in the dust and call upon the spirits. As the chanting intensified his gestures became more wild and his breathing more vigorous until he fell into a trance. Now he was the embodiment of a great warrior of history, and as such, demanded a sword to fight for his people. With closed eyes the man would begin to thrust and parry with the sword in a fight with an unseen enemy.

While some members of the group danced wildly and rehearsed martial moves, others began to hand out leaflets to the watching crowd. They claimed their movements made them invulnerable, and the leaflets claimed that Heaven was angry with the foreigners and especially the Christian missionaries.

> The scandalous conduct of Christians and barbarians is irritating our gods and geniuses, hence the many scourges we are now suffering... The iron roads and iron carriages [railways] are disturbing the terrestrial dragon and are destroying the earth's beneficial influences. The red liquid which keeps dripping from the iron snake [rusty water from the oxidised telegraph wires] is nothing but the blood of the outraged

spirits of the air… The missionaries extract the eyes, marrow and heart of the dead in order to make medicaments. Whoever drinks a glass of tea at the parsonage is stricken by death: the brains burst out of the skull… As for the children received in orphanages, they are killed and their intestines are used to change lead into silver and to make precious remedies.[1]

The roaming gangs were called the 'Righteous Harmony Fists', or in short, the Boxers. They were just one expression of the impact of Europe upon China in the nineteenth century. This impact cannot be overstated. As Ninian Smart writes:

> The Mongol conquests of Genghis Khan and his successors had been a shock, from China to Europe. But nothing ultimately has matched the effects of European conquest, for it introduced a whole variety of challenges across the world and spread ideas as heady as democracy, liberation, modernity, and the need for higher education in the Western mode. It was impossible that religious and other worldviews could be unaffected. It is out of the turbulences born of these conquests and of the two great wars of the twentieth century that the contemporary world has been created.[2]

The end of the Qing dynasty

The Opium Wars (1840–42) and the Taiping Rebellion (1850–64) left China weakened and vulnerable. The Emperors were young and ineffective. At this time there emerged the formidable figure of Dowager Cixi (1835–1908), who effectively ruled China for the fifty-year period from 1861 to 1908. She stands out as the second great female ruler in Chinese imperial history, but unlike Wu Zetian, she never became Emperor and ruled from 'behind the curtain'.

Dowager Cixi

Cixi was a concubine of the young Emperor Xianfeng (reigned 1851–61) who was unable to cope with the mounting problems of the Empire. He retired to the Summer Palace, leaving state affairs to his officials, and he died at the early age of thirty, weakened by drugs and debauchery. He had one son, who was by Cixi, and he was placed on the throne when he was only five years of age. Cixi secured Tongzhi's (reigned 1862–75) ascension through skilfully allying herself with the Empress and Xianfeng's younger brother, the Prince Kong. Kong was one of a small group of reformers who believed that cooperation with the Western powers was preferable to conflict. In an uneasy partnership with Cixi, he gave strength to the failing Manchu leadership.

The imperial system continued to rely on neo-Confucian orthodoxy, with its emphasis upon the Classics and the veneration for the Emperor. This led to imperial isolation, and the continual use of the traditional examination system was becoming increasingly irrelevant for the modern world. The system was overly centralized, with all major decisions requiring imperial approval. This meant the whole system was open to abuse and was riddled with corruption.

China's weakness merely further whetted the appetites of the foreign powers, and each defeat brought crushing indemnities leading to further loss of territories and finance. This resulted in an increasing stranglehold by the foreign powers on the economy and emerging industry. Foreigners had demanded extraterritoriality from Chinese laws, which infuriated the people. Their anger was particularly directed to the Christian missionaries, who could set up missions anywhere after the 1860s.

One incident that augmented the steady decline of China was the Japanese invasion. Korea had for a long time been a vassal state of China, but in 1885 Japan began to introduce a series of Japanese-style reforms. The Japanese ignored China's position as overlord and tried to force their plans on the Koreans. In 1894, China went to war with Japan, but they were no match against the Japanese, who were heavily armed with modern Western weapons. The Chinese were relentlessly pushed back while the Western powers did nothing to help. An angry Robert Hart, writing to England, described the provocation in the following words:

> China had given no offence, has done no wrong, does not wish to fight, and is willing to make sacrifices. She is a big 'sick' man, convalescing slowly from the sickening effects of centuries, and is being jumped on when down by this agile, healthy, well-armed Jap – will no one pull him off?[3]

On 21 November 1894, the strategic sea port of Port Arthur fell to the Japanese and China had to surrender.

This defeat merely underlined the weakness of the empire and a scramble began among the other foreign powers. Russian warships sailed into Port Arthur, as they were allowed by a secret treaty of 1896 to claim this all-year port. In 1890, 33 cities were open to foreign trade and residence, but in the period between 1894 and 1917, this increased to 93. Not all these cities housed foreign communities, but 16 did have significant concessions. In 1898 China granted more extensive concessions under leaseholds. To Germany, Jiaozhou Bay in Shandong, and over 500 square kilometres of the surrounding region was granted for 99 years. To Russia, the Liadong peninsula in southern Manchuria was granted for 25 years. To France, the port of Guangzhou in the south-east was granted for 99 years. To Britain was granted the New Territories opposite Hong Kong for 99 years, and also Weihaiwei port.

The young Emperor at that time, Guangxu, decided to support a group of reformers led by Kang Yuwei, and a series of reforms were introduced. These derived from the

Russian and Japanese models and sought to modernize the education system and check corruption. These changes were imposed in the face of opposition from the conservative element of the government. Cixi emerged from her retirement and acted quickly to imprison the Emperor and crush the so-called 'Hundred Days Reforms'. The conservative views of Cixi were, surprisingly, supported by the emergence of the growing anti-foreign movement in the country.

The Boxer Rising (1898–1901)

During the four decades when Protestant missionary work had been allowed in mainland China, there had been increasing tension between the Chinese villagers and Western missionaries. Missionaries were accused of interfering in disputes over land or water rights. If a Christian and a non-Christian argued over a matter, the missionary was often perceived as requiring the officials to favour the Christian. As drought devastated the countryside in the late 1890s, it was said that the ancient gods were not responding to their request for rain because the land was polluted by the Chinese Christians who refused to join their neighbours in what had traditionally been community rituals. The crops died in the fields, and rumours began to spread that Christians were poisoning the wells, and that they, with the missionaries, were taking the eyes and organs of the Chinese for use in evil magic.

The 'Righteous Harmony Fists' began in 1898 as a peasant rebellion resulting from poverty and dispossession, but it quickly acquired an anti-foreign complexion because they attributed China's misery to the reform element at court. Foreigners called them 'Boxers' because of the martial arts and callisthenic rituals they practised. The Boxers believed they had magical powers that could protect them from modern weapons. The movement was made up of several uncoordinated groupings united by a common hatred of all things foreign. The primary targets were Christian missionaries (called 'primary hairy men'), Chinese Christians ('secondary hairy men') and those who used foreign goods ('tertiary hairy men'). 'Hairy men' had to be killed.

The movement commenced in Shandong and swept across China. Although the military tried to contain it in some areas, the imperial court was initially undecided as to whether to support the Boxers or not. However, the anti-reform views of Cixi received the support of the Boxers, and they adopted the slogan, 'support the Qing, destroy the foreigner'. Cixi decided to support the movement, and appointed the pro-Boxer prince Duan as head of the Foreign Office.

In 1900, the Boxers moved into the capital. They entered Beijing chanting 'Burn, burn, burn! Kill, kill, kill!' and besieged the legation quarter of the city where all foreigners lived. Cixi's endorsement of the movement was effectively a declaration of war against Britain, the USA, France, Germany, Austria, Belgium, the Netherlands and Japan. Into the legation had come missionaries with many of their Christian converts. Parties were sent out to rescue more Chinese converts and bring them back to the safety of the compound because they were the most conspicuous targets of the Boxers' hatred. The siege was to last 55 days, with some of the worst fighting around the Catholic cathedral where Bishop Favier and 43 French soldiers defended over 4,000 Chinese converts who had sought refuge.

The siege was finally lifted by a joint expeditionary force of some 20,000 foreign troops who advanced from the coast to the capital. When the soldiers arrived, Cixi fled the city disguised as a peasant in a cart, and the Forbidden City was left to the foreign forces. After sacking the city, the Western nations went on to impose numerous demands upon China, including massive financial indemnity to be paid over forty years. In 1902, the court returned to Beijing and Cixi and her ministers began reluctantly to introduce modernizing measures. In 1905, the traditional examination system was finally abolished, and in 1908 Cixi announced a nine-year programme for constitutional reform. After a stroke, Cixi died on 15 November 1908. She had named her three-year-old great nephew Puji as heir, but his rule was to be short-lived. As the Qing dynasty struggled towards reform, it suddenly came to an end like a house of cards that finally collapsed. As Ann Paludan writes:

> After 2,000 years the imperial system had collapsed almost without a struggle. It had been one of the most successful political systems ever devised. Its extraordinary success had lain in its flexibility and cosmic nature, providing philosophical and moral basis for the relationship between human society and heaven. It provided a centralized form of government with a safety valve based on morality. If the emperor erred, he forfeited the divine mantle and could be replaced, but, until the late nineteenth century, the system as such was never questioned.
>
> It fell because it ceased to adapt and no longer presented an acceptable view of reality. The rise of the West shattered the notion of the Middle Kingdom with a special relationship to heaven; the modern age with industrialization created a society too large and complex for a system in which, theoretically at least, all power rested ultimately with one man...[4]

The Nationalist movement

After the crushing defeat of the 'Hundred Days Reform', many Chinese intellectuals had fled to Japan. One of the leading teachers was Dr Sun Yatsen (1866–1925) who was born near Guangzhou, but left the country at the age of twelve to continue his education in Honolulu. It was there that he became a Christian, received baptism in 1883, and graduated as a medical doctor in 1892 from a university in Hong Kong. In 1894, back in Honolulu, he founded the 'Society to Revive China', of which many members were either Christians or had been educated in missionary schools.

This Nationalist Republican movement started to develop underground branches in many parts of China. Sun attempted an uprising in his home area of Guangzhou. It was led by Protestants, and the chapel was their main base. The uprising failed and Sun had to leave China. He set up a base in Japan in 1905. Within a year many thousands of Chinese students gathered round him. On 9 October 1911, a bomb was accidentally detonated in Wuhan, and this became a trigger to anti-Manchu rebellions that spread across the empire. Sun Yatsen quickly returned to China and was elected provincial president of the Chinese republic in Nanjing.

The northern troops were commanded by General Yuan Shikai who negotiated a settlement with the Manchus, whereby Emperor Puyi recognized the loss of the Mandate of Heaven and stepped down as Emperor. He was allowed to remain in the Forbidden City with a stipend. In 1912, Sun Yatsen resigned as leader of the movement to allow Yuan Shikai to become the first president of China. Ahead of the national elections in December 1912, Sun Yatsen founded the Guomindang (GMD) – the National Party. The GMD gained a sweeping victory, but in June of the following year Yuan ordered the army to expel GMD members.

Beyond these bare facts, the revolution of 1911 is difficult to categorize and does not readily fit into the usual pattern of a revolution. The new 'Republic of China' was not actually republican because many of the old Qing bureaucrats merely remained in their positions, and neither was there a radical change in society and the economy. The most one can say is that the revolution stimulated the process of change that was already underway. Another difficulty in assessing the effects of the revolution is that the two contenders for power in China were both intent on fitting 1911 into their view of history. The first was the government of Taiwan that called itself the 'Republic of China' and traced its origins to Sun Yatsen. The second was the China Communist Party (CCP), which considered 1911 as a pivotal point in its view of the history of China. Zarrow calls these two views the 'heroic' and the Marxist interpretations.[5]

The so-called 'heroic' interpretation of the 1911 revolution focuses mainly upon the men who made the revolution. In this version, 1895 was important because it was when Sun Yatsen, the son of a peasant from near Guangzhou, organized his first uprising against the Qing. Sun left home to be educated in an Anglican school in Hawaii, and later completed medical studies in Hong Kong. Sun continued to raise revolts against the Qing until they put a price on his head, and that is when he fled to Japan. There he found modern cities and translations of exciting Western philosophers such as Rousseau and Marx, who stimulated his own thinking.

The anti-Qing Chinese students came together from various provinces in 1905 to form the National Alliance that elected Sun as leader. His 'Three People's Principles' of nationalism, republicanism and land reform were accepted as a revolutionary programme. Sun had a talent for raising money from the Chinese merchants of the diaspora, who saw massive business opportunities in a new, open China. By 1911 the National Alliance claimed a membership of 10,000. It particularly targeted the 'New Armies' that were being set up by the Qing to replace the old Manchu and peasant armies. It was on 10 October 1911 that a New Army mutiny broke out Wuhan, and the mutineers seized the arsenal, causing the Manchu governor to flee. Li Yuanhong was the commanding colonel of the New Army and, after intense pressure, he agreed to lead the revolutionaries. He was a good leader and by the end of the month, seven provinces seceded from the Qing Empire and established revolutionary governments.

244 THE SPIRIT OF CHINA

Although there was heavy fighting around Nanjing, and many Manchus in towns in the south were massacred or fled, a massive civil war was avoided. In January 1912, Sun Yatsen returned to China to be proclaimed provisional president of the new Republic of China. During the following few months the Emperor abdicated in return for guarantees of safety and a generous allowance. Yuan Shikai was the leader of the better-armed Qing forces in the north, and he negotiated peace with the revolutionaries in return for promises that he would become president.

Zarrow argues that this interpretation fails because in the final analysis, the Qing dynasty fell because its own army commanders were unwilling to continue to support it, and the Chinese elite saw no advantage in supporting the Qing rather than the new ideas of the republican movement.

The Communist interpretation of the revolution accepts the facts of the previous view, but puts the event into a Marxist framework of history. The 1911 revolution is seen as the revolution against the old feudal system, which introduced a bourgeois government that was a progressive phase towards the final socialist revolution. This was the view proposed by Mao Zedong and it is still found in the museums of China today.

> In the course of its history the Chinese revolution must go through two stages, first, the democratic [i.e. bourgeois] revolution, and second, the socialist [i.e. proletarian] revolution, and by their very nature they are two different revolutionary processes.[6]

Western historians have argued that the Chinese bourgeoisie was at this time numerically small and politically too weak to have played a significant role in the revolution. In some ways the 1911 revolution may be seen as a nationalist revolution, in which the ethnic Han Chinese revolted against the alien Manchus.

The May Fourth movement

On 4 May 1919, some 3,000 students assembled in Tiananmen Square in Beijing. The demonstration was well organized in its protest against the way that the imperial powers seemed bent on carving up China. The Versailles Treaty following the end of the First World War (1914–18) had awarded Germany's concessions in China over to Japan with the apparent cooperation of the Chinese politicians at the gathering. The following two weeks saw numerous student meetings and demonstrations. The anti-Japanese cause proved very popular and students and teachers began to organize their opposition.

Further demonstrations and arrests at the beginning of June brought traders and workers into the struggle. Soon temporary jails were overflowing. Students in Shanghai called for a 'triple strike' on 5 June of university classes, work and markets. This resulted in the city being virtually shut down for the day. The Beijing government decided to dismiss the three officials in Versailles who had agreed to the Japanese demands. The Versailles Treaty was finally concluded at the end of June, but without Chinese endorsement. This treaty marked a turning point in Chinese attitudes towards the West. Irrespective of all the humiliations caused by colonial powers upon China, the leading officials had continued to look to the West for its model. Now the intellectuals sought new alternatives and some formed anarchist groups, and others formed the Chinese Communist Party, which was established in the early 1920s with many anarchist members. Anarchists argued that the problems of the nations were rooted in the state, and so revolution was needed to destroy the state. Communists considered that it was the proletariat that was uniquely positioned to lead the liberation of all society. Thus, the appeal of Marxism in the 1920s was its promise to guide effective revolutionary action.

The May Fourth movement provides some important

insights into events that were to happen near the end of the twentieth century. The student movement of 1989 was a populist response to changes that were going on in China, but it was firmly crushed by the CCP after initial hesitation. Student movements in China have long been a force that has resulted in the overthrow of the state.

Confucianism and the fate of China

Following the collapse of the Qing dynasty, Chinese intellectuals undertook a desperate search for a way to save Chinese culture from disintegration. Two extreme trends evolved. The conservatives saw the answer in a revival of Confucian values and teaching, while the radicals wanted the elimination of Confucianism.

The first intellectual movement against Confucianism occurred in 1916–20 when many scholars returned from Europe and North America. They blamed China's failure on Confucianism with its ritual, morals and mysticism. This trend was carried forward into socialist China where Mao identified Confucianism with the exploitation of the working class. Condemnation and denunciation of Confucianism reached its peak during the Cultural Revolution (1966–76), when Confucianism seemed at the point of elimination.

At the other extreme were the Modern Confucians who advocated that China could only be saved if Confucian learning was propagated and Confucian values revived.

The Japanese invasion of China in the 1930s further strengthened the views of these scholars at this time. In 1938, He Lin wrote an article entitled 'The Future Development of Confucian Thought', in which he argued that the weakness of China resulted from the weakness of modern Chinese learning. If China was to be saved and avoid becoming a cultural colony, Confucian teaching and values must be promoted. But it was not Confucianism but a radically new philosophy that was to make its mark upon China in the second half of the twentieth century.

The Communist movement

One of the first Chinese intellectuals to write about the significance of the Bolshevik Revolution for China was Li Dazhao (1888–1927). He was a teacher of political science at Beijing University and established a society for the study of Marxism in the university. Li was also responsible for the university library, where one of the assistants was Mao Zedong. Mao was the son of a well-to-do peasant who had come to Beijing in 1918 after graduating from teacher training college in his home province of Hunan. Like many students of his time, he was attracted to the many new political ideas that were circulating among the Chinese intellectuals. Marxist study groups were formed in many cities in 1919–20, but these were loosely organized groups of students and intellectuals. The first congress of what was to become the Chinese Communist Party (CCP) met in Shanghai in 1921 and consisted of only twelve delegates, of whom Mao was one.

Following General Yuan's death in 1916, parliament was not able to restrain the growing rebellion of the local military governors, or 'warlords' as the historians have called them. China was pulled apart as warlords competed for control of various areas. In the face of the disintegration of the nation, the Guomindang (GMD) formed an alliance with the CCP to launch a military expedition into the north of the country to seek its reunification. During the course of this expedition the united front between the two forces broke apart due to irreconcilable differences over the issue of class revolution. The CCP gradually withdrew into the rural hinterlands, while the GMD sought to establish a modern state in 1928.

When the GMD declared itself the national government, it acted according to Sun Yatsen's principle that the party would have to guide the political destiny of the nation until the people were prepared for democracy. Although the government was established in Nanjing, large areas of China were outside its control. The government was beset with problems. In the north the Japanese were gradually encroaching, there was a series of revolts from disgruntled military leaders, and there was a growing Communist threat in the countryside. Chiang Kai-shek emerged as the dominant figure within the GMD.

By 1929 Mao Zedong had been relieved of his position on the Communist Party's central committee because of the failure of the Autumn Harvest Uprising in Hunan, and he had moved to the southern province of Jiangxi. Here he established his base and operated almost independently of the party leadership in Shanghai. From this base Mao instituted land reforms among the peasants and used guerrilla tactics against the Nationalists. In the next five years Chiang Kai-shek launched five campaigns against Mao's Communist base in Jiangxi. The first four failed, but the fifth, launched in October 1933, was more successful. The Communist forces suffered a series of defeats and in October 1934 it was decided to evacuate the region. Mao left behind the elderly, children and most of the women, and marched west with about 86,000 troops. All along the route the Communist forces were pursued and attacked by GMD forces. The march went through some difficult terrain and bad weather, so that only 4,000 survived the march. A year later they arrived in Shaanxi Province in the north-west. 'The Long March', as it became known, has achieved legendary status in Communist history and today many of the more notable sites have become tourist centres.

In 1937 full-scale war broke out between China and Japan. By the following year Japanese forces had taken Beijing, Shanghai, Nanjing, Guangzhou and Wuhan. The Nationalist government retreated west to Chongqing in Sichuan Province. For the first years of the war China virtually stood alone against Japan. The CCP forces in Yuhan opened a second front in the north to fight against the

Japanese. The pre-emptive strike on the American naval base at Pearl Harbor in December 1941, and the occupation of Hong Kong and Malaya, brought the US and Britain directly into conflict with Japan. US aid to China increased and was directed to the government in Chongqing, while Russian troops assisted the CCP in the north.

During this period Mao established himself as a major figure within the CCP. It was during this period that he was brought to the world's attention through the writings of the American journalist Edgar Snow, who visited Yun'an in 1936. His book *Red Star Over China* (1938) depicted the Communists as sincere revolutionaries dedicated to economic reform.

Christianity in China

The new intellectual climate at the beginning of the twentieth century not only introduced the ideas of Republicanism and Marxism, but also encouraged many to accept Christianity. This receptiveness to foreign ideas coincided with the rise of a new missionary zeal among the students of America and Europe. The Student Volunteer Movement (SVM) was founded by John R. Mott in 1888 with the watchword 'The Evangelization of the World in This Generation'. Between 1886 and 1919, around 2,500 student volunteers sailed for China.

In the nineteenth century, the Protestant missionary movement was mainly denominational missionary societies from North America and Europe. After 1900 there was an increase in the number of independent, so-called 'faith' missionaries from Holiness or Pentecostal movements. The established mission societies undertook massive building projects erecting schools, universities, and modern hospitals staffed by trained Western personnel assisted by many Chinese Christians. As Bob Whyte comments:

The Catholic Church had grown from 720,000 in 1901 to almost one and a half million in 1912. Amongst Protestants the number of missionaries had reached almost 5,500 by 1914 and the number of Christians was round 500,000. According to one source 253,210 of this number were communicant members – Presbyterians 65,786, Methodists 52,200, CIM 35,150, Baptists 33,256, Lutherans 24,422, Congregationalists 21,828, Anglicans 14,541 and others 6,027. The period 1900–14 therefore witnessed the most rapid growth of Christianity in China to date. This, combined with the apparent interest amongst China's intellectuals, seemed to confirm the optimism of the Missionary community.[7]

However, beneath this apparent success it was becoming clear that Christianity would have little real place in the lives of the young people of China. The World War of 1914–18 had not only caused changes in Europe, but had disillusioned many around the world. The missionary schools not only opened the minds of their young students to the Christian gospel, but also to new possibilities that were divergent to those of the fundamentalist Christian teaching. These Chinese students were looking for new institutions that would transform their nation, and for many Christianity was not sufficiently radical.

Missionaries in China were slow to perceive the changes that were going on in the thinking of the young intellectuals of China. Then, in May 1925 an incident happened that had significant repercussions for missionaries. British troops in Shanghai killed a number of unarmed students who were demonstrating over the killing of a striking Chinese worker in a Japanese factory. It led to widespread protests against foreigners in China, and many colleges were closed. The Guomindang launched their Northern Expedition in 1926, increasing the general instability in the region, and this resulted in more attacks upon missionaries. The unsettled situation resulted in a drop in the number of Protestant missionaries to 4,375 in 1928.

The Chinese church

Partly as a result of these events, there was a growth in the independence of Chinese Protestant churches. The so-called 'Three-Self Church' had been a matter of discussion among missionaries for many years. By this they meant local churches should aim to be self-governing, self-supporting and self-propagating. In preparation for a national Christian conference in 1922 with the theme 'The Chinese Church', a survey was made and published under the title *The Christian Occupation of China*.[8] It showed that in 1920 there were 130 Protestant missionary societies working in China, of which 65 were American and 35 were British. It is therefore not surprising that the conference made the public statement:

> We Chinese Christians who represent the various leading denominations express our regret that we are divided by denominationalism which came from the West.

The immediate result of the conference was the formation of the National Christian Council (NCC), whose first annual meeting was held in the following year. This was not only a response to the growing Chinese nationalism, but was to provide a positive response to the political process in China during the period. The Chinese church, however, still remained heavily dependent on foreign funding and personnel.

Another development from the 1922 conference was the formation of the Church of Christ in China (*Zhonggua Jidujiaohui*), which held its first assembly in October 1927. It brought together sixteen denominations representing about a quarter of the total number of Protestants in China. Initially most were Presbyterian or Congregational churches, but later some Baptists and Methodists joined. Although the aim was to unite all Protestant denominations, many resisted, mainly due to theological differences.

In North America and Europe there was a marked division between liberals advocating a 'social gospel' and fundamentalists (including evangelicals) who proclaimed the divine inspiration of the Bible and the priority for evangelism. This essentially divided the Protestants into two camps, which was reflected in China.

Chinese indigenous movements

Another indigenous development of the time was the growth of independent Chinese evangelists who bypassed the existing denominations. One example was Ni Duosheng, who became widely known in the West as Watchman Nee. He was born in Guangdong in 1903, and he studied at Trinity College in Fujian and attended a Methodist church. At the age of nineteen he rejected the teaching of infant baptism and helped establish an independent Christian community. He was greatly influenced by a former Church Missionary Society (CMS) missionary who had become associated with the Brethren Movement before returning to China as an independent missionary in 1920. Nee's key message was that there was one true church for each locality. In 1928 Nee settled in Shanghai and completed his book *The Spiritual Man* which was to gain much interest among Christians in the West.

Nee visited Britain in 1933 and established relations with various Brethren groups. It was, however, with Honor Oak Fellowship, led by Austin Sparks, that he gained the greatest support. Nee was a biblical literalist and taught a dispensational interpretation in which history is divided into distinct dispensations. In China, his movement, known as the 'Little Flock', continued to grow in the 1930s and 1940s, and later under Li Changshou ('Witness Lee').

Another Christian movement was the Jesus Family, which commenced in Mazhung in Shandong in 1921. The founder was a converted Buddhist monk, Jing Dianying, who modelled the community on strict spiritual discipline.

It stressed spiritual gifts, direct revelation through dreams and the importance of prayer meetings. By 1941 there were 140 communities with 6,000 members.

The Nanjing period (1927–37)

The emergence of the CCP as a credible force in China began to have an impact upon the church, especially as it had programmes of reconstruction among the rural communities. The conversion of Chiang Kai-shek to Methodism in 1930 meant that he gained support from both Protestants and Catholics alike. When he initiated his New Life Movement with its emphasis upon cleanliness and morality, it received widespread support from Chinese Christians. However, the Movement was rejected by most Chinese intellectuals who felt that Marxism provided a better intellectual foundation for the future of China than did the fascist nationalism of Chiang or the gospel of love advocated by Christianity. Thus, following the 'Long March', many Chinese intellectuals were drawn to support the Communists in Yan'an. Chaing had therefore lost the support of the two major groups that had influenced the government of China throughout the centuries: the peasants and the scholars.

The Japanese took advantage of the confusion in China and in 1931 invaded Manchuria and set up Emperor Puyi as the symbolic head of state. In 1937 this turned into a full-scale invasion that led to the Japanese occupation of much of the coastal areas and horrifying suffering for the Chinese people. The Guomindang (GMD) were forced to retreat to the West and set up their capital in Chongqing. Following the attack on Pearl Harbour in 1941, all mission property was taken over by the Japanese and many missionaries were interned. In many areas the churches were compelled to look after themselves, which was to provide preparation for the situation after 1949.

Soon after the end of the war against Japan the

cooperation between the Guomindang and the Communists broke down. In June 1946 the government launched an army of nearly 2 million against the Communist forces of the north.

Chiang was confident of success because he had more troops and they were better equipped. However, the Nationalist forces were poorly led and badly coordinated. Mao continued to push towards Beijing. In October 1949, from the gate of Heavenly Peace (*Tiananmen*) in Beijing, Mao proclaimed the establishment of the People's Republic of China (PRC). Although most Christians were shocked at the civil war, few expected the Communists to win. By the end of the year Chiang retreated to the island of Taiwan, taking with him the entire gold reserves of the country and what was left of his air force and navy. Some 2 million refugees and soldiers from the mainland settled on the island.

*   *   *

The twentieth century had commenced with the bloodshed of the Boxer rebellion, but this was but the prelude to many radical changes for China. The nation explored various ways by which it could transform itself as it faced the challenges of the contemporary world. The Republican views had mostly been rejected along with Christianity. It was Marxism in the form expounded by Mao Zedong that was to shape the future of China, and bring the missionary era to an end.

Further reading

Bailey, P. J., *China in the Twentieth Century*, London: Blackwell, 2001. A scholarly study of China during the twentieth century.
Preston, D., *The Boxer Rebellion: China's War on Foreigners, 1900*, London: Robinson, 2002. A new assessment of the impact of the Boxer Rebellion.

Tiedemann, R. G., 'Baptism of Fire: Boxer Uprising of 1900', *IBMR*, Jan. 2000, pp. 7–12. A Christian missionary perspective on the Boxer uprising.

Warner, M., *The Dragon Empress*, London: Vintage, 1972. A readable account of the life of Cixi and the end of the Qing dynasty.

Zarrow, P. *China in War and Revolution 1895–1949*, London: Routledge, 2005. A scholarly account of the history of China during this turbulent period.

DVD: *The Last Emperor* (1987).

Chapter 12

THE CHINESE DIASPORA

The migration of Chinese in the Qing and modern periods (1800–2000)

The Chinese did not have an equivalent to the concept of migration before the industrialization of China. In rural societies, males leaving home voluntarily resulted in a loss of labour for the family and village, and so this was perceived as an act of disloyalty. Only when they were posted on official business or sent to supplement family income through trade was it considered legitimate. Hence, journeying from home was only considered a temporary act, and the people away from home were therefore called *huaqiao* ('return-migrants').

The nineteenth century was a period of massive migration throughout the world. From Europe many were emigrating to the Americas and Australia, and at the same time many Chinese were journeying to South-east Asia.

As the Chinese migrated from their homeland they took with them much of their culture and religion. It was this that allowed them to keep their distinct identity as they made their impact on the world. This chapter seeks to explore the religious and cultural aspects of the Chinese Diaspora, but it is important to emphasize the diversity of religious expression in different areas of China as well as in the Diaspora. When one asks a Chinese person what is their religion, many will say 'Buddhist' or 'Christian', a few might say 'Daoist', but many will say they have none. Ancestor worship is not considered a religion as it is thought of as being a practice designed to show respect for those who have died. So-called 'popular religion' is merely considered superstition.

Although many national rituals such as the Spring Festival are common to all, local expressions vary in character and form. The rituals of the Diaspora depend much upon where the majority came from and at what time. As will be shown, it also depends on how they have sought to adapt to the majority culture in which they now live. Thus, although there are similarities among the Chinese communities of Taiwan, Hong Kong, San Francisco and London, there are also differences. Therefore in this chapter it is only possible to give an overview of festivals and beliefs, and to acknowledge the danger of making too many generalizations.

The history of Chinese migration

South-east Asia
From the Ming period, Chinese from the southern coastal areas of Guangdong (Canton) and Fujian had traded throughout South-east Asia. Many had settled in various places and formed growing communities. In Buddhist countries such as Vietnam and Thailand they had often intermarried and adopted the local language and customs so that they were assimilated into society. In contrast, in Muslim areas (Indonesia), Roman Catholic regions (Philippines) and tribal societies (Borneo), the Chinese community kept its own distinct identity. Because the people had mainly come from one region, they continued to speak their particular dialect and retained many of their local associations, such as the infamous Triads.

With the expansion of the European colonialists into Asia, new opportunities were created for many enterprising Chinese. Following the establishment of Singapore by the British in 1819, many Chinese entered and contributed to transforming the barren island into a thriving trading centre.

The discovery of tin in areas of Malaysia attracted thousands of Chinese to work in the mines. By 1850 there were some 10,000 Chinese in the city of Malacca, and they were the dominant ethnic group in Kuala Lumpur and Singapore.

Some Chinese fared better than others, and some were able to make great fortunes through trade and mining tin. However, in the Spanish-controlled Philippines and Dutch-controlled Indonesia, the Chinese suffered repeated persecutions. Early in the nineteenth century the Dutch seized the mines that the Chinese had been mining for centuries, which was to result in continuing hostility. When the Dutch conquered southern Sumatra in 1864 there was a massive migration of Chinese to work in the sugar and tobacco plantations. In Java, the Dutch used Chinese merchants to collect taxes, and some became very rich. By 1900 it is estimated that there were more than half a million Chinese living in the Dutch East Indies (now Indonesia).

The anti-slavery movement stimulated by the British evangelicals in the 1840s essentially ended the trade in African slaves. In the quest for cheap labour foreign contractors started coming to China, and through unscrupulous Chinese middlemen began signing up hundreds of thousands of Chinese to work in plantations and mines in South-east Asia and America. These workers were treated little better than slaves. The term 'coolies' comes from the Chinese kuli, meaning 'bitter labourers'. In 1852, sugar planters in Hawaii brought over the first Chinese workers on three- or five-year contracts that promised them three dollars per month, plus room and board, for a twelve-hour day, six days per week. Although most found the initial months terribly hard, many who finished their contracts chose to stay in Hawaii. Here they set up small businesses, and by 1900 there were some 25,000 Chinese in Hawaii.

California

The discovery of gold in California in 1848 led to large-scale voluntary migration to work in the gold mines. For the most part, these immigrants consisted of young male peasants in search of economic success. Fuelled by news of the California Gold Rush, they arrived in America hoping to strike it rich and so be able to send money back to their poor rural homes, or even return to China in a few years with newly acquired wealth. Approximately 15,000 Chinese were hired by Central Pacific Railroad as it stretched into the western frontier. Many moved to fill the void of low-paid labour created by America's rapidly expanding industries. Wool mills, as well as shoe and garment manufacturers, were among the most common employers of Chinese immigrants in the American West. By 1880, 25 per cent of California's workforce was of Chinese descent.

Even as they continued to contribute to the US economy, there were periods of friction with the white community triggered by comments about Chinese being depraved opium smokers. As the Chinese population in America increased, many of the immigrants came together to form Chinatowns in nearly every major US city. These became targets for anti-immigrant protests and riots that often resulted in violence. Chinese immigrants may have been targeted due to the increasing belief that immigrants were occupying too many jobs within the cities. Because Chinese Americans were living together in such close-knit communities within these cities, they drew the brunt of the anti-immigration sentiment. Pressure upon these immigrants became so fierce that some chose to leave the country altogether.

For those who remained, things began to normalize with time. However, new policies enacted by the government sought to prevent further immigration from China. In 1882, Congress passed the Chinese Exclusion Act, based upon the belief that, 'in the opinion of the Government of the United

States the coming of the Chinese labourers to this country endangers the good order of certain localities...'

It completely prevented Chinese without family already in the US from entering the country, thus effectively halting all immigration. The law was the first in US history to ban a specific racial group from entering America. Only diplomats, merchants and students were allowed access into the country, and Chinese Americans were denied the right to apply for naturalization. To enforce the law, the Angel Island Inspection Station was built in San Francisco in 1910. All Chinese entering the country went through an interrogation session and were then either allowed to enter the country, or detained in prison-like barracks, or deported. For 30 years Angel Island processed close to 175,000 Chinese who came to America only to find that the door had been closed on their people.

In time, America began to realize that this treatment of Chinese immigrants was contrary to the very foundations of the country. Awareness was raised by the protests and court challenges of Chinese Americans lobbying for their relatives who were still denied admittance. After a fire destroyed Angel Island in 1940, it was never reopened. Finally, in 1943 the Chinese Exclusion Act was repealed, allowing immigrants already in the US to bring over family members from China. 1952 saw the passage of the Walter-McCarren Act, allowing first-generation Americans to apply for citizenship. Throughout the 1960s, Chinese Americans made particular gains into professional arenas: medicine, corporations and politics. The 1964 Immigration and Nationality Act removed the last barriers to Chinese immigration, initiating a new era in the history of America's melting pot.

These scattered Chinese communities throughout Asia and America retained an interest in what was going on in China, where most of their families lived. Although the first migrants were illiterate, they saw to it that their children learned to read Chinese, and Chinese-language newspapers circulated in all areas. By the end of the nineteenth century some of these communities were beginning to play a significant role in Chinese politics, as will be seen in the following chapters.

Taiwan

Little archaeological evidence remains from Taiwan's early history, but the earliest settlers were probably from Southeast Asia, and are thought to have inhabited the island since 10,000 BC. It was in the fifteenth century that migration commenced from China. It was not until 1517 that Portuguese sailors reached the island, which they called *Ilha Formosa*, meaning 'Beautiful Island'. The Dutch invaded in 1624 and built a capital at Tainan, but just two years later they lost the island to a Spanish invasion. They managed to reconquer the island in 1641, only to lose it again in the 1660s when the new Manchu (Qing) Emperors gained control of the island and made it a county of Fujian Province. This resulted in a flood of Chinese immigrants from Fujian, of whom many were Hakka Chinese, largely from Guangdong. The descendants of these two migrations now make up by far the largest section of the population, amounting to 69 per cent and 15 per cent respectively.

In 1895, following war between Japan and China, Taiwan was given to Japan in perpetuity as a reward for its victory. The Taiwanese resented the proposal of being incorporated into Japan, and on 25 May 1895, with the assistance of disenchanted Manchu officials, the Taiwan Republic was established. The Japanese quickly quashed the rebellion and went on to establish a military base on the island and to promote education and economic development. After Japan's defeat at the end of the Second World War, Taiwan was handed back to China.

The US and Britain had agreed that Taiwan should be handed over to their ally, Chiang Kai-shek's Republic of China government, which was then in control of most of

China. During the next few years, Chiang's troops were beaten back by the Communist armies under Mao Zedong. Chiang and the remnants of his Guomindang (GMD) government fled to Taiwan in 1949. This group, referred to as Mainland Chinese, then numbered 1.5 million people, and they dominated Taiwan's politics for many years, even though they only account for 14 per cent of the population.

From 1952 to 1972, the GMD was able to build up Taiwan economically, thanks to the hard work of the Taiwanese, and the sound infrastructure built up by the Japanese. On the diplomatic front, they lost ground, and in 1971, their role of representing all of China disintegrated when Nixon and Kissinger made their 'opening' to China. Having inherited an effective dictatorship, Chiang's son, Chiang Ching-kuo, began a process of democratization, which eventually led to the election of the island's first non-GMD president, Chen Shui-bian, in 2000.

Britain

The earliest Chinese immigrants to Britain were recruited from the villages of the New Territories to serve as sailors aboard European ships. Several hundred Chinese seamen jumped ship and established communities in the East End of London and the docklands of Liverpool and Cardiff. Numbers increased during the Second World War, but many were subsequently repatriated. Those remaining formed the nucleus of, and the catalyst for, the much larger second-phase emigration from the New Territories.

This began with the 1948 British Nationality Act which accorded New Commonwealth citizens the right to live and work in Great Britain. People who were born in Hong Kong, especially indigenous citizens of the New Territories, were given a British passport. They could come to work and live in Britain freely until more restrictive immigration legislation in 1962 required employment vouchers or work permits.

The typical pattern of emigration was through chain migration, relying heavily on lineage ties at every stage. Lineage members from the first migration, already established in the UK restaurant trade, supervised immigration requirements, paid passage money and offered employment. Chain migration was also based on shared dialect, common district of origin or extended family.

Emigration from Hong Kong in this phase also included some 10,000 'stateless' China-born Chinese, some of the thousands who had crossed the borders from the People's Republic of China into the New Territories during the 1950s and 1960s and who were issued with Certificates of Identity. Many had lived for ten to fifteen years in villages of the New Territories as farmers before emigration. Emigration to the UK was for them a second experience of migration. Culturally they had much in common with New Territories villagers, with traditional Chinese lifestyles and customs.

Watson, in a classic study of Chinese in Britain, states that the Chinese are the 'least assimilated' among the various ethnic minorities, and they have prospered without changing their way of life to suit British social expectations. He writes:

> the migrants I have met are not particularly interested in making English friends or in changing their way of life. Chinese culture, in their view, is infinitely superior to the European cultures they encountered abroad. They have few illusions about their role as workers in an alien society, however, and prefer to maintain a low profile.[1]

Others, like Sinn, would question this view, arguing that there is a growing British Chinese identity.[2]

Chinese religion of the Diaspora

The Chinese of the Diaspora have not gone through the events of the Communist Revolution of 1949, nor the Cultural Revolution of 1966–67, and so have not experienced the anti-religious fervour. They have been more influenced by their contact with Western ideology, with its secularism and consumerism. Religious belief among the Chinese of the Diaspora crosses a wide spectrum. At one end, there are those who hold to many of the past traditions; these are usually the elderly and less educated. At the other, there are Western-educated young people who are a significant part of the growing global economy. Many have converted to Christianity, and Chinese churches can be found throughout the world. Between the two poles are a range of superstitions, customs and practices that even cross the generations of one family. The surprising thing, to the outsider at least, is that most are still eager to keep their Chinese heritage. They may live in different countries, speak different Chinese dialects or even don't speak Chinese at all, but they still see themselves as part of the great heritage of China.

Arthur Wolf makes a relevant comment:

> The most important point to be made about Chinese religion is that it mirrors the social landscape of its adherents. There are as many meanings as there are vantage points.[3]

Gods (shen)

Chinese popular religion has adapted itself to changing times and places, and so it is difficult to do more than draw out some common features. One of these is that all things are made of *qi*, including inanimate matter, humans, animals, gods and demons. *Qi* operates according to two basic patterns that have traditionally been known as *yin* and *yang*. Thus, in Chinese thought the term 'god' in the sense of 'superhuman being' does not have a straightforward meaning as suggested by the English word 'god'. The Chinese word *shen*, which is usually translated as 'god', has three distinct spheres of meaning. The first is the domain of the individual human being that may be translated as 'spirit' in the sense of 'human spirit'. The second meaning may be rendered in English as 'gods' or 'spirits'. The third meaning is more like that understood by the term 'spiritual'. As Teiser writes:

> The fact that these three fields of meaning ('spirit', 'spirits' and 'spiritual') can be traced to a single word has important implications for analyzing Chinese religion. Perhaps most importantly, it indicated that there is no unbridgeable gap separating humans from gods or, for that matter, separating good spirits from demons. All are composed of the same basic stuff, *qi*, and there is no ontological distinction between them. Humans are born with the capacity to transform their spirits into one of the gods of the Chinese pantheon.[4]

The word *shen*, 'spirit' relates to the *yang* and is opposed to the *yin* class of things known as 'ghosts' or 'demons'. These two terms cover all manner of spiritual beings, those that are benevolent and malevolent, lucky and unlucky.

There are two types of gods (*shen*) in Chinese popular religion: *fu* and *shi*. The *fu* are the spirits of charismatic people such as cultural heroes like the Yellow Emperor, Confucius and Mazu, and military heroes, such as Guandi, the god of war. Any of these gods may have a temple or an altar devoted to them.

The *shi* are temporary occupants of a position something like that of a local official. These include local earth gods, city gods, and the kitchen god in a household (*Zaojin*, 'Lord of the Stove'). The highest of this class is the Jade Emperor (*Yuhuang Dadi*), who is also called the 'Lord of Heaven' (*Tiangong*). Some of the more important *shi* may have previously been ancestors. All these *shi* are like officials holding positions in the spiritual bureaucracy modelled on the old imperial bureaucracy. The city god (*chenghuang shen*) corresponds to the local magistrate, and so each deity will have its own temple. Magistrates were men who had passed the highest levels of the civil service examinations and were appointed to certain towns on a rotating basis as the representative of the Emperor.

The earth gods (*Tudi Gong* – *gong* means an 'official') correspond more to local officers appointed by the magistrate. They usually have small shrines in public places or altars in larger temples, and are often depicted to be white-faced, with a black beard and a round neck. The deity is regarded as having two functions – to police the ghosts, and to spy on the affairs of his human charges. He will keep a record of their activities and report to his superiors. He serves localities, not kinship groups, so people owning land in more than one locality will worship more than one earth god.

The kitchen god (*Zaojin*) is not a god of culinary arts, but his location above the stove is not a matter of coincidence. The large brick cooking stove on which most meals are prepared stands as a symbol of the family as an independent entity. The family is the smallest corporate unit in society, and the kitchen god is the lowest-ranking member of the spiritual hierarchy. He is sent from Heaven to each family to take charge of their affairs. He makes a report to Heaven annually (on the twenty-third day of the last month of the Chinese year) on what the family has done in the past year. The kitchen god is usually depicted either by a picture on the wall or by a statuette on a shelf.[5]

Ghosts (gui)

A ghost is the spirit of a person who has died, and in the Chinese context, has no family to conduct the necessary rituals to help the ghost on its way. This is usually the result of a tragic death, especially if the body is lost. Ghosts therefore lack appropriate roles in the spirit realm and so are considered pitiful but dangerous. Malicious ghosts are those discontented spirits who are forced by their circumstances to prey on the living. They include the neglected dead and hateful souls who receive no sacrifices because they remain at the scene of death seeking revenge. Wolf comments, 'All ghosts are like bandits and beggars'.[6]

Offerings to ghosts are always made outside the house, and at the back of the house. The spirits of unmarried women are particularly likely to become ghosts, because women normally become members of their husband's family and are not worshipped as ancestors of their natal families. The natal family may set up a separate altar just for her, or even conduct a spirit marriage to an unmarried deceased man, or even, in some cases, to a living man who agrees to take her as his second wife. This allows her to become an ancestor in another family. Ghost marriage occurs in Taiwan today, as illustrated by the following newspaper report of 2002.

A man who died of complications after having a tooth pulled and his girlfriend who committed suicide from grief were married in a traditional 'ghost wedding,' it was reported yesterday. Some 30 family members attended the wedding ceremony of Chen Yen-jen, 26, and Chiang Chia-ling, 21, held at the city mortuary in Keelung on Sunday, a Chinese-language newspaper said. Chen's brother and Chiang's sister tied the knot on behalf of the dead, holding photographs of the deceased. Chen died of meningitis on Oct. 25 after he had a tooth removed a month earlier, the paper said. His girlfriend killed herself Nov. 3, the day of his funeral by burning charcoal in her college dorm room. She left a note asking to be married to Chen after her death and for them both to be buried together.[7]

The seventh month of the year is also a time when the ghosts are closer to the living, and so this is an inauspicious

268 THE SPIRIT OF CHINA

time for weddings. In Taiwan this is also a month for many colourful rituals that seek to appease angry ghosts.

Ancestors (zu or zuxain)

It has been shown that Chinese ancestor beliefs date back to the Shang period, and are still practised today. Gods and ancestors are both *yang* (deriving from the *hun*) phenomena, while ghosts are *yin* (deriving from the *po*). While ancestors are considered only to affect their own family, they may cause trouble for another. Becoming an ancestor is a process requiring certain specific rituals that may be conducted by either Daoist or Buddhist priests. At a Daoist funeral the priest often sends a messenger in the form of a paper drawing that is burnt to carry a message to the Ten Kings of Hell. This is a request that the spirit be allowed a quick ascent to Heaven rather than spending a long time in Hell being punished for past transgressions.

Most Taiwanese families have an altar table with images and name-plaques for ancestors and gods. Some people make ritual offerings every morning, but an increasing number of people do this only on birthdays or special occasions. Offerings include fresh fruit, cooked rice and burning incense. The ancestors are usually only recognized back two or three generations, until they are no longer remembered by any living member of the family. The plaque is then ritually burned. It is thought that once the rituals are no longer made the *qi* of the ancestor gradually disperses. A few larger, wealthier families may have an ancestral temple (*jiamiao*), containing a large cabinet with name-plaques of ancestors going back many generations. This may be within the compound of an extended family or in a village of related members. These temples used to be more common in China, but the turmoil of the twentieth century resulted in their destruction, as many families were fragmented.

A person worships his ancestors because he is obligated to do so as an heir and descendant, and he worships the gods in the hope of getting their good will. When people encounter misfortune they will usually turn to the gods for help and not to the ancestors, because the latter are regarded as being less powerful.

Christians have often struggled with the question of whether ancestor practices are essentially 'ancestor worship' or 'ancestor veneration'. The family altar will contain images of both ancestors and gods, and there is little distinction made between the two. The most significant distinction between them is that ancestors are only 'worshipped' by a single family, while gods are worshipped by a larger community. Both gods and ancestors can be appealed to for protection, but neither group is omnipotent and may take revenge on the living members of the family if neglected or insulted. Chinese Christians have therefore rejected such practices, usually in the face of much opposition from their families.

Festivals and rituals

Rituals and festivals are the main activities that join Chinese of the Diaspora together. How these rituals are understood varies from being seen as no more than Chinese traditional customs to being seen as significant religious activities. The Chinese scientist working in the West and fluent in English is probably an example of the first, while the grandmother in Hong Kong who speaks only Cantonese would be at the other extreme.

Temples are an important focus of Chinese communities. Here offerings to the gods usually consist of fruit or packaged food items. Fully prepared food is not offered to the gods, as this would imply the individual was assuming an equal status with the deity in sharing a meal with them. Ghosts may be offered cooked food, but only at a small table set outside the back door.

Spirit money is also burnt for gods, ancestors and ghosts. Gods should be given gold, ancestors silver and ghosts copper. Many temples have large ovens outside the main gate for this purpose. In Taiwan, businessmen often burn spirit money every fifteen days to ensure prosperity in their business ventures. This should not be seen merely as a means of bribing the deity, but as a Confucian principle of reciprocity in which the relationship between the parties is maintained.

All temples have birthday celebrations for their resident deity, and these are sponsored by community associations. Although a Daoist priest may be hired to perform the rituals during the celebration, it is the local community that organizes the event. The image of the deity is taken out of the temple for a tour of the area, traditionally carried on a palanquin, but more often today on the back of a small truck. This is the equivalent of the inspection that would have been conducted by the magistrate or high official in imperial times. The procession is often a long parade, with musicians and dancers and even children's groups.

For example, every year on a hot June day in an older section of Taibei City, Taiwan, the city god is brought out on a procession of his territory. At the start of the procession a portable image of the god passes through the temple precincts containing the incense brazier and out of the temple. The image is installed on the god's palanquin, which is now transported by a truck instead of shouldered by men. Youths with painted faces and wielding ancient weapons are at the head of the procession. Some of these young men are fulfilling a vow made when the god was petitioned for a cure or some other benefit during the previous year. Sometimes their martial dance becomes frenzied, indicating that they have been possessed by the deity. Most prominent in the retinue following the palanquin are the god's generals, some of whom are accompanied by their own entourage of divine soldiers. The general is a giant-sized puppet born atop a man's shoulders, while the soldiers are costumed, paint-faced youths.

Another major festival is *Qingming* ('clear and bright'), which takes place in early Spring 105 days after the winter solstice. This is popularly known as Tomb-sweeping Day. In the villages there may be traditional performances conducted outdoors, particularly for the earth god. He and the other gods are invited to attend a procession to the cemetery. Here the families gather to clear their ancestral tombs of any vegetation and rubbish, explode crackers to scare away ghosts, burn incense and pray to the ancestors. Today the families often have a group photograph and a picnic at the site. This is not so much a mourning ritual as a family reunion that includes both the living and the dead.

Divination

Divination is still commonly practised today. The three main forms are moon blocks (*bei*), divination slips (*qian*) and spirit mediums (*jitong*). Moon blocks are found in temples and are often used in conjunction with divination slips. Each petitioner chooses at random a long bamboo stick from a tall vase, sets it on the offering table and, from a kneeling position, casts the wooden moon blocks. If the moon blocks give an unsatisfactory response, the first bamboo stick is rejected and another is drawn from the vase. When the blocks fall so that one is facing up and the other is facing down three times in succession, the believer reads the number carved on the bamboo stick and selects the corresponding fortune slip from a frame hanging on the temple wall. These fortune slips are abstruse, and the worshipper often seeks aid from a temple overseer to interpret their relevance to his particular problem. When the fortune is 'accurate' – meaning that the god both understood the situation and gave advice that later proved beneficial – the divination slips are said to have 'spiritual efficacy'. Health problems, disharmony within the family, a string of bad luck or a dilemma in one's business or private life are all common reasons for visiting a temple and casting the moon blocks. The accuracy of the divination slips is often cited as evidence of a temple's efficacy. Divination, however, is a highly individualized affair, and some temples and their gods are better suited to particular needs than others. Temple overseers will not hesitate to recommend that a worshipper go elsewhere for assistance, and they do not see this as compromising the efficacy of their own temple.

Believers often visit temples for advice about their health, and some people have marvellous tales to tell. A miraculous cure is ready proof of efficacy. Within temples that specialize in healing, the god of medicine takes the prime place. The pattern for each patient is the same: the disease is often sudden and inexplicable, and it seems incurable even after a great outlay of money has been paid for modern medicine. At last the family comes to visit the temple, and a gradual cure results. The grateful recipients of the god's healing frequently return to offer prayers and gifts.

Spirit mediums (jitong)

In Taiwan, for example, spirit mediums are used both for divination and to manifest the presence of the god during a temple festival. Spirit mediums can be consulted at temples, or at home and some even have storefront offices. They may be male or female. Those who participate in community rituals or temple festivals are usually young men who enter a trance and cut their bodies with knives, drawing blood. This has all the expression of theatre that fascinates the crowds with spectacular feats like climbing a ladder of swords.

A diviner will similarly operate by entering a self-induced trance state. This is achieved by gradually rocking back and forth on a bench while chanting, and after twenty or so minutes the attendant will lead the client to the diviner. The client is then able to ask the spirit possessing the diviner specific questions, and the replies are written down by the attendant. After the consultation, the diviner jumps backwards to disconnect himself, or herself, from the spirit and is caught by the attendant. Spirit mediums most often identify the source of the misfortune as resulting from a particular ancestor or spirit.

Another form is the divination chair, or sedan chair, which is usually only about 45 centimetres high, and is considered to be the seat of the deity. It is held by two people, each holding two legs. They start to move rhythmically with the chair and enter into a light trance. Then together they bend the chair over and with one of the arms of the chair, trace out on a tabletop some Chinese characters. These are read and recorded by a third person sitting at the table, and are considered to be the response of the deity. The spirit medium may also be present to invite the deity to sit on the chair.

Exorcisms of troublesome ghosts are usually performed by Daoist priests known as 'red-hat', in contrast to the more highly trained 'black-hat' priests. The red-hat priests have less knowledge of the Daoist canonical literature, and represent more a mixture of Daoism and popular religion. A typical story comes from Taiwan:

> The medium came along, bearing with him the tools of his exorcism – a black triangular flag, a sword and seven sticks of incense. He set up an altar in the front of the house, calling on the gods to enter him before he went inside. He offered fruit and incense to the gods. Once the gods had entered him, he went inside the house, followed by a second exorcist. They went from room to room while the first exorcist recited incantations and hung written spells on each room as it was cleansed of spirits. Gradually the spirits were all driven into one small room and then the second exorcist came into action. He had a big ceramic jar with him and he went carefully over the whole room until he found the spot he wanted. There he started digging until he came to a collection of bones which

were tangled in the earth beneath the floor. It was those bones which had kept the spirits in the house, the bones of people who been killed long before. He dropped the bones into the jar and sealed the top with a written spell on yellow paper, and then dropped it into the depths of the ocean, leaving the family in possession of a new quiet little farmhouse.[8]

Feng Shui

The term *Feng Shui* (pronounced 'fung shway') literally means 'wind' (*Feng*) and 'water' (*Shui*). As we have seen earlier, *Feng Shui* is an elaborate form of geomancy that has a long history in China. It was banned in 1949 after the establishment of the CCP in China, but it has continued in Hong Kong, Taiwan and many areas settled by Chinese migrants. It is now undergoing something of a resurgence as part of the so-called 'New Age' movement.

Feng Shui is the belief and practice that for life to be auspicious, there needs to be a balance of the *yin* and *yang* elements of *qi*. Practically this is often expressed in the design of a house. A traditional Chinese house was built facing south with a wide view over water. Negative forces can result from something hindering the flow of *qi* through the house. Today this may be considered to be a tree or a lamppost set outside one's front door. To deal with this negativity, a mirror may be placed at the entrance to reflect it back. This has now become a complex skill of geomancy that may need one of the many self-appointed *Feng Shui* experts, who now offer their services in house design and decoration. They are often sought after a period of difficulty or misfortune to help remove the negativity, or simply to avoid such dangers.

*   *   *

Many Chinese of the Diaspora have converted to Christianity, which they have found meaningful and relevant to their life as global citizens. Even so, they have often retained their distinctive identity and have formed their own Christian fellowships in major cities around the world. Today, in the twenty-first century, many Chinese migrants are returning to China to take advantage of the economic boom in the country. The national newspapers humorously call such people 'turtles' who are swimming home. A man quoted in one newspaper said, 'What I want is not a stable and carefree life in a foreign country, but to be part of the sizzling economic development of my own country.'[9]

Further reading

Bloomfield, Frena, *The Book of Chinese Beliefs*, London: Arrow Books, 1983. A British journalist writes about the folk beliefs of people in Hong Kong.

Smith, R., *Fortune-Tellers & Philosophers: Divination in Traditional Chinese Society*, San Francisco: Westview Press, 1991. An excellent essay on different forms of divination, mainly in the Qing period.

Jordon, D. K., *Gods, Ghosts and Ancestors: Folk Religion in a Taiwanese Village*, Berkeley: University of California Press, 1972. An anthropological study of popular religion based on fieldwork done in the 1960s.

Wolf, A. P., *Religion and Ritual in Chinese Society*, Stanford: Stanford University Press, 1974. Although somewhat dated, this is an excellent collection of essays on popular religion.

Websites

Dimsum. The website of the British Chinese community. http://www.dimsum.co.uk/index.php

The Chinese in California. An American memories site. http://lcweb2.loc.gov/ammem/award99/cubhtml/cichome.html

Milefo's homepage. http://mi-le-fo.thetempleguy.com/index.htm

Chinese Paper Gods. Collected by Anne S. Goodrich in 1931, these have been digitalized by Colombia University. http://www.columbia.edu/cu/lweb/digital/collections/east asian/paper_gods/index.html

British *Feng Shui* **Society.** This website shows how the Chinese teaching on *Feng Shui* has been adapted for the British context. http://www.fengshuisociety.org.uk/

Chapter 13

MAO'S CHINA

Chairman Mao's political rule (1949–76)

This is a book about religion in China, but the wars and rev-
olutions of the twentieth century had such an impact upon
the people that the political events cannot be ignored.
Contact with the West brought many new ideas, but none
was to have such a major impact as Marxism, with its
underlying atheistic assumptions. It was Mao Zedong who
largely framed these ideas to suit the Chinese situation and
ruthlessly applied them. Many accounts have been written
of the life of Mao, and these have varied greatly in how the
man has been portrayed. The earliest account was that of
Edgar Snow, an American journalist caught up with the
events of China in the 1930s, who in 1937 published an
account of the life of Mao that placed him on the international scene.[1] A more recent biography that has achieved
fame in the Western world is that of Jung Chang and Jon
Halliday, *Mao: The Unknown Story*.[2] This is far more critical, and seeks to expose the intrigues and crimes of the
period. Perhaps the difference of opinion between these
two books illustrates the problems of analysing the life of
such a complex and influential personality.

The Communist government (1949–66)

The Communists came to power in China on 1 October
1949 and immediately launched needed reforms. Whereas
ancient China had been an empire, New China was
proclaimed to be a multinational state. The non-Chinese
peoples along its frontiers were seen as distinct but equal

ethnic groups. *Han* was considered to be the correct term for the majority people in the former heartlands of China, and 'Chinese' was used for all ethnic groups in the People's Republic. Stalin had enunciated a nationalities policy with four criteria for establishing nationality: common language, common territory, a common economic life and common cultural traits. Using these criteria, Chinese linguists finally recognized fifty-six minority nationalities. Some, like the Tibetans and Uyghurs, clearly fitted into this definition, but people like the Hui – Chinese-speaking Muslims scattered throughout the country – were more difficult to categorize. This policy also provided a further reason for the Chinese army in 1959 to incorporate (or 'liberate', depending on one's point of view) Tibet.

The Communist Party (CCP) ended hyperinflation, and began a massive land reform programme with the slogan 'Land to the Tiller!' At that time about 30 per cent of the tillable land was in the hands of a small minority of landlords, and the CCP aimed at reducing this, which would effectively destroy the old gentry-landlords as a class of people. The Party had widespread support among the peasantry, who at that time made up 80 per cent of China's population. The people wanted to rid themselves of the gentry-landlords who had dominated their lives for centuries. However, the land reform programme became chaotic and bloody as many peasants sought retribution from the landlords for past grievances. It is estimated that more than a million people died during this period.

Social organization
The Communist Party is the key organization in Chinese politics, and it is essential to have an understanding of how it works in order to appreciate Chinese politics. The usual explanation of the working of the inner Party's decision-making is to see the Party leadership functioning on a 'factional model'. Factions are informal groupings of leading

cadres (officials) centred around a main leadership figure, based on ties of *guanxi* (mutual benefits, the same place of origin and patronage). Such factions exist at all levels of Chinese society. In Chinese history since 1949 factional conflicts have been common and they have often been solved not through compromise but through purges, especially under Mao Zedong. The main policy question that has continually faced factions has been how to create a socialist society. The main options have been to follow either the Maoist model or that of the Soviet Union.

The social system that was established during the 1950s identified people as being of three classes: red, grey and black. 'Reds' were the cadres, revolutionary martyrs' family members, soldiers, workers, poor and lower-middle-class peasants. 'Greys' were *petit bourgeoisie* and middle-class peasants. The 'Black' class label was for landlords, rich peasants, counter-revolutionaries and those regarded as 'bad elements'. 'Rightists' were added to the list in 1957 for reasons that will be described later.

During the period 1949–79 social mobility was planned. This allowed about 13 per cent of those with worker status and 2 per cent of peasants to become cadres. This was based on political credentials and factional ties with those with upward social mobility. Downward social mobility was also notable and amounted to about 15 per cent of cadres being demoted to workers or peasants ('sending down') during political campaigns and purges.

Another important social institution enforced in the 1950s was the *Hukou* system, which discriminated between the rural and urban dwellers. This system of exclusion has deep roots in China and can be traced back centuries. Yet the system introduced at this time was qualitatively different from the imperial *hukou* system, since it introduced an unprecedented level of rigidity in its role and capacity of division and exclusion. As Fei-Ling Wang writes:

The PRC *hukou* system requires that every Chinese citizen register with the *hukou* authority (the *hukou* police) at birth. The categories of non-agricultural (urban) or agricultural (rural), legal address and location, and unit affiliation (employment), and a host of personal and family information are documented and verified to become a person's permanent *hukou* record. A person's *hukou* location and categorization or type was determined by his mother's *hukou* location and type rather than his birthplace until 1998, when a child was allowed to inherit the father's or the mother's *hukou* location and categorization. No one can acquire legal permanent residence and the numerous community-based rights, opportunities, benefits, and privileges anywhere other than where his *hukou* is. Only through proper authorization of the government can one change his *hukou* location and especially his *hukou* categorization from the rural type to the urban type.[3]

The majority of the Chinese population, who live in rural areas, have therefore been peacefully excluded under the *hukou* system. The much smaller urban population of about 20 per cent have had much better access to economic and social opportunities and benefits, and have also dominated Chinese politics. To a lesser extent, urban residents in smaller cities and in less developed regions have also been excluded compared with those living in major urban centres or regions more favoured by the government in terms of investment, subsidies, or policy flexibilities.

As a consequence of Chinese reforms since 1978, the *hukou* system has been adapted in a number of ways, and money has eroded some of the old edges of the system. However, in so doing it has created new divisions based on wealth. There has also been some controlled mobility for low-skilled or even unskilled labourers, as will be discussed in Chapter 15.

The first five-year plan (1953–57)
In 1953, the CCP launched its first five-year plan for industry. It was just at this time that China suffered a number of poor harvests resulting in many peasants migrating to the cities to escape hunger. At the same time, the Korean War had just ended, and many young men were being demobilized. Unemployment was rising in China's cities. Mao Zedong was disturbed that some family farmers were becoming more successful than others, and by the way that the successful farmers started lending money to the less fortunate. This resulted in the same debate that had arisen among the Communists in the Soviet Union in the 1920s: how far should they go in accommodating free enterprise as opposed to building socialism?

The CCP decided to launch a new programme of collectivized farming. China's peasantry saw Chairman Mao and the CCP as heroic leaders much more so than Russia's peasantry had seen Stalin and the Bolsheviks in this role. Therefore, throughout 1956 the peasants cooperated with the Party, and there was none of the resistance and warfare that had accompanied the collectivization of agriculture in the Soviet Union. By the end of the summer of 1956 nearly 90 per cent of China's farmers had joined a collective farm. The average collective consisted of around 170 families. The family unit remained, each family eating and living together under the same roof. Each family was allowed their own small plot of land and was able to sell the produce from these private plots as they pleased. Free enterprise remained, but it had been reduced, and socialism had been advanced.

Meanwhile, the birth rate among people in the countryside remained high, and people were still migrating from the countryside into the cities, where unemployment was growing. Peasant income remained low, which provided little in revenues for the government to invest in industrialization, and little with which to repay loans from the Soviet

Union. Manufacturing in 1956 and 1957 grew at an annual rate of 4 per cent, but Party strategists wished for more spectacular gains. They estimated that because of China's poverty, several years might pass before a more impressive rate in gains could be achieved. Seeing the growth in agricultural production as a part of the problem, the government sought to increase peasant incentives to grow more food by reducing taxes to 25 per cent of their income.

Mao was an egalitarian, with little respect for intellectuals and the educated. He had called intellectuals the most ignorant of people, and he had described China's common folk as the fount of wisdom and the hope of the future. Mao wanted economic advancement superior to what was taking place in other less-developed nations, and he believed he could accomplish this by turning the economy over to the spontaneity of the masses. To jump-start this spontaneity, Mao developed a new programme, which he called the 'Great Leap Forward'.

The Great Leap Forward (1956–59)

The Great Leap Forward was advertised as a technological revolution – as the proletarianization of the economy preceding mechanization of the economy. The development of agriculture was to be a priority, and in place of creating heavy industry, light industry was to be dispersed across the land. Relying on the masses, the government dismissed its economists and centralized economic planning. The government would continue to collect taxes and requisition grain, but the masses would mobilize themselves and run things spontaneously at the local level.

Mao wanted to move faster in the direction of the Communism of which Marx had spoken, with an abolition of differences between rich and poor and an abolition of divisions in labour.

Mao spoke of China achieving Communism sooner than the Soviet Union. He was displeased in 1956 when

Khrushchev denounced Stalin, and the Chinese Communists continued to praise Stalin to their nation. Mao characterized Khrushchev as a 'revisionist' – in other words, deviating from true Marxism. The ideological split between Mao and Khrushchev was aggravated by their different approaches to the power of the United States, the atomic bomb and provocations from Taiwan. Mao disliked Khrushchev's attempt at *détente* with the United States.

At the heart of the Great Leap Forward was the replacement of collective farms with People's Communes. Each commune consisted of 10,000 to 20,000 people – considerably larger than the collective farms. In the communes, peasants ate in mess halls. They surrendered their tools and farm animals to the commune and much of their personal property, including furniture and chickens. Women were encouraged to leave wifely duties and join the work brigades.

In addition to farming, in 1958 and 1959 new roads were built, new factories were constructed, dams were built, as were dikes, irrigation channels and lakes. Land was reclaimed, and new terraces were carved into mountains, most of them created by hand labour rather than modern earth-working machines. Then, in July 1958, the 'battle for steel' began. Communes were encouraged to build backyard furnaces to increase the national production of steel, but, in practice, the quality was poor and the effort merely withdrew labour from growing food. The outcome was a complete disaster.

No one in the countryside had time to tend their own plot of land. It has been estimated that these plots had accounted for 7 per cent of China's crop cultivation and 30 per cent of peasant income, but by the end of 1958 they were all but eliminated. It was now the commune that distributed whatever food there was to eat. It was the commune that organized everything, and it was the commune's responsibility to report to the government how much was being produced. It was the communes that had to fill production quotas and send the required percentage of what they produced to the government.

Some members emerged as leaders in the communes, but this was usually more by their enthusiasm and patriotism than their management experience or skill. Rather than the communal egalitarianism and spontaneity that Mao had envisioned, leadership developed into regimentation. Although 1958 was a year of good harvests, eager leaders wishing to enhance their prestige passed on to the central government inflated figures as to how much food they had produced. Some reported that their crop production had doubled in the year. As a result, based on these figures, the government set higher production goals and requisitioned even more food from the countryside. Rather than commune leaders confessing their error and refusing to send food that was needed to feed their fellow comrades, they distributed the inadequate supplies to those they favoured and left others to starve.

By the summer of 1959 much of the enthusiasm for the Great Leap was fading. It was another year of bad weather and bad harvests. Once again, too, little food was left for local consumption, and again people starved. In 1960, unusually dry weather brought drought in the north of China, and unusually wet weather, in the form of typhoons, caused flooding in the south. Agricultural production dropped further. Party leaders were only now becoming aware of the breakdown in the economy and the extent of the starvation in the countryside. By the end of 1961 it is estimated that as many as 20 million people had died from malnutrition.

Discovering how bad things were, the Communist Party struggled to put things right. Mao chose a devoted follower, Lin Biao, who was the defence minister and leader of the People's Liberation Army. Lin Biao began promoting Mao, and put together a little red book of quotations from

Chairman Mao for distribution within the army. Despite Mao maintaining his position within the Party, most high-ranking Party officials swung towards favouring a pragmatic retreat from Mao's Great Leap Forward. In 1963, at the age of seventy, an unhappy Mao diminished his participation in Party matters, leaving the Party to more pragmatic men.

Industry, large and small, was to remain state owned, but authority was given to trained managers as opposed to Maoist ideologues. Skilled technicians were promoted, and material incentives were created in the place of moralistic slogans. Control over commerce was returned to an economics ministry. The government closed thousands of small and inefficient factories. The industrial workforce was cut in half, and many were sent back to the countryside, where, it was hoped, they could find gainful employment.

In the countryside, more freedom was given to the communes to set their own production quotas. Attempts were made to make the communes work effectively. Party pragmatists encouraged the re-establishment of open markets in the countryside. Peasants were encouraged to trade locally, and for the sake of industrialization farming families were encouraged to buy goods made in urban factories rather than to engage in communal industries. With a good harvest in 1962 and a return to incentives over official altruism, came a rise in industrial production and productivity. In 1964, the Party leader second to Mao, Zhou Enlai, announced that the recovery from economic disaster was complete.

The Three-Self Movement

Through the turmoil of these years the Christian Church faced its greatest challenge. One of the most significant figures of the time was Y. T. Wu (1893–1979) who played a major role in forming what was to become the 'Three-Self Patriotic Movement' (TSPM). He is one of the most controversial figures in the history of the Chinese Church.[4] During May 1950, there were three meetings between Zhou Enlai and a group of Christian leaders headed by Y. T. Wu. Out of these meetings was to emerge what was to become known as 'The Christian Manifesto'. This document, less than 1,000 Chinese characters long, had as its principal themes anti-imperialism and the need to 'purge imperialistic influences from within Christianity itself'. To many Chinese Protestants, the manifesto was too radical and they refused to endorse it. However, with the outbreak of the Korean War and the intensified anti-American propaganda, the attitude of many changed. By 1953, some 400,000 Christians (half the entire Protestant community in China) endorsed the manifesto.

'The Three-Self Patriotic Movement' (TSPM) of Chinese Protestants was formerly inaugurated in 1951 with Y. T. Wu as President. The name came from the ideas of Henry Venn, a former leader of the Church Missionary Society who argued that all churches should be 'self-governing', 'self-supporting' and 'self-propagating'. Even in the nineteenth century Christian missionaries had spoken about the implication of this policy in China. Wu had made use of the idea to secure toleration of the Church by the Communist leaders.

1958 was the year of the 'Great Leap' forward and the formation of the People's Communes, and it seemed logical to the Party officials that the Church should follow a similar policy. Churches in various cities began to unite. This resulted in the abandonment of many distinctive denominational rituals and practices. For example, the Salvation Army had to give up all its military regulations and the Seventh-Day Adventists had to abolish their daily morning prayers and work on the Sabbath.

All the Protestant churches in China officially became Three-Self churches. The Three-Self Movement became the only bridge between the Chinese government and the Chinese Protestants, and it effectively became the means of control over the Church. An evaluation of the Three-Self Movement is still contentious. Today's leaders of the TSPM would say that it had three main achievements, namely: 'encouraging Chinese Protestants to become patriotic, helping the Chinese church to become self-governing, and urging Chinese Christianity to get rid of its foreign features.'[5]

Many evangelical groups felt unable to be involved with the process and were marginalized. In the 1950s there was an increasing hostility between the Communist regime and the TSPM on one side, and the evangelical leaders on the other. The government adopted a policy of repressing evangelical leaders like Wang Mingdao and Ni Tuosheng (Watchman Nee), and they were publicly denounced in 1955–56. The group outside the TSPM was to become what the West would call the 'underground church'.

As political changes escalated in the 1960s, Y. T. Wu proposed a 'socialist religion'. Wu argued that belief in God was not contrary to the philosphy of secular materialism, but that the two would eventually come together in a new synthesis. Such a view had little credence within the CCP, who held to the Marxist theory that 'religion is the opiate of the people'. Mao Zedong himself was hostile to all religious belief. All religious traditions in China were, however, about to go through an even greater trial.

The Cultural Revolution (1966–67)

The cult of Mao

Despite Mao's antagonism towards religion, during the 1960s he realized the Chinese people's need for a strong leader. Mao therefore encourged his own personality cult, following that of Lenin and Stalin in Russia. The new cult rearranged the old idea of the 'five relationships' of

Confucian teaching, and filial love, once directed to parents, was now directed to Mao. Perhaps this is best seen in Jung Chang's book *Wild Swans*. She was born in 1952, and reveals the effect that Mao had on one teenage girl.

> For two thousand years China had an emperor figure who was state power and spiritual authority rolled into one. The religious feelings which people in other parts of the world have toward a god have in China always been directed toward the emperor. My parents, like hundreds of millions of Chinese, were influenced by this tradition. Mao made himself more godlike by shrouding himself in mystery.[6]

The mass movement

In 1965, at the age of 72, Mao came out of seclusion. He complained about the rise of a new class of bureaucrats. China, he believed, was going the way of the Soviet Union and becoming a bureaucratic state. The Party, according to Mao, had been taken over by 'capitalist roaders', meaning people with a bourgeois mentality. Mao, like Trotsky, was advocating 'permanent revolution', although he did not label it as such. Mao began to create what was to become known as the Cultural Revolution.

Mao Zedong's wife, Jiang Qing, a former actress, belonged to a group of Maoists who wished for socialist purity in literature and the performing arts. In February 1966, the minister of defence, Lin Biao, still siding with Mao, invited Jiang Qing to establish cultural policy for the People's Liberation Army. Jiang Qing and her group were encouraged. They argued that China's garden of culture was infested with 'anti-socialist poisonous weeds'. Jiang Qing called for a revolution against bourgeois culture – a cultural revolution. Mao spoke of weeding from authority those who had chosen to lead China down 'the capitalist road'. Old comrades directly beneath Mao chose to accommodate him.

Mao moved again for the support of the masses and especially the young people. Young people, he said, were the most willing to learn and were 'the least conservative in their thinking'. Jiang Qing agreed with Mao's move, and she allied her group with student unrest in Beijing. China's students were more in tune with Mao's idealism than they were with the pragmatism practised by Mao's Party rivals. Jiang Qing's cultural revolutionaries distributed armbands to the students and declared that they were a new vanguard, the 'Red Guards'. Mao encouraged the student radicals to 'learn revolution by making revolution'. In Beijing their ranks swelled with disaffected youths from the provinces, attracted by the rhetoric, by their reverence for Mao as the father of China's revolution and by the excitement. During the autumn of 1966, Mao was reviewing gigantic parades at Tiananmen Square, his Red Guards chanting and waving the little red book of *Quotations from Chairman Mao* that Lin Biao had put together for the army. The cult of Mao was at its height.

The young people were with Mao in his attempt to prevent China from developing into a bureaucratic state, as had the Soviet Union. Backed by their government, they also demonstrated displeasure with US actions in Vietnam. Unlike protesting students in the United States at the time, China's Red Guards enjoyed the support of China's military, Lin Biao encouraging the students and describing Mao as 'the greatest genius of the present era' and as 'the great helmsman'. Lin Biao spoke of Mao as having created a Marxism-Leninism that was 'remoulding the souls of the people'.

All through 1966, secondary schools and colleges closed in China. Students, from nine through to eighteen years of age, followed Maoist directives to destroy those things of the past that they believed should be no part of the new China. These were called the 'Four Olds': old customs, old habits, old culture and old thinking. In a state of euphoria and with support from the government and army, the students went about China's cities and villages, wrecking old buildings, old temples and even ancient objects of art. In their wake, monasteries and places of worship were converted into warehouses, and leading Buddhist monks were sent off to do manual labour. To make the new China, the Red Guards even attacked their own parents, teachers, school administrators as insufficiently revolutionary. They even targeted 'intellectuals' and 'capitalist roaders' within the Communist Party.

In cities throughout China, Mao's movement was joined by a variety of people trying to prove they were as loyal to Mao as were the Red Guards. Politicians joined the movement in an effort to win against their political rivals. A mass hysteria had developed. Mobs of Red Guards grabbed prominent individuals whom they deemed insufficiently revolutionary, put dunce caps on their heads or hung placards around their necks, and paraded them through the streets. Officials were dragged from their offices. Their files were examined and often destroyed, and the officials were often replaced by youths with no managerial experience. The purges in the Party went higher and higher, until Deng Xiaoping and Liu Shaoqi were removed from their offices, and they and their families were humiliated. Filled with righteousness, the power of their numbers, and support from Mao, the campaigns for revolutionary change became violent. Anyone seen as evil was humiliated and beaten to death. Thousands of people died, including many who committed suicide.

The attack on religion

In the spring of 1966 the following poster was fixed to the wall of the YMCA in Beijing:

> There is no God; there is no Spirit; there is no Jesus; there is no Mary; there is no Joseph. How can adults believe in these

things?... Priests live in luxury and suck the blood of the workers... Like Islam and Catholicism, Protestantism is a reactionary feudal ideology, the opium of the people, with foreign origins and contacts... We are atheists; we believe only in Mao Zedong. We call on all people to burn Bibles, destroy images, and dispense with religious associations.[7]

Throughout the country bands of Red Guards destroyed images, closed temples, mosques and monasteries. In Tibet, the Red Guards blew up many of the most important religious centres in their belief that they were heralding a new Communist day. Buddhist monks were forced to return to what the Red Guards regarded as profitable labour as peasants on the land. Many religious leaders were beaten or killed, and scriptures were burned. Religious teaching and practice was halted throughout the nation. Premier Zhou Enlai fortunately saved many of the temples, palaces and other ancient buildings by putting them off limits to the Red Guards and placing military forces around them. In 1967, the last eight European nuns in China were deported to Hong Kong.

From the brink of chaos
By September 1967, the chaos was too much even for Mao. With differences of opinion being inevitable, violent battles erupted between Red Guard factions. Mao ordered the People's Liberation Army to quell the Red Guard factionalism, and Lin Biao called on the Red Guards to stop fighting each other and instead to study the works of Mao. The chaos and deaths continued, with the People's Liberation Army itself splitting into hostile camps. Mao was aware that some order was necessary, and he commanded that the Red Guards disperse.

By the summer of 1968, with the help of the army, the Red Guards were subdued. In large numbers, groups of young Red Guards were sent to labour in the countryside –

confused, as they were now cast down from the height of glory and political importance. Many of these students were not allowed to return to the cities until 1977, and they had to face privations and hard work among the peasants. Mao's romance with the masses was over, and he counted on the People's Liberation Army to bring order.

The last years of Mao Zedong (1969–76)

Mao wished to rebuild the Party, and the Ninth Party Congress was held in April 1969. Lin Biao was named Mao's successor, and at the Party Congress he denounced his old comrade and former rival, Liu Shaoqi. After the Party Congress, Mao moved to reduce the role of the military within the Party, and he moved against Lin Biao for reasons not easily ascertained. Perhaps Mao had come to see Lin Biao as too opportunistic and too powerful. Zhou Enlai was also opposed to Lin Biao, and Zhou also seemed to want to reduce the role of the military in Party affairs. While Lin Biao favoured unending class struggle, Zhou preferred to improve relations with the capitalist powers.

Mao visited regional military commanders and criticized Lin Biao, and Lin Biao was obliged to humble himself with public self-criticism. Reports suggest that Lin Biao's son, apparently outraged over treatment of his father, tried to strike back and to uphold his father's standing in the Party by instigating a military coup. Lin Biao was accused of intending to assassinate Mao, and the government moved against him. On 13 September 1971 Lin Biao and his wife fled to Russia in an aircraft that, surprisingly, crashed in Mongolia, killing all aboard.

With Lin Biao out of the way, Zhou Enlai was able to begin making overtures to the West. This commenced by what has become known as ping-pong diplomacy. A table tennis team from the United States was competing in Japan when it was invited to visit China. The friendliness expressed towards the team was a sensation in the US press, and a new atmosphere in relations arose between the two countries. In February 1972, President Richard Nixon and his Secretary of State, Henry Kissinger, journeyed to China. Mao was now seventy-nine and suffering from Parkinson's disease.

Conflict continued within the Party as to which direction China should take. Mao's wife, Jiang Qing, still favoured belligerence toward the capitalist powers. Her hostility was evident during the visit of President Nixon. She continued to advocate cultural purity, attacking even the artistic appreciation of Schubert, Beethoven and other Western composers.

Deng Xiaoping, who had been purged during the Cultural Revolution, was restored to prominence in the Party. Then, on 8 January 1976, Deng's ally, Zhou Enlai, died of cancer. Mourning for Zhou was widespread. Deng gave the eulogy, but it was a rival, Hua Guofeng, who was elevated to fill Zhou Enlai's position as Party leader. Deng was still thought of by many as a 'capitalist roader'.

Students in Beijing, still clinging to Maoist idealism, demonstrated in favour of rights for the poor and denounced 'revisionists and capitalist roaders'. Rival demonstrations also erupted, and on 5 April thousands of students rioted at Tiananmen Square after finding that tributes for Zhou Enlai that had been placed there the day before had been removed. The demonstrators displayed criticisms of Mao. Police cars were set afire. The outburst was quelled by security forces and an urban workers' militia, who arrested as many as 4,000 demonstrators. Deng was suspected of having encouraged the demonstration regarding tributes to Zhou, and those in the Party opposed to Deng rallied against him. Deng was purged again, but he was allowed to keep his Party membership.

Meanwhile, Mao's health was fading. Then came a major earthquake in which a quarter of a million people were killed. This was traditionally supposed to be nature's way of heralding the death of an Emperor. On 9 September 1976, almost twenty-seven years after he had declared the creation of the People's Republic of China, Mao died. A week of mourning was declared. The Soviet Union sent no condolences. Around 300,000 people filed by Mao's body and casket at the Great Hall of the People at Tiananmen Square, but there was less emotion than had been expressed with the death of Zhou Enlai. The ensuing power struggle resulted in Hua Guofeng being declared Mao's successor as Party Chairman, and Mao's wife, Jiang Qing, and three of her fellow cultural revolutionaries were imprisoned. They became known as the 'Gang of Four' and were blamed for the excesses of the Cultural Revolution, which effectively removed most of the blame from Chairman Mao.

*   *   *

The Cultural Revolution and its aftermath affected everyone in China, not only those who held to a religious belief. The young people who were members of the Red Guard have been called 'the Lost Generation' because they lost their chance of an education, and many of them lost their hope for the future. However, as we have seen, the Chinese have a long history with many peaks and troughs in their civilization. Soon after the Cultural Revolution, I remember sitting in a small eating house with a Chinese friend in southern China, quietly talking about the events of the previous years. I asked him how he thought these events would affect the history of China. On a piece of paper he drew a straight line, and at the end made a small blip. I understood! In the long history of China, the Cultural Revolution will eventually come to be seen as no more than a little blip. Even so, some forty years after the event, I still know of some older people who can't think about that time without visibly shaking.

Further reading

Chang J., and Halliday, J., *Mao: The Unknown Story*, London: Jonathan Cape, 2005. One of the most recent biographies, focusing upon the negative aspects of his life.

Chang, J., *Wild Swans: Three Daughters in China*, London: HarperCollins, 1991. A moving personal story of three generations living through the Cultural Revolution.

Mosher, S. W., *Broken Earth: The Rural Chinese*, London: Robert Hale, 1984. One of the first anthropological studies of the peasants in modern China, based on 18 months' field-work conducted in 1979–80 in a commune in southern China.

Whyte, R., *Unfinished Encounter: China and Christianity*, London: Fount Paperbacks, 1988. A major study of the history of Christianity in China, especially focusing on the twentieth century.

Wickeri, P. L., *Seeking the Common Ground: Protestant Christianity, the Three-Self Movement, and China's United Front*, Maryknoll: Orbis, 1988.

Xinran, *The Good Women of China*, London: Chatto & Windus, 2002. Fifteen moving stories of women who lived through the Cultural Revolution.

Websites

Virtual Museum of the Cultural Revolution. www.cnd.org/CR/english

The Mao Cult. An interesting section of a larger site on China. This part shows many posters of Mao from the 1960s. http://www.iisg.nl/~landsberger/cult.html

The Writings of Chairman Mao. This Marxist site provides an excellent collection of the writings of Mao, including some of his poetry. It also has a short biography. http://www.marxists.org/reference/archive/mao/index.htm

Chinese History Research Site at UCSD. A site maintained by students and faculty of the Modern History of China at the University of California, San Diego. http://orpheus.ucsd.edu/chinesehistory/

Chapter 14

DENG XIAOPING AND CHINA'S ECONOMIC REFORM

The opening up of China to the world (1976–97)

In late 1978, Deng Xiaoping emerged as China's top leader. He had been a Communist from the earliest days of the movement and was one of Zhou Enlai's closest allies, even though he had twice been purged and twice rehabilitated. The new leadership was faced with the challenge of reinvigorating the Party from the low point of Mao's final years. Deng was dubbed 'paramount leader' though he remained only a vice president in title.

Deng Xiaoping was a Hakka, born in the vicinity of Chongqing in the western province of Sichuan in 1904. In the summer of 1920, Deng graduated from the Chongqing Preparatory School where he and eighty schoolmates participated in a work-study programme for Chinese students. As a result they were allowed to go to France. Deng was the youngest of the Chinese students, and spent most of his time in France working in various industrial plants or helping in restaurants. He barely earned enough to survive, but while he was in France he came under the influence of his seniors and especially Zhou Enlai. Deng began to study Marxism, and in 1922 he joined the Communist Party of Chinese Youth in Europe. In the second half of 1924 he joined the Chinese Communist Party itself and became one of the leading members of the General Branch of the Youth League in Europe. In 1926 Deng had the opportunity to study in Moscow before returning to China in early 1927.

Two years later Deng led the Bose Uprising in Guangxi Province against the Guomindang (GMD) government. The uprising failed and Deng had to escape by going to the Central Soviet Area in Jiangxi Province. He later joined Mao Zedong in the south of the country and took part in the Long March in 1934, during which Deng served as General Secretary of the Central Committee of the Communist Party. While acting as political commissar for Liu Bocheng, he organized several important military campaigns during the war with Japan and during the Civil War against the GMD. In late November 1949, Deng led the final assault on GMD forces that were under the direct command of Chiang Kai-shek in his native Sichuan. Deng quickly moved into positions of leadership within Mao's China, but as was shown in the previous chapter, this was not without its difficulties.

Deng Xiaoping's reforms (1978–88)

A new day was heralded in foreign relations as Deng visited the United States in 1979, and China began to open up to the outside world. Soon thousands of Chinese academics were studying at Western universities, and tens of thousands of Western tourists began to explore China, bringing with them needed foreign currency.

To pre-empt any controversy about political reform, in March 1979 Deng issued the Four Cardinal Principles that China must follow in its future development:

1. The Socialist Path.
2. The dictatorship of the Proletariat.
3. The leadership of the Party.
4. Marxism–Leninism-Mao Zedong Thought.

The figure of Mao was, however, a problem to the CCP in that he had been both China's Lenin and China's Stalin. The USSR had denounced the excesses of Stalin, but a similar move could not be made in China without undermining the whole system. The solution was to divide Mao's rule into his good early phase and his bad last phase, influenced by the Gang of Four. He would be forgiven for the failings of the Cultural Revolution in the light of initiating the socialist revolution. Mao's thoughts from his early phase were still accepted as the essential guide for China's future. Gradually the pinnacle role of Mao was reduced. Copies of the 'Little Red Book' quietly disappeared, and most portraits of Mao were removed from public places, although not the one adorning Tiananmen Square. Even so, by 1990 a sort of Mao nostalgia, known as 'Mao fever', gripped many people, partially in response to the corruption revealed among some of the leaders of the time.

In order to regain public confidence in the CCP, the Party membership was sifted in order to bring more educated and gifted members to the fore. Deng introduced four modernizations for the country. The first was agricultural reform. Throughout the whole period of Mao's rule, agricultural production had lagged behind the hopes of the leadership, and it had even declined during the time of the Cultural Revolution. A new system was introduced that encouraged additional production on the farms that could be sold locally on the free market. Management of farms was moved from communes down to smaller family units, which provided great incentives and so increased production.

The second modernization was industrial development which under Mao had been focused upon heavy industry with few consumer items. Deng totally reversed the economic policy and opened the country to foreign trade. Light industry was to be helped by foreign investment for the production of consumer goods for sale abroad.

This allowed joint ventures between foreign firms and Chinese government agencies, which was the basis of the third modernization. Special Economic Zones (SEZ) were built in restricted areas where foreign firms could establish plants and house foreign personnel in international style. The first of these was at Shenzhen opposite Hong Kong, to be followed by Zhuhai and Shantou in Guangdong Province, Xiamen in Fujian Province, and the entire Province of Hainan. The modernization of science and technology was the fourth aspect of the programme. Mao's anti-intellectualism was replaced by Deng's pragmatism, and the country began to move towards increasing economic growth.

Since 1960 the emphasis had been upon large families, but in 1981 a State Family Planning Commission was established and laid down the norm of a one-child family. The aim was to restrict the population to 1.2 billion by the turn of the century. There was much opposition to the policy, especially in rural areas, where the traditional preference for sons remained strong. However, through a system of heavy fines and government pressure the policy was introduced. Dispensation was given to the minority nationalities, but for most of the country it was universally applied. This act was to result in social problems for the following generation, as will be discussed in the next chapter.

By the end of the 1980s economic innovations and growth were obvious throughout the country, and this raised the expectation of associated political reform. People began to wonder how far the 'Four Basic Principles' stated by Deng in 1979 could be pushed. The Democratic Movement began in October 1978 when 'big character' posters discussing politics were allowed, but during the 1980s satellite television was becoming a more effective means of communication. In May 1989 General Secretary Gorbachev of the USSR came to a summit meeting in Beijing, and the world's TV companies came to report the event. They found Tiananmen Square a colourful campsite filled with many thousands of students and other peaceful demonstrators for democracy. The demonstrators demanded political reform, and on some days up to 1 million people were involved. As the world watched, two or three thousand protestors staged a hunger strike. The CCP leaders refused to negotiate, and after some hesitation they called in the tanks of the People's Liberation Army. Eventually, on 4 June they opened fire and killed at least 200 demonstrators and wounded thousands.[1] The world was stunned!

The Democracy Movement was denounced as a conspiracy to ferment chaos and undermine the CCP. There began a relentless pursuit of everyone connected with the event, with students being jailed and workers' leaders executed. It was evident that Deng's reforms, whilst wide ranging, did not cover the political arena.

Officially, Deng decided to retire from top positions when he stepped down as Chairman of the Central Military Commission in 1989 due to ill health. He retired from the political scene in 1992, but China was still in the era of Deng Xiaoping until he died on 19 February 1997, aged ninety-two. Bonavia writes that ultimately Deng's influence on China may be even greater than that of Mao.

> As a revolutionary, he may lack Mao's extraordinary charismatic effect, but over the long term he will probably be seen to have built more than he destroyed, whereas it can be argued that Mao destroyed more than he built. Mao was the demolition expert, but Deng is the architect.2

Document 19

One area of the life of the Chinese people that was influenced by the changes was that of religious freedom. In March 1982 the CCP set forth its new policy concerning religious affairs, known as 'Document 19'. This thirty-page circular originated from the highest echelons of Chinese government – the CCP Central Committee. The final section states:

Strengthening Party leadership is the basic guarantee for dealing properly with religious questions. The Party's religious work is an important component part of the Party's United Front Work and mass work and involves many areas of social life. Therefore, our Party committees at all levels must powerfully direct and organise all relevant departments, including the United Front departments, the religious Affairs Bureaux, and Minorities Affairs departments and the Trade Unions, Youth League, Women's Federation and other people's organisations, to unify their thinking, understanding and policies and to share work responsibility, cooperating closely resolutely to take this important task in hand and conscientiously fulfil it satisfactory.[3]

The Three-Self Patriotic Movement (TSPM) and other religious bodies are classified as 'people's organizations' and technically separate from CCP control. However, as the paragraph shows, they were to be under the close direction of the CCP.

Classic Marxism saw religion as an epiphenomenon that supported the status quo of the class structure, and so hindered the socialist revolution. Religion acted, in the famous phrase of Marx, as the 'opiate of the people'. The leftists saw religion as something that had to be exterminated, but the new leaders considered the forceful destruction of religion as anti-Marxist. The CCP still regarded religion as a relic of the old society that would eventually disappear. For pragmatic reasons the CCP was therefore willing to tolerate and make use of religious believers, but in the long term it could see no place for religion in a true socialist society.

The vast majority of the citizens in our country will be able consciously to adopt a scientific attitude towards the world and life and will no longer need to look for spiritual support from the illusory world of gods.

Both 'Document 19' and the Constitution of the PRC guarantee freedom of religion:

> Every citizen has the freedom to believe in religion, and the freedom not to believe in religion.   (Document 19)

> Citizens of the People's Republic of China enjoy freedom of religious belief. No State organ, public organization or individual may compel citizens to believe in, or not to believe in, any religion.   (Article 36 of the 1982 Constitution)

There were, however, certain limitations on this right. First, the Party must still 'resolutely propagate atheism'. Second, in allowing religion the State only protects what it considers to be 'normal' religious beliefs and activities. A line is therefore drawn between acceptable and unacceptable religion, which, as we shall see later, becomes important when some groups are defined as 'dangerous cults'. Third, religion is essentially relegated to the private domain. All religious activities are strictly limited to designated religious buildings, which are under the control of the government's Religious Affairs Bureau. In addition the government forbids religious believers to spread their religion in society at large.

The CCP recognized that it was not possible to regulate the individual's personal life in the way experienced during the Cultural Revolution. Document 19 therefore specifically allows certain religious practices in the home such as prayer and scripture reading. This freedom is for the family and the home should not be turned into a regular house meeting. Evangelical house meetings are singled out for mention:

> So far as (Protestant) Christians undertaking religious activities in home-meetings are concerned, these should not, in principle, be permitted. But they should not be rigidly

prohibited. The religious masses should be persuaded, through the work of the patriotic religious workers, to make other suitable arrangements.   (Section 6)

Document 19 was sufficiently ambiguous to provide a variety of interpretations. Leftist Marxists were often strong in their suppression, while more liberal members were more tolerant. Thus, while at a national level there was toleration of religion, this varied widely at the local level.

For thirteen years (1966–79) Chinese Christians had to worship in secret, but with the change in law in 1982 there was soon growth, within the house churches especially. The TSPM began to open churches in the major cities. It also began the process of amalgamating or closing down existing house-church gatherings. Although in theory this process was voluntary, in some cases force was used. In 1983 the persecution of the independent house-churches intensified with the launch of the national campaign against 'spiritual pollution'. Hundreds of house-church leaders were arrested, especially in Henan Province, but most were released after a few months.

Even so, during the 1980s the Protestant church grew rapidly, especially within the rural areas. In 1987, the Shanghai Academy of Social Sciences concluded the reasons for the rapid growth were:

1. The attraction of novelty.
2. The decline in prestige of the Party and of Socialism because of the Cultural Revolution.
3. The creation of an ideological vacuum, which allowed the revival of religion.
4. The role of healing in attracting new converts.
5. The lack of education and of social knowledge.
6. The provision of strong social bonds, comfort, encouragement in this life and hope of happiness in the next.[4]

In 1979, the Catholic Patriotic Association was reformed and Catholic churches began to re-open across the country. Within ten years there were more than 1,000 churches, 1,100 priests, and some 3.4 million Catholics, according to official figures.

According to some house-church leaders Deng Xiaoping was 'an instrument of revival'. One leader said that 'he was God's unwilling instrument to help bring revival to China.' Another house-church leader from Shanghai explained: 'Under too much oppression, the Gospel does not spread. With too much freedom, the gospel is never tested.' A house-church leader in Guangdong said: 'Deng replaced Maoist ideology with a materialistic philosophy: get rich quick. It is astonishing that this started many people on a spiritual quest, asking if they are only there to buy a larger television or a better fridge.'[5]

The reawakening of Buddhism

The resurgence of Buddhism was slower than that of Christianity; however, temples gradually began to be restored. By the 1990s, the restoration process increased as the temples and shrines took on the additional role of tourist centres. Money was provided from local govern-ments to rebuild some of the major sites in order to encourage both internal and international tourism. However, as local people became more wealthy they too started contributing to the restoration of their local temple until by 2000 massive restoration programmes were occurring all across the country.

One of the major statues found in the Buddhist temples is that of the Bodhisattva Guanyin. One often sees peasant farmers bowing to the image of Guanyin, and even educated businessmen and women, although their self-consciousness is evident as they bow. Older women come and fervently pray for the success of their grandson or granddaughter in their examinations, or that they will get to a good university. In 2004, one of the world's tallest statues was completed on Hainan Island. This 108-metre statue of Guanyin is taller even than the Empire State Building, and is set in what is essentially a giant Buddhist theme park.

One politically contentious aspect of Buddhism in China has been that of Tibetan Buddhism. Here religion is closely associated with social identity, and the Han Chinese control over the region that used to be independent Tibet is still resented by many Tibetans.

The Panchen Lama is the second highest ranking figure in the Gelukpa school of Tibetan Buddhism after the Dalai Lama. In 1964, the Tenth Panchen Lama was arrested after a speech supporting the exiled Dalai Lama, and he spent most of the next fourteen years in prison or under house arrest in Beijing. He was released in 1978, but continued to be an outspoken advocate of liberalization laws and policies to ensure the survival of Tibetan culture and religion. He sought laws to make Tibetan the official language of the Tibetan Autonomous Region, which were passed in 1987. The Tenth Panchen Lama died on 20 January 1989 under mysterious circumstances, three days after consecrating a *stupa* containing the remains of many of his predecessors, which had been desecrated by the Red Guards. The Tenth Panchen Lama was then also interred in the tomb, which was completed in 1992.

Upon the death of the Tenth Panchen Lama, both the Tibetan government-in-exile and the CCP initiated searches for his reincarnation. The search, ordered by the Fourteenth Dalai Lama, proceeded according to the traditions of Tibetan Buddhism. On 14 May 1995, after a six-year search, the Dalai Lama recognized Gendhun Choekyi Nyima as the Eleventh Panchen Lama of Tibet. Three days later, the young boy and his family, together with Chadrel Rinpoche and his secretary, who both led the search, were all taken to Beijing. In December 1995, the

Chinese announced they had discovered the incarnation of the Panchen Lama in the son of one of their security officers, and the boy, Gyaltsen Norbu, was installed during a private ceremony.

Meanwhile, little is known of the whereabouts of Gendhun Choekyi Nyima. Some of his supporters claim him to be the world's youngest political prisoner, whereas the CCP claim that they are protecting him from publicity so that he can get on with his studies. The political importance of the disagreement revolves around the fact that the Panchen Lama bears part of the responsibility for finding the incarnation of the Dalai Lama and vice versa. Thus, upon the death of the current Dalai Lama, China would be able to direct the selection of a successor, thereby creating a schism and leadership vacuum in the Tibetan independence movement.

Recent news reports from Chinese authorities claim that Gendhun Choekyi Nyima is intelligent, a good student, and is able to recite more than 400 pages of sutras, adding that he has an unusual understanding of the sutras.

Dangerous cults

As mentioned earlier, one problem with 'Document 19' concerned the clause as to what makes for normal religious practice. Although the government can state that it allows freedom of religion, it would also argue that it must protect its people from unacceptable religious movements designated as 'dangerous cults'. The most notable example is the Falun Gong.[6]

Falun Gong (Falun Dafa)
Falun Gong can be translated as 'the practice of the wheel of law'. It is a branch of traditional *Qigong*, which has never been seriously disturbed by the regime.

The founder of Falun Gong is Li Hongzhi who claims to

have been born on 13 May 1951. However, the Chinese authorities say he was born on 7 July and fraudulently altered his recorded date of birth to 13 May, which was, in that lunar year, the birthday of Gautama Buddha. Li Hongzhi lived as a child in the remote mountainous province of Jilin. He grew up in relative poverty like many ordinary Chinese, and graduated from high school during the Cultural Revolution when higher education was essentially closed. He later served in the army working with horses at an army stud farm, and he later worked as a clerk for the Municipal Cereals and Oils Company.

He claims to have started to learn about *Qigong* when he was four years old, but he refuses to name his teacher in order to protect his identity. He says that his teacher told him, 'You are the one I have been looking for.' However, none of his school friends seem to have been aware of his involvement with *Qigong* and even doubt that it actually happened. It was during the 1980s that Li began to develop his ideas of *Qigong*, and in May 1992 he made his teaching public. His first book, *China Falun Gong*, described his discoveries. A second book, *Zhuan Falun*, was published illegally in January 1994. Between 1992 and 1994, Li went on a national speaking tour. He seems to have started by making his ideas accessible and affordable to the poor, and began by teaching in the public parks. Reports say that the China Qigong Research Society charged fees, but Li would say that they were not for him. Quickly a disagreement began between Li and the Qigong Society, which was soon to result in a political dispute.

His teaching immediately became popular in China, with a following that finally included more people than the Chinese Communist Party itself. The Party began to refuse to approve requests by the Falun Gong to hold conventions, and finally Li Hongzhi felt he had best leave for the USA, which he did in 1996. Li moved first to Dallas and then to New York City, from where he oversees the expansion of

Falun Gong internationally. Small groups now exist in the main metropolitan areas of the USA and Canada, and also in some thirty other countries.

Falun Gong claims to be a radically more effective form of Qigong. In addition to being a powerful mechanism for healing and stress relief, it is able to cultivate enlightenment. The reason for this is that whereas other Qigong methods are beneficial only when you do the exercises, Falun Gong continues to refine the practitioner even though he or she is not continually practising. This, it is claimed, makes Falun Gong unique. Everyone is welcome to practise Falun Gong and no previous training is needed. People can learn from tapes or video, and the internet. Falun Gong simply teaches five exercises specially designed to complement one's process to enlightenment.

Practitioners claim that there is a 'law wheel' called *fa*, which is rotating in another dimension in the lower part of our abdomens. Drawing upon its power offers personal benefits such as the ability to cure disease and prevent deterioration of the body. The exercises influence the life forces circulating on the inside that then intersect with this wheel. The practice stimulates the function of *qi*, increases the delivery of oxygen to the tissues, speeds up the elimination of waste material from the body, and stimulates the immune system. Li suggests that the more one practises, the more one's body actually changes. Many people claim that practising Falun Gong has cured them from various illnesses including chronic fatigue syndrome.

To this point the beliefs of Falun Gong do not differ radically from traditional ideas of *Qigong*. However, there is an aspect that is less spoken about that goes far beyond traditional ideas. In accordance with traditional Chinese beliefs, both benign deities and demonic forces are considered to exist and influence human life. However, according to Li these beings are aliens from other planets, and have come from dimensions that humans have not yet discovered.

They have corrupted humanity by introducing machinery like computers and aeroplanes. Li describes this aspect of his beliefs in the following words:

> The aliens have introduced modern machinery like computers and aeroplanes. They started by teaching mankind about modern science, so people believe more and more science, and spiritually, they are controlled. Everyone thinks that scientists invent on their own when in fact their inspiration is manipulated by the aliens. In terms of culture and spirit, they already control man. Mankind cannot live without science.
>
> The ultimate purpose is to replace humans. If cloning human beings succeeds, the aliens can officially replace humans. Why does a corpse lie dead, even though it is the same as a living body? The difference is the soul, which is the life of the body. If people reproduce a human person, the gods in heaven will not give its body a human soul. The aliens will take that opportunity to replace the human soul and by doing so they will enter earth and become earthlings.
>
> When such people grow up, they will help replace humans with aliens. They will produce more and more clones. There will no longer be humans reproduced by humans. They will act like humans, but they will introduce legislation to stop human reproduction.[7]

The world media paid little attention to the movement until 25 April 1999. On that day some 10,000–15,000 Falun Gong practitioners quietly surrounded Zhongnanhai, the government headquarters in the heart of Beijing, not far from Tiananmen Square. They lined the streets quietly without placards, and simply stood or sat quietly for twelve hours. Some meditated and others read books. This was meant as an appeal against what they considered inaccurate and even slanderous attacks on Falun Gong made by He Zouxiu, a physicist and member of the Chinese Academy of Sciences. This right of appeal was within the constitution, but it came as a shock to China's rulers to see that Falun

Gong could mobilize so many thousands of people to quietly stand around their residence. Massimo Introvigne comments: 'The regime was particularly scared by the failure of its intelligence services to prevent the demonstration and by membership in Falun Gong by some medium-level political and military leaders'.[8] Unofficial sources think that so many civil servants were practitioners of Falun Gong that they could have closed down the workings of government.

In July 1999, the Chinese regime formally reversed the legal status of Falun Gong, and launched a press campaign against spiritual and religious groups. Newspaper articles, comics and booklets were written presenting Falun Gong as a dangerous cult.[9] An arrest order was then issued for Li Hongzhi. Interpol refused to serve the warrant because there was no criminal wrongdoing, and considered it blatantly political.

The CCP focused upon four main criticisms of the movement. First, that it has fabricated heretical ideas and practises mind control. Li Hongzhi is accused of inventing a series of fallacies, such as the 'doomsday of the world' in order to frighten his disciples into following his instructions without question. This is the same argument used by many in the West in the 1970s and 1980s, that 'cults' brainwash their members. In much of their literature the CCP place Falun Gong alongside other violent religious movements like Aum Shinrikyo in Japan (1986), Branch Dravidians in the USA (1993), Solar Temple in Canada and Switzerland (1994), and Movement for the Restoration of the Ten Commandments of God in Uganda (2000).

Second, Falun Gong is accused of collecting money by illegal means. The sale of books and videos on their teaching is especially noted. 'They purchased villas and cars, obtained visas for entry to foreign countries and bought green cards, frequented gambling dens and other places of ill repute abroad and spent money like water.'[10] The New

Star Publishers has produced thousands of illustrated leaflets containing what is claimed to be photographs of Li's home in Beijing and his new car.

Third, Falun Gong is accused of disturbing public order:

> Since 1996, the 'Falun Gong' organisation illegally besieged schools, media and publishing establishments and government organizations or held sit-ins with more than 300 'Falun Gong' practitioners participating on each of 78 occasions. In April 1999 more than 10,000 people besieged Zhongnanhai, the seat of the Central Government, which seriously undermined the normal public order and gravely disrupted the normal life of citizens.[11]

Fourth, a more dramatic accusation is that over 1,500 people have died from practising Falun Gong. Many Falun Gong practitioners are said to have refused to receive treatment after becoming ill, and have then died as a result. Others are said to have suffered from mental disorders, and some have committed suicide. Horrific pictures of those who hanged themselves, or burnt themselves, or committed murder accompany these accusations. On 23 January 2001, on the Eve of the Spring Festival, seven Falun Gong practitioners entered Tiananmen Square and set fire to themselves. Of the seven, two were stopped before they could seriously harm themselves, but the other five suffered horrific burns, one dying on the spot.

Although the persecution has scared many followers and driven them underground, millions remain in China and several thousands around the world. Exactly how many 'members' Falun Gong has is a matter of dispute; the government uses a figure of 2 million while Li claims 100 million. Although the movement recommends a nine-day introduction course and frequent contact with local centres, it also states that anybody can start practising Falun Gong by following the instructions from one of the many

books, cassettes and websites. The web pages present a
message of non-aggression, health, human rights and openness. If people want to attend a group they can e-mail to
find the nearest one. Before they join they are often asked
to read the basic text called *Zhuan Falun*. In the past press
censorship was the means by which the ruling authorities
could restrict any dissenting voice. The internet now proves
to be a powerful means of global communication that
enables a small organization to challenge state authority.

Eastern Lightning

A different type of movement is 'Lightning from the East'.
Whereas Falun Gong originated from traditional Chinese
beliefs, Eastern Lightning has Christian origins and has
had a devastating impact on the church in China, especially
in the rural areas. According to Bi Rongsheng, Deputy
Director of the Religion Section of the Public Security
Bureau, Eastern Lightning was founded by Zhao Weishan
in Acheng City, Heilongjiang Province, in 1989. Zhao was
originally a member of 'The Shouters' – a movement
founded by Witness Lee – but he broke away to form a
group calling itself the 'Church of the Everlasting
Fountain'. Zhao began to call himself 'Powerful Lord'. This
group grew rapidly, mainly through selling booklets and
tracts. By 1991, they had thousands of members, and this
resulted in a government crackdown. They fled to Henan
Province and took the name 'Church of Real God', and
claimed that they had a special revelation on the text
Matthew 24:27: 'For as lightning that comes from the east
is visible even in the west, so will be the coming of the Son
of Man'. Following another government crackdown, Zhao
fled to the USA with a woman alleged to be the female
Christ. No pictures have ever been published of them, even
though some reporters have tried to do this.[12]

  According to their website, God has spoken to them
more than a million words in Chinese, but this is now

translated into English. The teaching is rather confused, but it appears that God has become incarnate on two occasions, first as a male and second as a female. The first Christ was conceived by the Spirit, but the second was from human life. The first performed the work of redemption while the second will perform 'the work of perfecting and conquering'.[13] This is set within the teaching that God is at work in three stages:

	Age of the Law	Age of Grace	Age of the Kingdom
God's form in the world	In Spirit	In flesh as the male Jesus who was conceived by the Spirit as a sinless human being.	In flesh as the female Christ from human life, but not belonging to sin.
Purpose of God's work	Guidance	Redemption	Perfecting & conquering
Names	Yahweh	Jesus	Female Christ
Place of work	Israel	Judea	Among the Gentiles (China)

The Bible is regarded as the historical record of God's first two stages of work in the world, so it is more important than any other book in the world. However, God's words today are even more significant, so that people who rely only on the Bible cannot know redemption. Nevertheless, nearly all articles from the group continually quote Bible passages.

Eastern Lightning use a number of unacceptable methods of recruitment. Members of the movement have been known to attend existing churches and even help with Bible studies. Eventually they will start speaking of special revelation and so encourage uneducated members to follow their teaching. Money may also be offered to entice leaders to join the movement. There have been accounts of male leaders of house churches being seduced by young female members of Eastern Lightning. If they refuse the enticement, they have been known to be drugged, and photographs have been taken of them in bed with women.[14]

In other cases, housegroup leaders have been asked to cast spirits out of members said to be possessed. When they have failed, a member of Eastern Lightning would apparently succeed in the name of the female Christ. There have even been reports of house church leaders being kidnapped and beaten. The most notable case occurred in April 2002 when thirty-four house church leaders were kidnapped.

*   *   *

Deng Xiaoping's reforms and open-door policy have radically transformed China's economy, but the government's conservative approach on religion contrasts with its reformist economic policy. In the spiritual vacuum left by the failure of Marxism there has been religious revival, but this has also resulted in the emergence of many new religious movements. China's eighteen state-sanctioned Protestant seminaries cannot graduate enough ministers to teach the new believers. Spiritually hungry young people and uneducated peasant farmers are therefore vulnerable to new religious movements.

Further reading

Aikman, D., *Jesus in Beijing*, Oxford: Monarch, 2003. An optimistic account of the Church in China, including interviews with many leading Christians.

Lambert, T., *The Resurrection of the Chinese Church*, London: Hodder & Stoughton, 1991. A short account of the Church in China.

Bonavia, D., *Deng*, Hong Kong: Longman, 1989. A readable account of the life of Deng Xiaoping.

Wei Liang, Diane, *Lake with no Name*, London: Review, 2003. A love story set during the events leading up to the Tiananmen Square demonstration of 1989.

Websites

US Department of State. This site gives a review of the US view of religious freedom within China. http://www.state.gov/g/drl/rls/irf/2003/23826.htm

Panchen Lama Official Website. http://www.tibet.ca/panchen lama/index.html

Falun Dafa Official Website. http://www.falundafa.org/

CESNUR. Professor Massimo, an expert in new religious movements, discusses Falun Gong. http://www.cesnur.org/testi/falung101.htm

Chapter 15

SOCIAL CHALLENGES IN THE TWENTY-FIRST CENTURY

The period of Hu Jintao (from 2003)

Recently a tour guide showed me around a temple in Luoyang and the conversation turned to religious practice today. 'Religion is not popular in China today', was his well-practised comment. Yet just a few minutes earlier he had remarked that many of the villages we had travelled through this Sunday morning were empty because the people were at church.

One cannot visit China today without being aware of a spiritual and moral vacuum. The Marxist ideology that drove the country for the last decades of the twentieth century has turned into a quest for wealth. Consumerism has become the new ideology, best illustrated by a generation of students with computers, cell phones and DVDs. The quest for wealth alongside the political challenge was expressed in a BBC commentary in 2006:

> Today, the excesses of Mao's Red Guards seem a long way from China's consumerism and new social freedoms. China has changed beyond recognition. But today's leaders seem gripped with fresh resolve to maintain public respect for Mao. One of the greatest challenges facing the Communist Party now is to oversee rampant reform and economic boom without losing political control. Mao and his stature is a key part of that. In his New Year's speech this week, President Hu Jintao emphasised the need to bear Maoist principles in mind as China faces its current challenges and the threat of fragmentation and social unrest.[1]

Five generations

In recent years many personal accounts have been pub-
lished about experiences during the Cultural Revolution.
These have expressed in graphic terms the pain and trauma
many people in all walks of life faced during that period.[2]
The term 'generation' has become a useful way for modern
scholars to seek to understand the social issues of modern
China. 'Generation' provides a shorthand way of describing
Chinese society in the same way as 'baby boomers' and
'generation X' have been used of Western society. *Mao's
Children in the New China* tells the story of the Red Guard
generation that are called the 'Third Generation'.[3] Today,
there is a shared awareness of the times that parents and
grandparents lived through. The term 'generation' therefore
provides a useful means of understanding how China has
been shaped.

The first of the five generations are those who, through
various armed conflicts, founded the People's Republic of
China on 1 October 1949. The most well-known members
of this generation were Mao Zedong, Zhou Enlai and Deng
Xiaoping. This was the generation that broke with the old
traditions of China in order to create something radically
different, and for this reason they are frequently referred to
as 'the Rebel Heroes'. They believed that human will could
be transformed into material power and virtually anything
was possible. This generation still has immense respect
from the people of China because of its revolutionary
achievements.

The second generation are those who came of age during the first seventeen years of Communist rule in China
(1949–66). They accepted the leadership of the first generation and responded with loyalty and enthusiasm to the call
of the Party, and for this reason they are often called 'the
Loyal Soldiers'. This was a time when Mao's version of
Marxism was dominant, and there was little access to

alternative thought, be it Western or traditional. Politics was dominant in the lives of this generation of young people, and many sought to enter the Communist Youth League and then the CCP. They put state interests above individual interests, and were proud of their frugality. They read Soviet books and sang revolutionary songs.

The third generation is, as we have seen, the young people of the Cultural Revolution – 'The Red Guards'. They were born in the 1950s, and imbibed the enthusiasm of their parents during the early years of New China. There was some criticism of the failure of the 'Great Leap Forward', but the sense of heroism and idealism was deeply engrained in their lives. As with the second generation, they accepted state ideology and especially the oratory of Chairman Mao. As Stanley Rosen writes:

> With the coming of the Cultural Revolution they transferred their complete devotion to Chairman Mao, competing to be the most loyal followers of the Chairman. Under these conditions they could commit the most violent crimes with the purest of hearts. Objectively, therefore, these Red Guards should be seen as victims as well as criminals.[4]

After the euphoria of the Cultural Revolution in 1967, the young people of the cities were exiled into the countryside with the aim that they should learn from the peasants. For many almost a decade passed before they were allowed to return to the cities, but there they found there were no jobs and often no homes. Nevertheless, they were a realistic group who had learned to adapt to rigorous conditions in order merely to survive in the countryside. Some of them were able to take the lead in the market reform introduced by Deng Xiaoping.

The fourth generation were those born in the 1960s, and although they have childhood memories of the Cultural Revolution, they themselves were not involved. They saw their own family members being persecuted and their education was often little more than the teaching of Chairman Mao quotations and performances of model operas. However, when China was opened up to the world in 1979, they were able to respond to new ideas and opportunities. Many of them have become the pioneers of market reform and speculators of the new economy. They responded to Deng Xiaoping's acclamation, 'To grow rich is glorious'. It is their children who are the students of today.

The fifth generation grew up in the 1990s, and are the ones most influenced by films, television and the internet. As any Westerner travelling in China knows, they are eager to learn English and meet a foreigner. They watch the latest Western films on DVD, follow the National Basketball Association games on television and desire to graduate with an MBA. They mainly come from one-child families and feel the pressure of their parents for them to succeed in their studies and to gain good jobs. They are also marked by a strong tendency towards self-interest, and success is measured according to wealth, status in society and the number of people over whom you have authority. However, this individual pragmatism does not mean that they are not patriotic; they do have a deep love for China.

In the first decade of the twenty-first century, one meets up with three generations. Grandparents, who are the 'third generation', grapple with the changes of the last forty years. Some are willing to talk or even write about their past experiences, but most struggle to find the words and remain silent even to the probing questions of foreigners. The former Red Guards defend their actions, arguing that they were idealistic and enthusiastic for the cause. They also remind the young that they had little choice, and tears often come as they remember how they suffered in the countryside. Their children have little by way of ideology, and are focused upon acquiring wealth and social position. The grandchildren are kept busy working long hours in the schools in order to get good grades, and obtain lucrative positions in the future.

In 2005, the *Chinese Journal of Education* had on its front cover a telling photograph of three people sitting on a bus. In the middle was an old man dressed in what was a slightly modified Mao suit that was standard dress in the 1960s. His wrinkled face was marked by years of work and suffering, and his eyes were closed as if he had seen too much and did not want to see any more. On either side of him were two young students, apparently coming home from college. They were dressed in the latest fashion, hair tinted and cut with style. Their bright young faces were eagerly looking at their cell phones as they texted their friends. The picture summarizes much of what China is today. The difference between the period of the Cultural Revolution and the beginning of the twenty-first century is that money has replaced ideology as the social commodity.

This has caused immense pressure for young people to succeed, and parents encourage their children to work hard for long hours:

> On average, China's children spend 8.6 hours a day at school, with some spending 12 hours a day in the classroom. The survey also claimed that the majority of children spend longer hours at school than their parents spend at work.[5]

No wonder recent reports have acknowledged that many children are overworked and depressed.[6]

Those who get to the leading universities and gain the top grades can find lucrative jobs in America or some other Western country. A recent survey showed that 70 per cent of graduates from Beijing University, the 'Cambridge University' of China, went overseas. Those from the top 100 Chinese universities can usually find jobs in the bigger cities, but here competition for jobs is vigorous. Since 2005, graduates have found it increasingly difficult to find jobs, and they have to spend much of their final year at university going for interviews. Often it comes down to a matter of *guanxi*: Is your father an official, or do you have influential friends? Those who fail can only find jobs in the distant villages where they may struggle with the local dialect, working with poor facilities and having to survive on a minimal salary. No wonder some resort to suicide.

Following the death of Deng Xiaoping, Jiang Zemin (1926–) became President of the People's Republic of China. He had come to the fore in 1985 when he became mayor of Shanghai, a high-profile position which gave him an international reputation. He became General Secretary of the Communist Party of China in June 1989, cementing his position as heir apparent to Deng Xiaoping. Upon Deng's death in 1997 he assumed full leadership, but there were various political movements as a new generation of political leaders began to emerge. Jiang Zemin finally stepped down as President in March of 2003 and was succeeded by Hu Jintao.

Hu Jintao (1942–) was trained as an engineer, joined the Communist Party in 1964 and quickly worked his way up, gaining notice in Beijing as a leader in the Communist Youth League. Most of his career was spent in western China, overseeing Gansu, Guizhou and Tibet. Picked for the Central Committee's Political Bureau in 1992 by Deng Xiaoping, Hu was the first modern Chinese leader to start his political career after the 1949 Communist revolution. In 2002 all other senior leaders of the Central Committee stepped down to make way for a 'fourth generation' of Party officials, but Hu remained to take over as President.

Hu and Premier Wen Jiabao have inherited a country wrought with social, political and environmental problems. One of the biggest challenges Hu faces is the large wealth disparity between the rich and the poor, which could result in discontent and anger that could wreak havoc on Communist rule. Furthermore, the cronyism and corruption plaguing China's civil service, military, educational, judicial and medical systems could destroy the country. At the beginning of 2006, Hu launched the 'Eight Honours and Eight Disgraces' movement in a bid to promote a more selfless and moral outlook amongst the population. It contains eight poetic lines which summarize what a good citizen should regard as an honour and what to regard as a shame.

The population of China is currently over 1.3 billion, and so it is not surprising that the nation is facing massive social issues exacerbated by the rush for economic riches. These final two chapters attempt an analysis of the current social and religious situation of China in the twenty-first century.

The rural/urban divide

The social unrest of the first half of the twentieth century meant that there was little migration to the cities, but after the establishment of the Communist regime the people began to migrate to new opportunities in the cities. An estimated 20 million peasants went to the cities between 1949 and 1957 looking for jobs in the new industries.[7] At that time migrants were not considered a distinct category, and neutral terms such as *yimin* ('migrant') were used.

By the mid 1950s, the number of migrants was so great that they could not be fully absorbed into the new industries, and the voluntary migration became considered a national problem. As a result, the state passed new laws to restrict the flow of migrants, enforced through the 1958 Housing Registration Stipulations that required every Chinese citizen to register at birth with the local authorities as either an urban or a rural householder of a particular location. This *Hukou* system, mentioned in Chapter 13, resulted in the division of the entire Chinese population into two different categories: urban and rural. Rural householders were prohibited from migrating to the cities and not entitled to receive state-subsidized housing, food and education. Rural and urban residents were placed under different forms of state control. In the countryside there was a far-reaching grassroots network, while in the cities there were the work units and neighbourhood committees.

During the 1960s many skilled urban workers were sent to the far western regions of China to promote economic and technical development. During the Cultural Revolution millions of Red Guards travelled to the country, destroying temples and many ancient sites. Millions of urban youth and intellectuals were later sent by Mao into the countryside to be 're-educated' by the poor. These events were not seen as migrations, but more as political events.

With the reforms of the late 1970s the situation was to change dramatically, and peasants began to reappear on the city streets. This was due to many reasons. First, the agricultural reforms improved farming efficiency, and so fewer farm workers were required. Second, the rapid growth in new industries required a large amount of cheap labour, and these migrants provided the necessary resource. Although the government tried to control the migration, they could not stop millions of peasants coming into the cities. By the end of the 1980s these workers came to be known as 'the floating population'. The term itself suggests that these people will eventually leave the cities and return to their villages.

No one knows how large the floating population really is. There are gross differences in estimates: official sources speak of 2 or 3 million for each of the larger cities, such as Beijing or Shanghai. However, in 2007, China Television stated that the total floating population could be as many as 200 million. The floating population problem is an example of China's tendency to ignore or underestimate trends that are not consistent with the official state doctrine. With the strict Chinese household registration system, it should be easy to identify and control the floating population. In principle, the floating population from rural areas remains registered in their home villages as part of the agricultural population. They are not entitled to the privileges of subsidized food and housing reserved for urban residents. Employers must get permission from the ministry of labour or their local labour offices to hire migrant workers, and they must register these workers. In other words, the state authorities have legal and administrative means to send migrant workers back to rural areas once they are no longer needed. One notable result of this is that one does not find the sprawling slums so common in the cities of other developing nations.

Inequality between urban and rural areas rose steadily over the 1990s. The ratio of urban–rural per capita income (urban disposable income to rural net income) increased from 1.86 in 1985 to 3.11 in 1990. While there was a short period of declining differences between 1995 and 1997, there was a dramatic and continuous increase in this ratio between 1997 and 2002, from 2.47 to 3.11. It is likely, however, that these are still underestimates of the actual urban–rural income gaps. As the *China Human Development Report (CHDR)* 2005[8] points out:

> if public housing subsidies, private housing imputed rent, pension, free medical care, and educational subsidies were included, the actual per capita income of urban residents in 2002 would increase to between 3,600 and 3,900 RMB per month, bringing the urban–rural income ratio to about four-fold instead of the 3.2-fold acknowledged by official figures.

A World Bank report comments:

> Today, China has one of the highest rural–urban inequalities in the world and various social indicators suggest that the recent growth is largely bypassing the remaining poor, who tend to be isolated from the market economy in remote locations, ethnic minorities, or are disabled.[9]

The World Bank estimates that over 500 million Chinese peasants live in poverty, struggling to maintain shelter, food and education. Few are able to pay for medical care that may cost them many years' income. This means they either enter into debt to family and friends, or they simply wait for death to claim them. Many peasants are facing additional problems. Often their land is being acquired to provide water and electricity to the resource-hungry cities. Over 1 million people were relocated from the valley of the Yangzi River in the construction of the world's largest dam. Many of these people have been provided with new houses in the new towns along the banks of the Yangzi, but with no jobs. Changing climatic conditions have also meant that many areas of China continue to face water shortages and crops fail.

Many older farmers are worried about the effects of migration on agricultural production in the years to come, since they believe their children will never return to farm the land. A country as large as China cannot afford to leave large tracts unfarmed because its people are unwilling to live as farmers. Mechanization is not a realistic substitute, since in most areas the land is too hilly.

There is a massive widening gap between the rich and the poor. Many urban dwellers live in nice complexes with security guards, and they drive quality cars. Beijing alone has 3 million private cars in 2007. In contrast, peasants struggle to survive in New China. No wonder China's leaders worry about possible social unrest.

Population control

In 1969 China's population reached 800 million. From 1962 to 1972 China's annual average number of births was 26.69 million. It is therefore not surprising that the government called for the use of contraception. However, in the early 1970s family planning entered a new phase, and the state encouraged later marriages, late childbirths, and one child per couple. Massive propaganda was used to change the Chinese view of the family. Posters advertised *wan-xi-shao*, meaning 'later, longer, fewer'. Then in 1980 the 'one child' policy was introduced. Couples who followed this policy received many privileges:

- birth coupons
- monthly financial rewards
- extended maternity leave
- increased land allocation
- preferential treatment in education
- housing and employment
- pension benefits.

These 'benefits' were lost after the second child was born. Fines of up to 15 per cent of the family's income were imposed and the child was denied free education or health care. In many cases the child was not even registered as a member of the Chinese population. The only exceptions were in rural areas suffering from a shortage of labourers, where a couple were allowed to have a second child after a break of several years. Similarly, two or more children were permitted if one or both parents were from an ethnic minority.

This policy had the desired effects. It checked the trend to over-population. It created favourable conditions for the development of China's economy and improvement of the people's living standards. It helped to improve the quality of education, medical services, and maternal and health care. It has been estimated that the working population will peak in 2009 at some 925 million and thereafter decline to 835 million by 2024.

The policy also had some less desirable effects. It promoted a radically different view of marriage, birth and family. It resulted in many abortions, some of which were very late. It resulted in a gender imbalance in the population.

Today, there are 117 boys for every 100 girls registered as born. This seems to have resulted from the Chinese continued preference for boys, both for economic and social reasons. Boys were traditionally regarded as the ones to look after their elderly parents while girls married out into other families. Today ultrasound scans can identify the gender of the foetus, and so this influences whether the pregnancy is continued or terminated. This has resulted in a shortage of young women suitable for marriage. This is not particularly obvious in the cities, because the girls can migrate to the cities and marry out of the peasant lifestyle. In the poorer rural areas of the country the shortage of women is resulting in some horrific stories of girls being bought as wives and even kidnapped. By 2020, China could be short of around 40 million women, leaving many young men unable to find wives.

The uneven application of the family planning policy has caused disquiet. The newly rich families are now willing to pay the fines and in some cases pay bribes to have a second or even third child. Another option is the DINK family ('Double Income No Kids'), which some city high-fliers follow in order to gain the most from the modern economic boom.

Today many aspiring young couples are facing the problem of their responsibilities to two sets of elderly parents, many of whom have little or no pensions. A question I have been asked by many modern students is who is responsible for their parents – they as young people or the state? What do you do in America or Britain? It is a familiar issue in the West, where the government and individuals have had time to build up at least a modest contribution to support their ageing population. In China, the finances are not there for most families, and with an ever-increasing elderly population, the country is facing major financial problems in the future. The population may have aged before the country is sufficiently developed.

Frequently the young children are left with ageing grandparents to look after them while both parents work. In the cities grandparents may live in a large house or apartment with their family while caring for the children. The Chinese jokingly call these sometimes obese children 'little emperors', as they are spoiled by two parents and four grandparents. In contrast, in rural areas parents may leave their children with grandparents while they join the floating workforce in the cities, going home only once a year at Spring Festival. Those who do bring their children with them to the cities are faced with other problems. Their jobs as builders or cleaners mean they have to move frequently from site to site. This means that even if they can afford schooling, the children often have to move with their parents.

Single children are now growing up without siblings, and they in turn may produce children who will grow up without brothers and sisters. The result of this will be that the second generation will also have no cousins, no aunts or uncles. Individuals will have no kinship network. Together with the increasing divorce rate, this must have a devastating effect on the family structure that has been the foundation of Chinese society throughout its long history.

Women in New China

During the period of Mao, the socialist notion of women's liberation and gender equality through participation in social production was accepted. In the cities the woman's income was important for the family, as illustrated by one of the slogans of the Cultural Revolution: 'Women hold up half the sky'. In practice, however, men tended to be assigned to 'technical' work and women appointed to service and auxiliary work that was considered more suitable. Gendered job assignment was not seen as discriminatory towards women.

Urban women had substantial gains compared with their rural counterparts. A nationwide survey conducted by the Women's Federation in 1990 found that 82.6 per cent of urban women had pensions compared with 5.6 per cent of rural women; 71 per cent had medical cover compared with 9.2 per cent.[10] However, the reform of the labour system in the 1980s has eliminated some of the advantages that urban women enjoyed. The state no longer guarantees urban employment, and due to the need for more efficient businesses, many more women than men have been made unemployed. Some reformers criticized the Maoist gendered employment policies for impeding economic growth and argued that women should return home.

In response there was a rising feminine voice during the 1980s. The Women's Federation played a prominent part in blocking the proposal that 'women return home'. In 1992, the Law on the Protection of Rights and Interests of Women was passed, which reiterated the equal rights of women in all areas of life.

According to World Health Organization statistics, China is the only country in the world where more women commit suicide than men. Every year, 1.5 million women attempt to take their own lives, and a further 150,000 succeed in doing so. The problem is worse in rural areas, where the suicide rate is three times higher than in the cities. The pattern of suicide in China is different from that of the West, where suicide is more common in men and in urban areas. Fifty per cent of all female suicides in the world occur in China, which can partly be accounted for by the accurate reporting system of the Chinese. Among Chinese women aged sixteen to twenty-six, the suicide rate is particularly high. Xu Rong, head of the Suicide Prevention Project at the Beijing Cultural Development Centre for Rural Women, says one of the reasons is the ready availability of poisons in agricultural areas. 'It's all too easy to get hold of pesticides,' she says. 'Some women commit suicide impulsively. A husband and wife may have a bitter fight. When it's over, the woman just grabs some poison and drinks it.'[11]

Xu Rong believes this results from emotional problems for young wives who leave their own family and friends to enter an alien environment. 'They have their father-in-law to deal with, their mother-in-law, various uncles, sisters-in-law and so on. She's got to gain everyone's acceptance. When there are conflicts, she's the weakest.' Particularly in arranged marriages, where the husband may sense his wife is unwilling to be with him, resentment can build up, leading to arguments and violence.

Another surprising element of the suicide pattern in China is that both women and men aged fifty-five and older are at increasing risk, even though Chinese society has always been thought of as valuing the elderly. Part of the reason may be that the elderly themselves, in a very Confucian way, respond to the burden that they are on young people by committing suicide as a way of controlling resources that are scarce. Additionally, as economic and social forces change, some elderly people in China are being isolated and uncared for.

Information technology

It wasn't so long ago that the internet was seen as a trap for the Chinese authorities. The country desperately needed to foster economic growth, and in the early 1990s much of the globe was plugging itself into the worldwide network. Sooner or later, the thinking went, China would have to plug into the web too, and however efficiently its leaders might have controlled information in the old days, they would be no match for this new democratic beast, decentralized and crackling with opinion and information from the four corners of the earth.

Things didn't exactly turn out that way. In 2005,

Microsoft was still defending itself for having acquiesced to Chinese demands over the New Year's holiday that it shut down the MSN Spaces website of a popular Beijing blogger, whose postings had apparently run foul of censors. This has led to the following assessments by two leading experts: 'Our best hope for political change in China is a growing middle class that is tuned in and economically independent,' said Dan Griswold, a trade policy expert at the Cato Institute. 'Clearly it's a two-edged sword,' said Allen Miller, the Senior Vice President for Global Affairs of the Information Technology Association of America, a trade group representing dozens of companies. 'On the one hand, it is a wonderful market and everyone wants to jump into it and on the other, it's a bit of a threat.'

China's leaders were savvy about their internet strategy almost from the moment they began permitting global connections in 1994. Rather than trying to tame the web through sheer technology, they instead created a multilayered regime of filtering and surveillance, vague legal regulations and stringent enforcement that, taken together, effectively neutralized the internet in China.[12]

Moral collapse

The government recognizes that in the rush for wealth there has been a moral collapse in China. Confucian philosophy, emphasizing high personal morality and a strict hierarchy of social relationships, was endorsed by China's imperial rulers over the past two millennia and still has huge influence in other East Asian nations. Market reforms since the late 1970s have brought dazzling growth and greatly improved living conditions. The shattering of Communist ideals has resulted in wealth being considered almost the sole indicator of success. This has left many feeling lost or resentful.

Corruption in all circles is unfortunately common.

People's ability alone is not enough and they need to develop *guanxi* (relationships) in order to gain advancement. This dark side of *guanxi* results in cronyism and competing factions.

Violent crime is still generally less than in many other parts of the world, but this sort of crime is increasing. Car drivers find it prudent to ensure their doors are locked at night, especially as they halt at traffic lights. They know some have been attacked at knife-point and have been robbed or had their cars stolen, but foreigners are, however, still generally safe.

Adultery is common, and divorce has become a major problem in society. In 1985 the divorce rate was only 45.8 in 10,000 each year, but in 2005 it reached 178.5.[13] This has left young people looking for romantic love. This is being fed by Western movies and love songs by pop idols from Taiwan, Hong Kong and South Korea.

Lying and cheating at work and school is commonplace. At universities plagiarism is sadly all too common, with students merely copying homework from sites on the internet and passing it off as their own. Students know that teachers can't fail too many of them, as it will be the teacher who will be dismissed for being a poor teacher. The universities also know that they can't risk too many students failing as it will lower their ranking, or even worse, cause the students to riot.

Classes in Moral Education were introduced in the schools in about 1992 with the aim of improving moral behaviour in society. I recently heard an eminent Chinese professor of education criticizing the basis of moral education as taught in schools. These classes, he stated, are merely based on being patriotic to one's country and supporting the CCP. The professor argued that all that happens is that the children behave nicely before the teacher, but not in his or her absence. China is facing a moral vacuum and all it has to offer is patriotism. As Becker writes:

This deterioration in relations between the governed and those who govern has many ramifications. China is now a society in which everyone seems to be engaged in deceiving and cheating one another. In such circumstances, the transition to a market economy has not led to any fairness. Hard work and honesty are not rewarded; corruption is. The privatization process in a dictatorship such as China has brought about the criminalization of the state. Party members, who are beyond the law, have been free to engage in the theft of state assets on a grand scale. The cynicism and hypocrisy which this has fostered are destructive, particularly so in a society that has abandoned a once fanatically held ideology. A society in which no one is prepared to tell the truth, whether about historical events, small or large, or commercial transactions, individual or corporate, cannot prosper.[14]

After this stark assessment of China in the year 2000, Becker asks, 'How then does China get from where it is now to where it should go?'

*   *   *

The central force in Chinese politics remains the Communist Party, with the support of the army. Its tentacles reach into every aspect of Chinese society and economy, where it controls most of the energy production, health care, education, banking and communications. Never in human history has anyone tried to govern 1.3 billion people from a single centre and it is still uncertain if this can be done. Criticisms may be in the minds of many people, but few give them expression in spoken words or writing. If the rapid economic growth falters, and increasing numbers of students and labourers are unable to find jobs, perhaps the unwritten agreement that the CCP continues in power will come to an end.

The Eight Honours and Eight Shames has been widely regarded as one of Hu Jintao's ideological solutions to the increasing lack of morality in China. In 2005, the Chinese premier, Wen Jiabao, warned the National People's Congress in Beijing of 'deep-seated conflicts', and promised to spend more to ease the urban–rural divide. The Chinese government hopes that continued rapid economic growth will permit their continued hold on power, but they are now caught between the resentment of those left behind and the aspirations of the new middle class. The Oxford political scientist Steve Tsang says China is a 'brittle' place. It may look strong on the outside, but the situation could disintegrate very quickly.

The West continues to remain fascinated by what it sees of China, and political leaders from all backgrounds seek to establish good relations with the growing economy. It is certain that China will be an increasingly important player on the world scene, but there are a growing number of voices warning that the economic bubble may burst.[15] However, as Gelber writes, 'America still seems torn between the view that China could in time become America's most important geopolitical rival – which therefore needs to be contained – and the belief that market-driven economic growth will, of itself, compel democratic moderation in China.'[16]

Further reading

Becker, J., *The Chinese*, London: John Murray, 2000.
Jiang, Y., and Ashley, D., *Mao's Children in the New China*, London: Routledge, 2000.

Websites

China View. A useful website available in different languages (including English), giving national and international news. http://www.xinhuanet.com/english/index.htm

Official website. The official Chinese government website opened on 1 January 2006. http://english.gov.cn/

Women of China. A remarkably open magazine dealing with many of the issues facing women and families in modern China. http://www.womenofchina.cn/magazine/

Chapter 16

THE FUTURE OF RELIGION IN NEW CHINA

The period of Hu Jintao (from 2003)

The Marxist view of religion is that with the emergence of a socialist society, religion will eventually disappear of its own accord. In practice this has not occurred, and religion has remained a social phenomenon in all socialist societies. The ruling Communist Party is therefore faced with a dilemma in formulating practical policy in order to deal with religion. The government can either use all possible methods to eliminate religion, or champion religious freedom as a way of uniting religious believers with the Party until religion eventually dies out. It has been shown that since the formation of New China in 1949, the CCP's policy has swung between these two alternatives.

Adaptation to religion

By the mid 1980s the CCP had basically abandoned the view that 'religion is the opiate of the people', with religion now being seen as a reactionary ideology. The Party has come to realize that religion will continue to remain an important part of Chinese socialist society for many years to come. At the national conference that was held in 2000, Jiang Zemin affirmed that religion is a phenomenon that will have a 'long-term existence' in China. The government should not therefore equate religion with political opposition, or try to restrict normal religious activities through administrative means. Nevertheless, the Party continues to hold that atheism remains an essential tenet of Marxist philosophy and membership of the Party.

This raises the question of whether religion is beneficial to social progress. Even if the policy is one of maintaining religious freedom in order to ensure the support of believers, there is the problem of denying the positive value of religion. Xing Fuzeng has helpfully discussed the attitude of adaptation in three broad levels.[1]

First, no matter what religion people adhere to, the most important thing is that they should love the motherland and uphold the leadership of the CCP. In the 1990s, moral education was introduced into schools with the intention of deepening this way of thinking. This teaching was based upon patriotism as a means of continuing to unite the nation following the collapse of official Marxism-Leninism. Scholars have criticized this form of moral teaching based solely on patriotism as lacking any real content. Most people in China now realize that Marxism has not produced the promised 'New Man' who works for the benefit of others. Today everyone is chasing after wealth and few care who they push aside to gain this.

Second, with regard to economic development, all religions are obliged to guide believers to support the construction of socialist modernization. People are therefore not required to abandon their religious beliefs, but they must love their country and uphold the socialist system under the leadership of the CCP. This will require them to respect the laws and regulations of the country, and carry out religious activities only for the highest interest of the nation. Religions must therefore not merely be other-worldly, but should show active participation in economic development.

Third, as we have seen, although economic reform has brought increased wealth to most of the population of China, people have a spiritual hunger. Marxism-Leninism used to form the core of spiritual culture, but since the 1980s this has become less and less significant. The role played by religion has been increasingly affirmed by the Party. As many studies have shown, it is the places with a higher proportion of religious believers where the crime rate is lower. Religious belief provides a basis for morality in a society facing the impact of secularization. Pragmatism has therefore become the basis of the Party's policy on religion. Religion is recognized as serving a positive social function. For example, as we will show, religious freedom for Muslims has increased in order to court the oil-rich nations of the Middle East.

Since the formation of New China, the CCP has made a distinction between the five legitimate religions, feudal superstitions and 'evil cults'. The five religions are Buddhism, Daoism, Roman Catholic Christianity, Protestant Christianity and Islam. Confucian teaching has been regarded as an ancient Chinese philosophy. The government, just like the imperial court throughout Chinese history, will classify a religious organization as a superstition or cult if they think that it may threaten law and order. It is therefore immediately attacked, as with Falun Gong in the 1990s.

The CCP has established 'patriotic religious associations' for each of the five religions. With reform and the opening up of the nation, the main function of these organizations has come to be assisting the Party in raising the patriotic awareness of ordinary members and to run the practical affairs of the religion. Currently there are seven patriotic religious associations at national level, with two each for Roman Catholics and Protestants, and one for each of the other religions.

The constitution of 1982 states that religion must not interfere in state administration, civil law or education. This is presented as a 'separation of church and state'. However, this does not mean that religious bodies have complete freedom, but that religious bodies are not to interfere with government. The CCP has defined legitimate religious services and the locations for them. All locations must have a recorded membership of believers, a fixed area for meetings, qualified leadership and a regular income. Those which qualify under these conditions must register with the government and can enjoy the protection of the law. Those who are not registered are considered illegal. In response to accusations from the USA that it does not allow religious freedom, the CCP can vigorously argue that China enjoys 'full freedom of religious belief'. Seeking personal salvation is allowed, but public displays of religion outside the confines of state-controlled institutions are not. As we have seen in previous chapters, China's history is filled with religious uprisings against the state, and the current leaders have not forgotten the lessons of history. As a result, the twin issues of minorities (*minzu*) and religious communities will remain important issues for the government of New China.

Minorities and development

In *Cultural Encounters on China's Ethnic Frontiers*, Harrell describes the efforts of China concerning development as typical of many so-called 'civilizing projects'.[2] He defines these as:

> A kind of interaction between peoples, in which one group, the civilizing centre, interacts with other groups (peripheral peoples) in terms of a particular kind of inequality. In this interaction, the inequality between the civilizing centre and the peripheral peoples has its ideological basis in the centre's claim to a superior degree of civilization, along with a commitment to raise the peripheral people's civilization to the level of the centre, or at least closer to that level.

While Harrell is particularly interested in China, he emphasizes that civilizing projects are to be found around the world where there is a dominant civilization and distinct minority communities at the periphery. For example, they are found in the history of North American native peoples, the Canadian Inuit and Australian Aborigines. According to Harrell, the main effect of civilizing projects is that they seek to rid the minority society of what the majority community considers to be inferior cultural features.

Harrell writes that in response, the minorities 'develop an ideology of ethnicity, or ethnic consciousness', which has two features:

> First, it [the minority group] sees itself as a solidarity, by virtue of sharing at least common descent and some kind of common custom or habit that can serve as an ethnic marker... Second, an ethnic group sees itself in opposition to other such groups, groups whose ancestors were different and whose customs and habits are foreign, strange, and sometimes even noxious to the members of the subject group.[3]

Members of such minorities therefore respond by active resistance to civilizing projects that the majority community seeks to implement. Herein lies the nature of the conflict between the dominant Han Chinese and the minority Tibetans. Stalin's four nationality criteria still define minorities in China today: a language, cultural life, economic life and common territory. Most of the minority groups are found in the far south-west in Yunan Province, and do not constitute large numbers. The largest communities are the Tibetans and the Muslims. These two groups have been more troublesome for the government because of their connections with strong religious traditions.

The Tibetans

The construction of the Qinghai–Tibetan railway is part of the economic development that central government is bringing to the Tibetan highlands. The historic sites that were destroyed during the Cultural Revolution have largely been rebuilt and have become major tourist sites for both Han Chinese and international tourists. Half the population of Lhasa is now made up of Han Chinese who administer the region. The government speaks much about the preservation of the heritage of Tibet, and has sought to encourage the exhibition of Tibetan songs and dances.

In contrast, an illustration of Tibetan feelings can be seen from those who have graduated from high school and are generally frustrated and angry. They are convinced that the Chinese authorities have failed with regard to equality and human rights for ethnic Tibetans in the communities in which they live. For them the problem is the attitude of the Chinese government, which, they say, neither accepts Tibetan culture nor understands that it is a valid alternative to Chinese culture. In practice, Tibetans therefore do not feel they have the same rights and privileges enjoyed by Han Chinese. These young people feel very pessimistic regarding the current situation for Tibetan culture, and see no signs of any improvement in the economic, educational or linguistic situation for those who are unwilling simply to abandon their cultural heritage and 'become Chinese'.

These educated young people consider that there are three essential points that must be addressed: First, the environment must be protected. This is essential not only for the protection of the unique natural habitat of the Tibetan plateau, but because it is the context within which the Tibetan culture emerged and upon which it depends. Tibetan culture has much in common with the North American Indian views relating to the partnership that exists between human beings and the natural environment in which they live. Second, it is essential that the economic situation of the average ethnic Tibetan be improved. Particularly among the younger people, there is a strong conviction that the Tibetan way of life is one among many valid options in the modern world. They see no incompatibility whatever between living one's life according to the cultural principles of the Tibetan heritage and other people living a lifestyle like a modern Japanese, North American or European citizen. Third, these Tibetan young people consider that traditional Tibetan philosophy and thought must be retained. Tibetan thought, they hold, is the storehouse of the Tibetan cultural heritage and must be passed on to the next generation.

Many of the young Tibetan people struggle to find jobs. Some have had free school education for anything up to nine years, but even after that they are still way behind the urban children. Only a few manage to get sponsorship to attend university. The remaining young people have to choose between continuing to work on the farms or herding yaks, or going to the cities to sing and dance for the entertainment of the tourists.

The Dalai Lama, who has widespread support from world leaders, says he faces increasing criticism from his own people over his peaceful push for more autonomy instead of fighting China for full independence. 'Criticism about my approach, not seeking separation, is growing, increasing and my response to them is to be patient. More patience, more patience,' he said. 'Otherwise, we have nothing positive to show them from our approach. So we find it more and more difficult to answer them.'[4]

Muslim minorities

Today it is difficult to be precise about the demography of Islam in China. There were only 10 million muslims according to the 1953 census, and a little less than 20 million in 1990. However, this is as many as live in Syria or Yemen, and in practice there are probably many more. The ten Muslim minorities (*minzu*) can be separated into three groups, as done by Jean Berlie.[5]

The first group is composed of the Hui (Chinese Muslims), the Uyghurs and the Kazakhs. The second group includes the Mongolian Muslims (*Dongziang*) who form an autonomous district in Gansu and the Kyrgyzs residing in Chinese Turkistan. The third group consists of the Baoan, the Tajiks, the Tatars and the Uzbeks. The Tajiks are the only Shiites in China.

The Hui do not fit into the normal criteria of *minzi* because they live throughout China. They are distinguished because of religion rather than ethnicity. A Muslim who violates Muslim ethics is considered a 'bad Hui', but he, or she, cannot become a Han. On the other hand, a Han may become a Hui, but this is very rare. In the 1980s at the ancient port of Quanzhou in Fujian Province numerous Han succeeded in reconstituting their genealogies and re-established their identity as Muslims.

China has not been immune from the ethnic tensions that have occurred in other parts of the world. One of the worst in recent times occurred in Nanbei, Henan Province, in 2004. Each day, the call to prayer goes out from the mosque to the Hui residents, while nearby is the village of Weitang, inhabited by Han. A local traffic dispute between the villagers of Nanbei and Weitang spiralled out of control and members from both sides attacked each other with farmers' tools and Molotov cocktails. It took more than 10,000 People's Armed Police and other military personnel to restore order. They found 148 people were dead.[6]

Most of the Muslim minorities live in Xinjiang Province and related areas in the north-west of China. However, the top government officials are mainly Han Chinese, and the region's vast oil, gas and coal fields are exploited almost entirely by outside agencies. A similar pattern is seen with tourism, where well-connected Han Chinese have cornered lucrative markets, which has exacerbated the mistrust between Han and local people.

The Uyghurs also mainly live in Xinjiang Province. Recently they have illustrated a growing problem for minorities in China. Domestic tourism is booming in

China, and during the holiday times (the so-called 'golden weeks') millions of wealthy tourists from the East Coast visit the poorer regions of the West. Beijing argues that tourism will boost the local economy, but the Han dominance in the tourist industry means that the visitors who peer across the cultural divide do little for the local economy. The main involvement is the employment of young people to sing and dance as entertainment for the tourists, and the older people to make handicrafts.

In 2006, there was something of a reaction in the mountain town of Tuyoq in Xinjiang. This small town, whose main occupation is growing vines, has few attractions apart from a Muslim shrine and a few defaced Buddhist grottoes. Since the town was placed on the tourist map in 2004, the numbers of tourists have increased, and they pay a 30 yuan (£2) fee for the visit. However, none of the money gets to the local people, so in 2006 tension erupted and they blocked the road for three days.[7]

Beijing's control is so firm that it is hard to imagine the region spiralling into the type of violence that destroyed the tourist industry in India's northern region of Kashmir. Experts are, however, warning the authorities of possible dangers. Nicholas Bequelin, a Xinjiang expert at Human Rights Watch in Hong Kong, says: 'The peace and calm we see in Xinjiang today is not equilibrium, it's a stability enforced from above'.[8]

The growth of all religions

As was mentioned earlier, each of the five officially recognized religions has a bureaucratic link to the government. Popular Chinese religion is regarded as 'superstition' and so is generally disregarded. Confucianism is regarded not as a religion but as an ideology, and Confucius is seen as an early Chinese philosopher.

Confucian learning

The views of Chinese intellectuals of the twentieth century have resulted in two extremes with regard to Confucius. The conservatives wanted to see a revival of Confucianism, while the left-wing radicals wanted to see its total destruction. It was the radicals adhering to the form of Maoist socialism who appeared to have won when, during the Cultural Revolution, Confucianism was almost destroyed. For most Chinese, Confucian ideas became no more than a shadow of the past feudal age and the reason for the failure of China in the world. Mainland China became the least Confucian country in East Asia. One writer comments:

> As a result, three irreversible changes have taken place in relation to Confucianism: Confucian organizations and institutions have disappeared, Confucian scholars have lost their social identity, and Confucian rituals no longer have spiritual values.[9]

Since the 1980s, however, Confucian teaching has been on the rise, despite some criticism of its relevance to modernity. Statues of Confucius now have pride of place in most Chinese universities. Confucianism has not yet achieved a new identity, but its ideas are becoming increasingly popular. People in all walks of life are again reading the *Analects* and other Confucian texts. In October 2006 Professor Yu Dan of Beijing Normal University gave a series of lectures on state television on the *Analects* of Confucius and his disciples. This brought her instant fame, and in 2007 her book based on the transcripts of the series became China's best-selling book in recent years. In a single day, 15,000 autographed copies of her latest book were bought.

Confucian values are being linked with the cultivation of moral standards and beliefs in a society that has gone through major transformations in recent decades. Tian Na, a 25-year-old teacher who bought the book on the internet, said:

We were taught Marxism and Leninism in school. But when I became independent and went to college, I saw professors take bribes and I felt the old slogans like 'serve the people' were no longer relevant.[10]

The simplicity of the message written by Yu Dan has charmed readers from across the generations. Tian Na was brought up in a relatively prosperous family in the 1980s and 1990s, but the book is being read by the older generations that experienced the turmoil of the Cultural Revolution. Nevertheless, the book has been criticized by established Confucian scholars who argue that Yu offers little more than a mixture of ancient teaching from Zhuangzi and anecdotes on how to handle stress and relationships. Guo Shipeng says:

> Writer Zha Jianying said Yu's book had found a frantic audience in the ideological vacuum following the collapse of Communism as the 'state religion' which has made China the world's 'largest soul market' with its 1.3 billion population.[11]

Folk religion

As was mentioned previously, Buddhist temples and monasteries are now receiving greater support than they have had for many years. Buddhist monasteries now house an estimated 200,000 monks, and they are reporting an influx of children whose parents think the religious life is the best way for their children to be fed and educated. Along with the Daoist temples, they have become a mixture of places of worship and tourist attractions. Around these centres are tea houses, snack shops and many types of vendors, especially at the times of national holidays. Although Buddhist and Daoist temples are considered more buildings of cultural interest, people can often be seen ardently praying as they face some family crisis.

In contrast to the formal patterns of Buddhist and

Daoist temples, folk religion takes on many expressions and is especially found in rural areas. These diffused religious practices are not restricted to one source, but are a combination of ideas from magic, Confucianism, Daoism and Buddhism. In recent years, ancestral halls and temples have been rebuilt and statues of deities, particularly Guanyin, have been installed on many altars.

Pui-lam Law made a study of twenty-eight villages in the Pearl River Delta.[12] At the end of 2002, thirty-eight temples had been rebuilt or renovated to serve the local community. Temples are continually being rebuilt and initiated with ceremonies of spiritualization. Women go in large numbers to worship at the temples. There are temples in every village, and the various deities have differing abilities and characteristics. For example, Xuantian Shangdi is the chief of all deities, Yi Ling is the god of healing, and Guangong is the god of justice and bravery. Guanyin is popular with women, as she is considered to protect women and give them sons.

When women want to communicate with the deities, they have to find shamans to do this for them. Law tells of the case of Ah Kiu, one of the most famous shamans in the region. She became a shaman when she was about forty-three after suddenly falling ill after returning home from a temple. She consulted doctors but she did not recover. It was a shaman who diagnosed that she had been chosen by a deity to be a spirit medium. Now Ah Kiu becomes possessed by her deities and is able to identify the causes of misfortune that often are the result of the neglect of ancestral duties.

Following her study of this rural area of south China, Law suggests that:

> Many Chinese turn to revived religions for support when they feel overwhelmed by the changes that have taken place in the post-Mao era. Thus, the emergence in the 1990s of the

phenomenon of women flooding the temples during temple fairs and important festivals may suggest that women are feeling helpless as their lives are engulfed by rapid social changes and unfair treatment, and that they are seeking spiritual support in pre-1949 local traditions.[13]

Islam

'Marxist in mind, Muslim in heart' characterizes the attitude of many Muslims in China towards the state that has cultivated a loyal Muslim elite that is useful in its international diplomacy. Berlie considers mosques as the single most important marker of Muslim presence in China and estimates there are some 40,000 mosques in the country.[14] Not surprisingly, mosques became targets for destruction during the Cultural Revolution. Since the 1980s many mosques have been reconstructed and they have become the centre of community for the Hui, Uyghurs and Kazakhs. However, some of the reconstructed mosques have followed the pattern of Middle Eastern religious buildings. This is encouraged by Chinese Muslims who, returning from Mecca, want their own mosques to resemble those they have seen in Arabia. The Islamic Association has received generous gifts from international donors to build new mosques, and these have followed the tastes of the benefactors. This is resulting in the disappearance of the historic 'pagoda style' of mosque. This change in architecture shows the underlying tension between the Sinicization of the past and the *Umma* of the modern world.

The Chinese authorities also want to strengthen trade links with the Middle East, especially to meet China's increasing demand for oil. The control over Chinese Muslims is gradually being relaxed and some are beginning to learn Arabic. The increasing number of Muslim tourists and businesspeople is causing an increase in observance of their faith among the Hui people.[15]

Another important development is the increasing

number of Chinese Muslims participating in the pilgrimage to Mecca. In 2007, for example, 10,000 Muslims went on *Hajj* on specially chartered aircraft. Generally Muslims who have been on *Hajj* tend to return with a more fundamentalist perspective. Considering China's fear of Islamic radicals, there is a question as to whether increased Islamic allegiance will be tolerated.

Until the coming of the internet there was little possibility for communication, but now they are beginning to take sides on global issues. The attack on the United States on 9 September 2001 led to some Chinese Muslims talking about their Iraqi 'brothers'. Twenty-two Uyghur 'terrorists' were detained by the USA in Guantanamo. The movement for independence in the Muslim region of Xinjiang remains too divided to trouble Beijing at the moment, and currently most imams are pro-China. However, the government is faced with the dilemma of either lining up with the USA's anti-Islamist policy or appearing to support Islam.

Some ten years after it was written, Berlie's conclusion of her study of Islam in China seems to be correct:

> In 1998 religion has a promising future in China, as the political, economic, social and cultural sectors display improvement... In a country where economic pressures are great and the population gigantic, humans seek reassurance when solving their problems. Islam by its simplicity can appear to resolve them. The future of Islam in China is certain, if it is able to adjust itself to the modern socio-political context merging religion and culture.[16]

Christianity

China is a vast country and the application of the law on religion tends to vary from place to place. Thus, especially with regard to Christianity, one sees different policies being applied in different places. In some places the authorities take a laid-back approach to religious meetings, while in others they are anxious that no group steps out of line. Christians throughout the country find it almost impossible to get into positions of leadership and the CCP holds doggedly to an atheistic position.

China cut ties with the Vatican in 1951, leaving the Roman Catholic community divided between the official state-backed church and an underground church loyal to the Holy See. Three Self Churches (TSPM) are full, with many services throughout the week. Some of these services are mainly attended by the elderly, but other meetings draw large numbers of young people. The TSPM in many areas has an effective ministry in reaching out to many of the poor and those in social need. In many areas of the countryside people attend the local churches in large numbers. One can only assume that these sections of the Church will continue to grow, especially those sections in which Christianity is associated with miracles.

Christianity, and in particular evangelical Protestantism, tends to be more alluring to the Chinese than either Buddhism or Islam. With its emphasis on a personal relationship with God, evangelical Christianity is flexible enough to provide a message to both the poor and the wealthy. In 2007, the China Christian Council (CCC) said that the number of people claiming to be Protestant Christians in China had now reached 16 million, an increase of 6 million over a decade ago.[17] There are about 55,000 churches and meeting points in the country and more than 36,000 pastoral personnel, including 3,700 pastors and assistant pastors.

Many of the house churches are not so visible, and people take care not to be conspicuous as they are meeting in unregistered places. However, some of these meetings are now becoming registered. The line between the TSPM and the house churches is not, therefore, as distinct as some writers suggest. The dividing line is becoming more porous, with some Christians appreciating the religious worship of both communities.

It is often the educated students and professionals who now have the greatest difficulty in making a Christian commitment and joining a fellowship. However, throughout the country there is a steady stream. In 2001 the Christian Culture Research Institute of the China People's University carried out a survey of university students.[18] There were 306 sample groups including 6,184 undergraduates from 22 different departments. Of the students given questionnaires, 3.6 per cent explicitly acknowledged belief in Christianity, while 61.5 per cent agreed with the statement, 'I don't believe in Christianity, but I'm interested in it'.

The survey showed that university students rarely came into contact with Christianity through a church, but mainly through reading and lectures. Approximately 50 per cent said they became interested in Christianity through studying Western culture, art and philosophy. About 30 per cent became interested after thinking about questions relating to their outlook on life and work. As may be expected, few mentioned the influence of parents or family. The Bible is a major influence upon Christian students. According to the survey, 50 per cent of the Christian students participate in 'home meetings' and another 25 per cent 'go to church'. Christianity seems to be touching all sections of society, but it still remains too small to have a profound influence on society as a whole.

Edmond Tang, from the University of Birmingham, comments:

> Today it is an open secret that Christian fellowships – a new kind of 'house church', run by Chinese professors and students, are active in most Chinese universities. More than 30 academic faculties and research centres are devoted to the study of a once maligned religion.[19]

It is clear that Christianity is growing in every section of society and is having a positive influence upon society. Christians do love their country and want to serve their people. Questions remain as to whether the Christian presence can emerge into the political arena.

*   *   *

So, our journey to explore the spirit of China comes to an end. In so few pages it is only possible to draw out a few themes from the rich history of China. Through more than two millennia empires have risen and fallen, but the indigenous philosophies of Confucianism and Daoism have continued to have a great influence not only on social structure but on the popular beliefs of the people. The introduction and adaptation of Buddhism was historically one of the most surprising features of the Chinese religious story. It was transformed from Indian Buddhism to become a distinctly Chinese form that is seen today. Christianity came much later and has only slowly become established among the people. As we have seen, amidst these major traditions there have arisen many new religious movements of various beliefs, some of which have threatened to destabilize the nation as a whole.

In the twentieth century it has been the secular philosophies of Marxism and later consumerism that have dominated the people. Although materialism is still the dominant spirit of the age, one cannot but be aware of the spiritual hunger of the majority in New China. Despite the rapid economic growth, there is widespread gnawing anxiety over the future. China in 2006 had more that 200 million worshippers of all faiths, double the number of just nine years ago. People ask questions about religion with an interest rarely found in the West. It is hard to predict where China will be in ten or twenty years' time, but one thing is clear: the spiritual quest of the people of China will still be there.

Further reading

Berlie, Jean A., *Islam in China*, Bangkok: White Lotus Press, 2004.
Aikman, D., *Jesus in Beijing: How Christianity is Transforming China and Changing the Global Balance of Power*, Washington DC: Regnery Pub., 2003.

A TIMELINE OF CHINESE HISTORY

Dates	Period/Dynasty	Major events
c. 5000–3000 BC	Langshao culture	Farming in Yellow River valley, pottery, divination and ancestor rituals.
c. 3000–2200 BC	Three Rulers and Five Emperors	Mythical rulers credited with invention of farming, building, medicine and silk.
c. 2200–1766 BC	Xia civilization	Little historical evidence.
1766–1045 BC	**Shang civilization**	First known civilization concentrated along lower reaches of Yellow River. Ritual bronze vessels, oracle bones used in divination.
1045–771 BC	Western Zhou	Capital city Chang'an, near Xian. 'Mandate of Heaven' was the political basis.
771–476 BC	Eastern Zhou: *Spring and Autumn Period*	Capital moved to Luoyang. Confucius (551–479). Classical literature and art. Laozi – Daoist teaching.
403–221 BC	Eastern Zhou: *Warring States Period*	Increasing warfare. Mencius (373–289).
221–207 BC	**Qin dynasty**	States united under Shi Huangdi (259–210). Capital Chang'an. Building of Great Wall. Standardization of weights and measures. Destruction of books.

206 BC–AD 6	Han Dynasty (Western)	Capital at Xian. Adoption of Confucian ideas. 51 BC and AD 79, conferences held on content of Confucian Classics.
AD 25–220	Han Dynasty (Eastern)	Capital at Luoyang. Beginning of Confucian civil service. Celestial Masters movement (142f.). Yellow Turbans (184f.). Buddhism enters China from India.
220–80	Three kingdoms: Wei, Shu, Wu.	Empire divided. Era is romanticized in later literature.
265–316	Western Jin	
316–420	Eastern Jin	311 Luoyang conquered by Xiongnu. China divided into North and South. Kumarajiva (344–413), translator of Buddhist scriptures. Mao Shan movement (370f.). 399 Fa-Hsien goes to India.
420–589	Series of southern and northern dynasties.	Bodhidarma arrives in China.
589–617	Sui dynasty	North conquers South and unites China. Capital at Chang'an.
618–907	Tang dynasty	A period of great scholarship and art. Chinese Buddhist schools emerge: Pure Land, Chan, Tiantai, Huayan. Xuanzang goes to India in 627. Nestorian Christians arrive in 635. Muslim traders arrive via Silk Route in about 638.

907–60	Five kingdoms in the North, ten kingdoms in the South.	A period of war and fragmentation.
960–1229	**Song dynasty**	China united, leading to period of high culture. The Jin invade the North, and Song capital is moved from Kaifeng to Hangzhou. White Cloud Society (1108f.).
1279–1368	**Yuan dynasty** (the Mongols)	Mongol invasions of China and Europe under Chinggis Khan (1167–1227). Kublai Khan (1215–94) conquers the whole of China and builds a new capital at Beijing. Marco Polo visits China in 1266–69 and 1271–95. Arrival of Franciscan missionaries (1305). White Lotus Society rebellions against Yuan dynasty (1337).
1368–1644	**Ming dynasty**	Mongols defeated. Strong emperors rebuild Beijing and the great wall. Arrival of the Jesuits. Matteo Ricci (1552–1610).
1644–1911	**Qing dynasty**	Han people subjugated by Manchus. Kangxi (r. 1661–1722). Qianlong (r. 1736–95). Coming of Protestant missionaries, incl. Robert Morrison (1782–1834). Opium War (1840–42). Hudson Taylor arrives in China 1854. Cixi (1835–1908). Hong Xiuquan and the Taiping Rebellion (1851–64). Boxer Uprising (1898–1901).

1911–49	Republic of China	1911 Emperor Puyi deposed. 1911 Revolution – attempted democratic government. Sun Yatsen first president of GMD. 1921 Chinese Communist Party founded. 1931–45 Japanese invasion. 1934–35 Communist Long March. 1946–49 Civil War.
1949 onwards	**People's Republic of China –** Chairman Mao	1949 CCP assumes power. Republic of China in Taiwan. 1951 Three-Self Movement inaugurated. 1958 Great Leap Forward. 1967–77 Cultural Revolution. 1972 Nixon visits China.
	CCP – Deng Xiaoping (1904–97)	1979 opening of China to the world. 1982 Document 19 adopted. 1989 Tiananmen Square. 1992 Deng retires from politics. 1997 Hong Kong returned to China.
	CCP – Jiang Zenmin (1926-) Hu Jingtao (1942–)	1997 Jiang Zemin becomes President. 2003 Hu becomes President.

MAPS

The following maps have been taken from *A Visual Sourcebook of Chinese Civilization* (www.depts.washington.edu/chinaciv); prepared by Patricia Buckley Ebrey and used by permission.

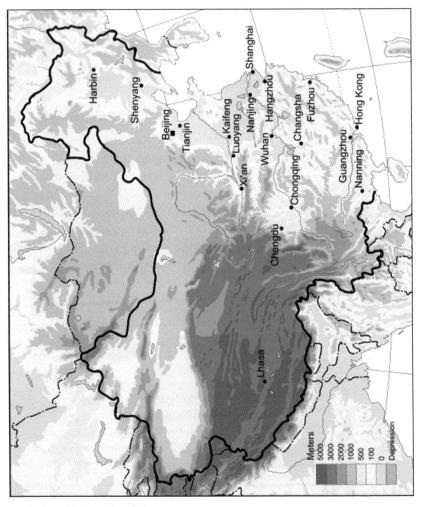

The People's Republic of China

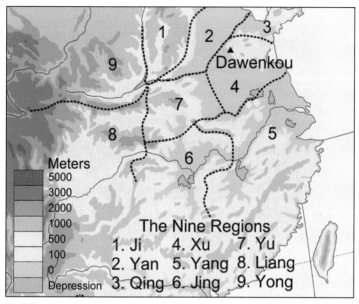

Neolithic China, showing the legendary Nine Regions.

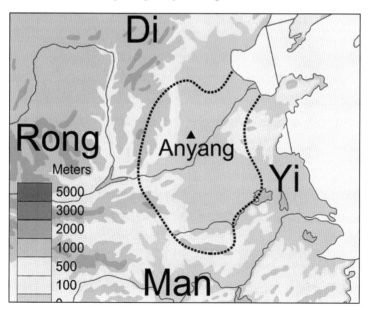

Shang dynasty China, showing the traditional terms for the non-Han peoples of the north, south, east, and west.

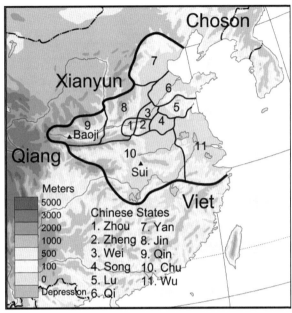

Zhou dynasty China during the Spring and Autumn Period, showing the royal domain and ten major fiefs.

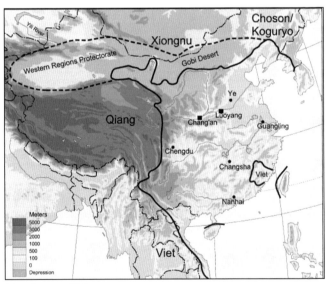

Han dynasty China.

China during the Period of Division circa 500, showing the non-Han Northern Wei dynasty and the Han Southern Qi dynasty as well as the surrounding kingdoms and peoples.

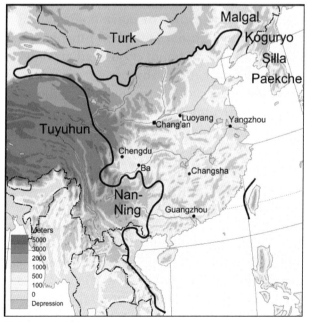

Sui dynasty China.

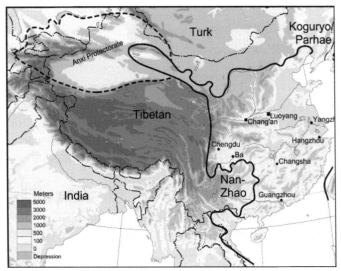

Tang dynasty China circa 742.

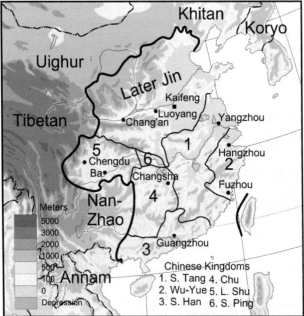

Five Dynasties China circa 936, showing the Later Jin dynasty and six of the Ten Kingdoms as well as the surrounding kingdoms and peoples.

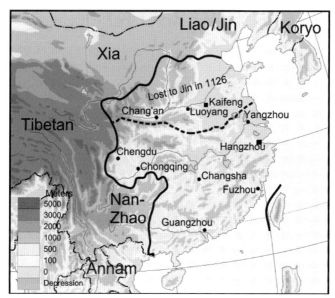

Song dynasty China, showing the approximate borders of the Northern Song in 1100 and indicating the area lost to the non-Han Jin dynasty in 1127.

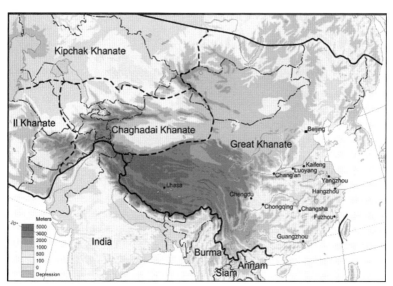

The Mongol empire, showing the Four Khanates and the surrounding kingdoms and peoples. It was the Great Khanate that was known to the Chinese as the Yuan dynasty.

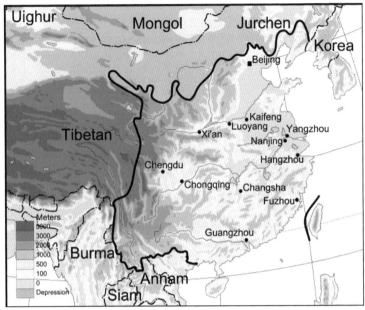

Ming dynasty China.

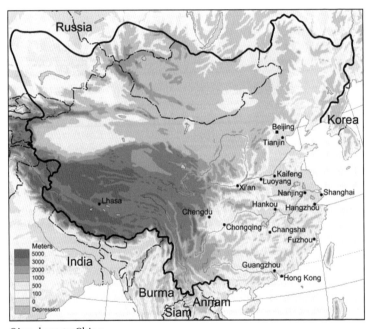

Qing dynasty China.

GLOSSARY

The modern Pinyin system of transliteration of Chinese has been used throughout the text. As the Wade-Giles system is found in many of the older books to which reference is given, this has also been added in parentheses below.

Amituo (A-mi-t'o): The Buddha Amitabha, important within Pure Land Buddhism.

Anatman [Sanskrit]: Literally 'non-self'.

Avatamsaka Sutra [Sanskrit] *(Hua-yen-ching)*: Literally 'Flower Garland Sutra', the main text of Huayan Buddhism.

Ba: Ancient civilization in the region of modern Sichuan and the Yangzi River that came to an end about 220 BC.

Baopuzi (Pao-p'u-tzu): 'The Master who embraces simplicity'. This is both the name of a Daoist master and the title of the book he wrote.

Benxing (pen-hsing): In Neo-Confucianism this means 'original (moral) nature'.

Bodhi [Sanskrit]: Enlightenment in Buddhist teaching.

Bodhisattva [Sanskrit], *pusai*: An enlightened being who has vowed to stay in *samsara* to help sentient beings attain enlightenment.

Buddha [Sanskrit], *Fuo (Fo)*: An 'awakened being', but more specifically the historical Sakyamuni Buddha or one of the many other Mahayana Buddhas.

Caodong (Ts'ao-Tong): One of the major lineages in Chan Buddhism.

Celestial Masters: An orthodox Daoist sect founded by Zhang Daoling in AD 142.

Chan (Ch'an): One of the main schools of Chinese Buddhism, known as Zen in Japan.

Channa (Ch'an-na): Meditation used by the Chan school of Buddhism.

Cheng: 'Sincerity' enables a person to develop their nature.

Chun Qiu: 'Spring and Autumn Annals' – one of the five Confucian Classics, this book tells the history of the Lu state from 722 to 481 BC.

Dao: 'Way' – an important philosophical concept in Daoism, seen as a transcendent source of all things. It is always good and it is the origin of heaven and earth.

Daode Jing (Tao Te Ching): The major text of Daoism, believed to have been written by Laozi.

Da Xue: 'Great Learning' – the shortest of the Four Books of Confucian learning, which provides eight steps to effective government.

De: 'Power' or 'virtue'.

Di: Earth.

Fajia: 'Legalism' – one of the three major philosophical traditions of China, this was employed by the First Emperor. It required central government to rule with power, as human nature was essentially evil and needed to be controlled.

Fashi: 'Ritual Master' – a Daoist official that emerged in the Song Dynasty.

Feng Shui: A form of geomancy.

Fu: 'Blessedness' – a common symbol for blessing.

Gui: A ghost.

Guanxi: Mutual relationships.

Hanhua: 'Becoming like the Han' – a series of reforms to Buddhism introduced during the reign of Emperor Xiaowen in about AD 480.

Huahu: A theory concerning the relationship of the Buddha and Laozi that was widely debated in AD 520.

Hun: The *yang* element of the soul, which is the spiritual element of a person and after death becomes a spirit or ancestor.

Hukou: The system that required every Chinese citizen to register with the authorities and be designated as rural or urban dwellers.

Junzi (Chun-tzu): The notion of a superior person that, in Confucian teaching, referred to a person dedicated to the cultivation of *ren*.

Jitong: Spirit mediums.

Keyi: 'Concept-matching' – a mode of translation used by Buddhists to explain Indian Buddhist teaching.

Li Ji: 'Book of Rites' – one of the five Confucian Classics, this deals with the principles of conduct.

Li: A term originally used for religious rituals, but widened to include personal conduct.

Lingbao: A Daoist school, usually translated as 'Numinous Treasure'.

Lunyu: Known in English as *The Analects*. It is a collection of sayings of Confucius on ethics and philosophy.

Neiye: 'Inward training' – a Daoist text that encouraged a mystical tradition.

Minzu: The 55 official minorities in contemporary China.

Po: The element of the human soul that corresponds to *yin* and stays with the body after death to become a ghost.

Qi: Life force or vital energy that flows through the body. It is an important concept in Chinese medicine.

Ren Xing: 'Human nature' – a term widely used by Mencius, who assumed that human nature was inherently good.

Ren: Confucius saw this as a cardinal virtue. It can be understood as loving kindness to other people. It also means human beings.

Ru: At the time of Confucius the *ru* were experts of the texts and rituals that governed the conduct of the ruling aristocracy.

Shang Di: The moral ruler of the universe.

Shangqing: 'Highest Clarity' – the text of a fourth-century Daoist movement also called by this name.

Shang Shu: 'Ancient (above) book' – one of the five Confucian Classics
and the earliest known book of history. It provides the basis of
Confucian historiography.

Shen: A spirit or deity.

Shiji: 'Historical Records', written about 100 BC by Sima Qian.

Si Shu: 'Four Books' – compilations of the sayings of Confucius and
Mengzi widely used by Confucian scholars.

Shijing: 'The Book of Poetry' – one of the five Confucian Classics, this
is a collection of writings from the Zhou dynasty.

Tian: 'Heaven' or 'sky' – traditionally understood as the supreme ultimate.

Tianming: 'The Mandate of Heaven' – a concept that developed in the
early Zhou period that came to be understood as a principle that a
bad ruler would be deposed by heaven.

Taiping: 'Great Peace' – a term implying an era of great peace that was
used by both the Yellow Turban movement and the Taiping
Rebellion.

Tu shen: Earth god.

Wang: A king.

Wu: A Daoist philosophical concept meaning 'emptiness'. It is also used
of a shaman.

Wudi: The first five emperors of a Chinese legend that was popular in
the Han dynasty.

Wu Jing: The 'Five Classics', considered by Confucius to be records of
the ancient culture.

Xiao (Hsiao): 'Filial piety' – respect for elders and parents.

Xinzhai: 'Fasting the mind' – a concept used by Zhuangzi Zhou. This
was a mental technique to free the mind from preconceived ideas.

Yi: One of the innate sources of morality.

Yijing   (I Qing): The 'Book of Changes' – a manual of divination composed before the time of Confucius.

Yin-Yang: The differing expressions of the force of *qi* expressed as light
and darkness.

Yu-zhou-kuan: 'Concepts of *yu* and *zhou*' – cosmology.

Zhang Yong: 'The Doctrine of the Mean' – one of the Four Books of
Confucian learning, which explores the way to cultivate one's own
character.

Zhi: 'Duty' – one of the innate sources of morality.

BIBLIOGRAPHY

Becker, J., *The Chinese*, London: John Murray, 2000.

Berlie, Jean A., *Islam in China*, Bangkok: White Lotus Press, 2004.

Bloomfield, F., *The Book of Chinese Beliefs*, London: Arrow Books, 1983.

Boardman, E. P., 'Millenary Aspects of the Taiping Rebellion (1851–64)' in Sylvia L. Thrupp, ed., *Millennial Dreams in Action*, The Hague: Mounton, 1962.

Bodde, Derk, 'Myths of Ancient China' in S. N. Kramer, ed., *Mythologies of the Ancient World*, New York: Doubleday Anchor Books, 1961.

Bol, Peter K., *This Culture of Ours: Intellectual Transitions in T'ang and Sung China*, Stanford University Press, 1992.

Bonavia, D., *Deng*, Hong Kong: Longman, 1989.

Broomhall, A. J., *Hudson Taylor*, London: Hodder & Stoughton and OMF, 1981–88.

Burnett, D., *The Spirit of Hinduism*, Oxford: Monarch, 2006.

Burnett, D., *The World of the Spirits*, Tunbridge Wells: Monarch, 2000.

Ch'en, K., *Buddhism in China: A Historical Survey*, Princeton: Princeton University Press, 1964.

Chamberlain, J., *Chinese Gods*, Malaysia: Pelanduk Publications, 1995.

Chang, C., *The Development of Neo-Confucian Thought*, London: Vision Press, 1958.

Chang, Gordon G., *The Coming Collapse of China*, London: Arrow Books, 2002.

Chang, J. and Halliday, J., *Mao: The Unknown Story*, London: Jonathan Cape, 2005.

Chang, J., *Wild Swans: Three Daughters in China*, London: Harper Collins, 1991.

Chen, K., *Buddhism in China: A Historical Survey*, Princeton: Princeton University Press, 1972.

Clissoid, T., *Mr China*, London: Constable and Robinson, 2004.

Corwin, C., *East to Eden?*, Grand Rapids: Eerdmans Publishing Co., 1972.

Craig, Mary, *Kundun: A Biography of the Family of the Dalai Lama*, London: HarperCollins, 1997.

Daisaku Ikeda, *The Flower of Chinese Buddhism*, trans. Burton Watson, New York: Weatherhill, 1986.

Davis, E., *Society and the Supernatural in Song China*, Honolulu: University of Hawaii Press, 2001.

De Bary, T. and Bloom, I., *Sources of Chinese Tradition: From Earliest Times to 1600*, New York: Columbia University Press, 1999.

Dobson, W. A. C. H., *Mencius: A New Translation Arranged and Annotated for the General Reader*, Harmondsworth: Penguin Books, 1963.

Ebrey, P. B., *Chinese Civilization: A Sourcebook*, 2nd edn, New York: Free Press, 1993.

Ebrey, P. B., *China: Cambridge Illustrated History*, Cambridge: CUP, 2003.

Fei-Ling Wang, *Organizing through Division and Exclusion: China's Hukou System*, Stanford, CA: Stanford University Press, 2005.

Fenby, J., *Dealing with the Dragon: A Year in the New Hong Kong*, London: Little, Brown & Co., 2000.

Findling, J. E. and Thackeray, D. C. W., *The History of China*, Greenwood Press, 2001.

Gao Wangzhi, 'Y. T. Wu: A Christian Leader Under Communism' in D. H. Bays, ed., *Christianity in China: From Eighteenth Century to the Present*, Stanford: Stanford University Press, 1996.

Gelber, H. G., *The Dragon and the Foreign Devils*, London: Bloomsbury, 2007.

Gernet, J., *Buddhism in Chinese Society: An Economic History from the Fifth to the Tenth Century*, NY: Columbia University Press, 1995.

Gernet, J., *China and the Christian Impact*, Cambridge: CUP, 1985.

Goldin, P. R., *Rituals of the Way: The Philosophy of Xunzi*, Chicago: Open Court Pub. Co., 1999.

Hansen, V., *Changing Gods in Medieval China, 1127–1276*, Princeton: Princeton University Press, 1990.

Harrell, S., *Cultural Encounters on China's Ethnic Frontiers*, Seattle: University of Washington Press, 1995.

Hawkes, D., *Ch'u Tz'u: Songs of the South*, Oxford: Clarendon Press, 1959.

Hoff, Benjamin, *The Tao of Pooh and the Te of Piglet*, London: Egmont, 2002.

Hsu, Cho-Yun and Linduff, K. M., *Western Chou Civilization*, New Haven: Yale University Press, 1988.

Jaspers, K., *Way to Wisdom*, Yale University Press, 1954.

Jiang, Y. and Ashley, D., *Mao's Children in the New China*, London: Routledge, 2000.

Keightley, D., 'The Religious Commitments: Shang Theology and Genesis of Chinese Political Culture', *History of Religions*, 17.3–4 (1978).

Kohn, Livia, *God of the Dao: Lord Dao in History and Myth*, Ann Arbor: University of Michigan, 1998.

Kohn, Livia, *The Taoist Experience: An Anthology*, NY: State University Press, 1993.

Lambert, T., *The Resurrection of the Chinese Church*, London: Hodder & Stoughton, 1991.

Malatesta, E. J., *The True Meaning of the Lord of Heaven (T'ien-chu Shih-i)*, Taipei: The Ricci Institute, 1985.

Mao Zedong, 'On New Democracy', in *Selected Works of Mao Tse-Tung*, Beijing: Foreign Language Press, 1967, vol. 2, p. 339.

Menzies, Gavin, *1421: The Year China Discovered the World*, London: Bantam, 2003.

Michael, Franz, *The Taiping Rebellion: History and Documents*, Vol. 1, Seattle: University of Washington Press, 1966.

Miller, J., *Daoism: A Short Introduction*, Oxford: Oneworld, 2003.

Moffett, S. H., *A History of Christianity in Asia. Volume One: Beginning to 1500*, San Francisco: Harper, 1992.

Mote, F. W., *Intellectual Foundations of China*, New York: McGraw Hill, 1993.

Mungello, D. E. (ed.), *The Chinese Rites Controversy: Its History and Meaning*, Nettetal: Steyler Verlag, 1994.

Nomachi, K., *Tibet*, Hong Kong: Local Colour, 1994.

Onon, Urgunge, *The Secret History of the Mongols: The Life and Times of Chinggis Khan*, Curzon, 2001.

Osade, Y., Allwright, G. and Kanamaru, A., *Mapping the Tibetan World*, Tokyo: Kotan Publishing, 2004.

Palmer, M. I., *The Jesus Sutras: rediscovering the lost religion of Daoist Christianity*, London: Piatkus, 2001.

Paludan, A., *Chronicle of the Chinese Emperors*, London: Thames & Hudson, 2003.

Perry, E. J. and Selden, M., *Chinese Society, 2nd Edition: Change, conflicts and resistance*, London: Routledge, 2002.

Reigert, R. and Moore, T., *The Lost Sutras of Jesus*, London: Sovereign Press, 2003.

Bagley, R., *Ancient Sichuan: Treasures from a Lost Civilization*, Princeton: Princeton University Press, 2001.

Robinet, I., translation by Brooks, P., *Taoism: Growth of a Religion*, Stanford University Press, 1997.

Rustichello, *The Book of Marco Polo, wherein is recounted the Wonders of the World*.

Ruthven, Malise, *Islam in the World*, Oxford University Press, 2000.

Shryock, J. K., *The Origin and Development of the State Cult of Confucius: An Introductory Study*, New York: Paragon, 1966.

Sima Qian, *Records of the Historian*, translated by Burton Watson, Hong Kong: Columbia University Press, 1993.

Sinn, E., *The last half century of Chinese Overseas*, Hong Kong: Hong Kong University Press, 1998.

Siu-Chi Huang, *Essentials of Neo-Confucianism: Eight Major Philosophers of the Song and Ming Periods*, Greenwood Press, 1999.

Smart, N., *The World's Religions*, Cambridge: CUP, 1993.

Snellgrove, D., *The Nine Ways of Bon*, London: 1967.

Snow, Edgar, *Red Star over China*, Harmondsworth: Penguin Books, 1972 (new enlarged edition of first edition of 1937).

Stauffer, M. T., *The Christian Occupation of China*, Shanghai: China Continuation Committee, 1922.

Strassberg, R. E., *A Chinese Bestiary: Strange Creatures from the Guideways through Mountains and Seas*, Berkeley: University of California Press, 2002.

Swanson, P. L., *Foundations of T'ien-T'ai Philosophy*, Berkeley: Asian Humanities Press, 1989.

Teiser, S. F., 'The Spirits of Chinese Religion' in Lopez, D. S., ed., *Religions of China in Practice*, Princeton: Princeton University Press, 1996.

Thompson, L. G., *Chinese Religion: An Introduction*, Belmont: Wadsworth, 1989.

Ting, K. J., *A Rationale for Three-Self*, Neesima lecture, Doshisha University, Japan, 28 September 1984.

Trons, N. J., *The Last Emperor: The Life of the Hsuan-tung Emperor Aisin-Gioro Puyi, 1906–1967*, London: The House of Fans, 1983.

Turnbull, S., *Genghis Khan & the Mongol Conquests, 1190–1400*, Routledge, 2003.

Von Glahn, R., *The Sinister Way: The Divine and the Demonic in Chinese Religious Culture*, Berkeley, CA: University of California Press, 2004.

Waddell, A., *Buddhism and Lamaism of Tibet*, Kathmandu: Educational Enterprises, 1985.

Waley, A., *The Analects of Confucius*, London: Allen & Unwin, 1938.

Warner, M., *The Dragon Empress*, London: Vintage, 1993.

Watson, Burton, *Chuang Tzu: Basic Writings*, New York: Columbia University Press, 1964.

Watson, J. L., *Between two cultures: migrants and minorities in Britain*, Oxford: Blackwell, 1977.

Weinstein, S., *Buddhism under the T'ang*, Cambridge: CUP, 1987.

Whyte, B., *Unfinished Encounter: China and Christianity*, Glasgow: Collins, 1988.

Wolf, A., 'Gods, Ghosts & Ancestors' in Wolf, A. P., *Religion and Ritual in Chinese Society*, Stanford: Stanford University Press, 1974.

Xinran, *The Good Women of China*, London: Chatto & Windus, 2002.

Yao, Xingzhong, *An Introduction to Confucianism*, Cambridge: CUP, 2002.

Yu, Chun-Fang, *Guanyin: The Chinese Transformation of Avalokitesvara*, New York: Columbia University Press, 2002.

Zarrow, P., *China in War and Revolution 1895–1949*, London: Routledge, 2005.

Zhang Li, *Strangers in the City*, Stanford: Stanford University Press, 2001.

NOTES

Chapter 1. The People of the Yellow Earth

1. Bodde, Derk, 'Myths of Ancient China' in *Mythologies of the Ancient World*, ed. S. N. Kramer, New York: Doubleday Anchor Books, 1961.
2. Burnett, D., *The Spirit of Hinduism*, Oxford: Monarch, 2006, ch. 2.
3. *People's Daily*, 13 December 2003.
4. Keightley, D., 'The Religious Commitments: Shang Theology and Genesis of Chinese Political Culture', *History of Religions*, 17.3–4 (1978), pp. 211–55.
5. Hsu, Cho-Yun and Linduff, K. M., *Western Chou Civilization*, New Haven: Yale University Press, 1988, p. 103.
6. Hawkes, D., *Ch'u Tz'u: Songs of the South*, Oxford: Clarendon Press, 1959, pp. 104–7.
7. Mote, F. W., *Intellectual Foundations of China*, New York: McGraw Hill, 1993, p. 15.
8. Ibid., p. 21.
9. Hsu & Linduff, op. cit., p. 382.
10. Jaspers, K., *Way to Wisdom*, Yale University Press, 1954.
11. Bagley, Robert, *Ancient Sichuan: Treasures from a Lost Civilization*, Princeton: Princeton University Press, 2001.

Chapter 2. Early Confucian Teaching

1. Mote, F. W., *Intellectual Foundations of China*, New York: McGraw Hill, 1993, pp. 28–9.
2. Waley, A., *The Analects of Confucius*, London: Allen & Unwin, 1938, p. 21.
3. Yao, Xinzhong, *An Introduction to Confucianism*, Cambridge: CUP, 2000, p. 143.
4. Dobson, W. A. C. H., *Mencius: A New Translation Arranged and Annotated for the General Reader*, Harmondsworth: Penguin Books, 1963, 6.20, p. 141.
5. Ibid., 6.24, p. 143.
6. Goldin, P. R., *Rituals of the Way: The Philosophy of Xunzi*, Chicago: Open Court Pub. Co., 1999, p. xv.

Chapter 3. Early Daoism

1. Mote, F. W., *Intellectual Foundations of China*, New York: McGraw Hill, 1993, p. 60.
2. Kohn, Livia, *God of the Dao: Lord Dao in History and Myth*, Ann Arbor: University of Michigan, 1998.

3. Ibid., p. 275.
4. Quotations are from GNL translation, see website.
5. *Huai Nan Tzu*, ch. 18.
6. Hoff, Benjamin, *The Tao of Pooh and the Te of Piglet*, London: Egmont, 2002.
7. Watson, Burton, *Chuang Tzu: Basic Writings*, New York: Columbia University Press, 1964, p. 23.
8. Watson, *Zhuangzi*, ch. 6, 'The Great and Venerable Teacher'.
9. Ebrey, P., *Chinese Civilization: A Sourcebook*, 2nd edn, New York: Free Press, 1993, p. 30.
10. Watson, *Zhuangzi*, op. cit., ch. 4, 'In the World of Men'.
11. Ibid., ch. 19, 'Mastering Life'.
12. Miller, J., *Daoism: A Short Introduction*, Oxford: Oneworld, 2003, p. 54.
13. Ibid., pp. 1–3.
14. De Bary, T., and Bloom, I., 1999, *Xunzi*, ch. 23, 'Human Nature is Evil', p. 179.
15. De Bary, T. & Bloom, I., 1999, *The Book of Lord Shang*, 'Reform of the Law', p. 104.

Chapter 4. Religion in the Qin and Han Dynasties

1. Sima Qian, *Records of the Historian*, translated by Burton Watson, Hong Kong: Columbia University Press, 1993.
2. Ibid.
3. Shryock, J. K., *The Origin and Development of the State Cult of Confucius: An Introductory Study*, New York: Paragon, 1966, p. 57.
4. Strassberg, R. E., *A Chinese Bestiary: Strange Creatures from the Guideways through Mountains and Seas*, Berkeley: University of California Press, 2002, pp. 48–56.
5. Von Glahn, Richard, *The Sinister Way: The Divine and the Demonic in Chinese Religious Culture*, Berkeley, CA: University of California Press, 2004, p. 45.
6. Burnett, D., *The World of the Spirits*, Tunbridge Wells: Monarch, 2000.
7. Morgan, E. S. (trans.), *Tao, The Great Luminant: Essays from the Huai Nan Tzi*, ch. 7, 'Jingshen', pp. 59–60, http://www.sacred-texts.com/tao/tgl/tgl3.htm
8. Wang Shanshan, 'Stones indicate earlier Christian link?', *China Daily*, updated: 2005-12-22, http://www.chinadaily.net/english/doc/2005-12/22/content_505587.htm

Chapter 5. Buddhism Comes to the Middle Kingdom

1. Ch'en, K., *Buddhism in China: A Historical Survey*, Princeton: Princeton University Press, 1964, pp. 29–31.

2. De Bary, W. M. Theodore and Bloom, I., *Sources of Chinese Tradition: From Earliest Times to 1600*, New York: Columbia University Press, 1999, pp. 421–6.
3. Daisaku Ikeda, *The Flower of Chinese Buddhism*, trans. Burton Watson, New York: Weatherhill, 1986, p. 48.
4. Gernet, J., *Buddhism in Chinese Society: An Economic History from the Fifth to the Tenth Century*, NY: Columbia University Press, 1995, pp. 4–14.
5. Ibid., p. 15.
6. Kohn, Livia, *The Taoist Experience: An Anthology*, NY: State University Press, 1993, p. 204.
7. Ibid., p. 45. Pp. 44–8 contain the first English translation of the *Lingbao Lueji*.
8. Robinet, I., *Taoism: Growth of a Religion*, Stanford: Stanford University Press, 1997, pp. 149–83.
9. Thompson, L. G., *Chinese Religion*, Belmont: Wadsworth, 1989, p. 113.

Chapter 6. Religion During the Tang Dynasty

1. Findling, J. E. and Thackeray, D. C. W., *The History of China*, Greenwood Press, 2001, p. 72.
2. Reigert, R. and Moore, T., *The Lost Sutras of Jesus*, London: Sovereign Press, 2003, p. 5.
3. Weinstein, S., *Buddhism under the T'ang*, Cambridge: CUP, 1987, p. 72.
4. Yu, Chun-Fang, *Guanyin: The Chinese Transformation of Avalokitesvara*, New York: Columbia University Press, 2002.
5. Swanson, P. L., *Foundations of T'ien-T'ai Philosophy*, Berkeley: Asian Humanities Press, 1989.
6. Reigert & Moore, op. cit., p. 3.
7. Palmer, M. I., *The Jesus Sutras: rediscovering the lost religion of Daoist Christianity*, London: Piatkus, 2001, p. 42.
8. Reigert & Moore, op. cit., p. 120.
9. Moffett, S. H., *A History of Christianity in Asia. Volume One: Beginning to 1500*, San Francisco: Harper, 1992.

Chapter 7. Neo-Confucianism and New Religious Movements

1. http://www.lingshidao.net/hanshi/baijuyi.htm
2. Bol, Peter K., This Culture of Ours: Intellectual Transitions in T'ang and Sung China, Stanford University Press, 1992, p. 22
3. Chang, C., The Development of Neo-Confucian Thought, London: Vision Press, 1958, p. 43.
4. Siu-Chi Huang, *Essentials of Neo-Confucianism: Eight Major Philosophers of the Song and Ming Periods*, Greenwood Press, 1999.

5. De Bary, W. T. and Bloom, I., *Sources of Chinese Tradition: From Earliest Times to 1600*, New York: Columbia University Press, 1999, pp. 330–31.
6. Ibid., p. 683.
7. Siu-Chi Huang, op. cit., pp. 171–88.
8. Robinet, I., translation by Brooks, P., *Taoism: Growth of a Religion*, Stanford University Press, 1997, p. 94.
9. Even today the character *fu* is found on the doors of houses in China as a token of good fortune.
10. Hansen, V., *Changing Gods in Medieval China, 1127–1276*, Princeton: Princeton University Press, 1990.
11. Chamberlain, J., *Chinese Gods*, Malaysia: Pelanduk Publications, 1995, p. 90.
12. In 2007 this was 9 May, but note that the date is not fixed as it is based on the lunar calendar.
13. Davis, E., *Society and the Supernatural in Song China*, Honolulu: University of Hawaii Press, 2001, p. 1.

Chapter 8. The Tibetans and Mongolians
1. Waddell, A., *Buddhism and Lamaism of Tibet*, Kathmandu: Educational Enterprises, 1985, p. 382.
2. Ibid., p. 34.
3. Snellgrove, D., *The Nine Ways of Bon*, London: 1967, p. 200.
4. Ibid., p. 207.
5. Onon, Urgunge, *The Secret History of the Mongols: The Life and Times of Chinggis Khan*, Curzon, 2001.
6. Turnbull, S., *Genghis Khan & the Mongol Conquests, 1190–1400*, Routledge, 2003, p. 17.
7. Waddell, op. cit., p. 37.
8. Rustichello, *The Book of Marco Polo, wherein is recounted the Wonders of the World*.
9. See Henson, V., *The Open Empire*, New York: Norton, 2000, pp. 344–7.
10. Ruthven, Malise, *Islam in the World*, Oxford University Press, 2000, p. 279.
11. 'China Struggles with Tibetan Buddhism', NewsMax.com Wires, Thursday, 11 August 2005.

Chapter 9. The Ming Dynasty and the Jesuit Missionaries
1. Menzies, Gavin, *1421: The Year China Discovered the World*, London: Bantam, 2003, p. 75.
2. Ibid., p. 154.
3. Chen, K., *Buddhism in China: A Historical Survey*, Princeton: Princeton University Press, 1972, p. 443.

4. Malatesta, E. J., *The True Meaning of the Lord of Heaven (T'ien-chu Shih-i)*, Taipei: The Ricci Institute, 1985.
5. Quoted in Zurcher, E., 'Jesuit Accommodation and the Chinese Cultural Imperative', in Mugello, D. E. (ed.), *The Chinese Rites Controversy: Its History and Meaning*, Nettetal: Steyler Verlag, 1994, p. 51.
6. Ibid., p. 52.
7. Matteo Ricci, *Letters*, translations by MRL from *Lettere*, ed. Francesco D'Arelli, Macerata: Quodlibet, 2001.

Chapter 10. The Rule of the Manchus and the Growing Impact of the West
1. Gernet, J., *China and the Christian Impact*, Cambridge: CUP, 1985, p. 137.
2. Mungello, D. E., *The Chinese Rites Controversy: Its History and Meaning*, Nettetal: Steyler Verlag, 1994, p. 94.
3. Quoted by Bishop K. H. Ting, *A Rationale for Three-Self*, Neesima lecture, Doshisha University, Japan, 28 September 1984.
4. *Kangxi: Great Emperor and True believer of Christ*, see website section.
5. Ebrey, P. B., *China: Cambridge Illustrated History*, Cambridge: CUP, 2003, p. 234.
6. Broomhall, A. J., *Hudson Taylor*, London: Hodder & Stoughton and OMF, 1981–88.
7. Michael, Franz, *The Taiping Rebellion: History and Documents*, Vol. 1, Seattle: University of Washington Press, 1966, pp. 26–7.
8. Ibid., Vol. 3, p. 1517.
9. Corwin, Charles, *East to Eden?*, Grand Rapids: Eerdmans Publishing Co., 1972, p. 67.
10. Boardman, Eugene P., 'Millenary Aspects of the Taiping Rebellion (1851–64)' in *Millennial Dreams in Action*, ed. Sylvia L. Thrupp, The Hague: Mounton, 1962, pp. 70–79.
11. Ruthven, Malise, *Islam in the World*, Oxford University Press, 2000, p. 279.

Chapter 11. China in Revolt and Revolution
1. Quoted in Warner, M., *The Dragon Empress*, London: Vintage, 1993, pp. 179–80.
2. Smart, Ninian, *The World's Religions*, Cambridge: CUP, 1993, p. 28.
3. Warner, op. cit., p. 149.
4. Paludan, A., *Chronicle of the Chinese Emperors*, London: Thames & Hudson, 2003, pp. 216–17.
5. Zarrow, P., *China in War and Revolution 1895–1949*, London: Routledge, 2005, p. 31.

6. Mao Zedong, 'On New Democracy', in *Selected Works of Mao Tse-Tung*, Beijing: Foreign Language Press, 1967, vol. 2, p. 339.
7. Whyte, B., *Unfinished Encounter: China and Christianity*, Glasgow: Collins, 1988.
8. Stauffer, M. T., *The Christian Occupation of China*, Shanghai: China Continuation Committee, 1922.

Chapter 12. The Chinese Diaspora
1. Watson, J. L., *Between two cultures: migrants and minorities in Britain*, Oxford: Blackwell, 1977, pp. 193–4.
2. Sinn, E., *The last half century of Chinese Overseas*, Hong Kong: Hong Kong University Press, 1998.
3. Wolf, A., 'Gods, Ghosts & Ancestors' in Wolf, A. P., *Religion and Ritual in Chinese Society*, Stanford: Stanford University Press, 1974, p. 131.
4. Teiser, S. F., 'The Spirits of Chinese Religion' in Lopez, D. S., ed., *Religions of China in Practice*, Princeton: Princeton University Press, 1996.
5. See the interesting collection of Chinese paper gods collected by Anne Goodrich.
6. Wolf, op. cit., p. 172.
7. *Taipei Times*, Tuesday, 19 November 2002.
8. Bloomfield, F., *The Book of Chinese Beliefs*, London: Arrow Books, 1983, pp. 101–2.
9. Rong Jiaojiao, 'The Turning Tide', *China Daily*, 30 May 2007, p. 20.

Chapter 13. Mao's China
1. Snow, Edgar, *Red Star over China*, Harmondsworth: Penguin Books, 1972 (new enlarged edition of first edition of 1937).
2. Chang, J. and Halliday, J., *Mao: The Unknown Story*, London: Jonathan Cape, 2005.
3. Fei-Ling Wang, *Organizing through Division and Exclusion: China's Hukou System*, Stanford, CA: Stanford University Press, 2005, p. 23.
4. Gao Wangzhi, 'Y. T. Wu: A Christian Leader Under Communism' in D. H. Bays (ed.), *Christianity in China: From Eighteenth Century to the Present*, Stanford: Stanford University Press, 1996, pp. 340–52.
5. Ibid., p. 348.
6. Chang, J., *Wild Swans: Three Daughters in China*, London: HarperCollins, 1991.
7. Whyte, R. *Unfinished Encounter: China and Christianity*, London: Fount Paperbacks, 1988, pp. 290–91.

Chapter 14. Deng Xiaoping and China's Economic Reform
 1. Estimates of civilian deaths which resulted vary: 400–800 (*New York Times*), 1,000 (NSA) and 2,600 (Chinese Red Cross). Student protesters maintained that over 7,000 were killed.
 2. Bonavia, D., *Deng*, Hong Kong: Longman, 1989, p. 248.
 3. Lambert, T., *The Resurrection of the Chinese Church*, London: Hodder & Stoughton, 1991, p. 53.
 4. Ibid., p. 116.
 5. http://www.jesus.org.uk/dawn/1997/dawn9710.html
 6. *People's Daily*, 1 March 2001.
 7. 'Interview with Li Hongzhi', *Time Magazine Asia*, 10 May 1999.
 8. Introvigne, Massimo, 'Falun Gong', http://www.cesnur.org/testi/falung101.htm (accessed 14 April 2007).
 9. *'Falun Gong' is a Cult*, Beijing: New Star Publishers, 1999.
10. Ibid.
11. Ibid.
12. Forney, M., 'Jesus is back and she is Chinese', *Times Asia*, Vol. 158, 5 November 2001, p. 18.
13. Hidden-advent, 'The mystery of the incarnation 2', *Christ's Utterances*, 2006, 1–2 (website).
14. Hattaway, P., 'Christians wish they were in prison: An examination of the Eastern Lightning Cult in China', *Asia Harvest*, 30 April 2002.

Chapter 15. Social Challenges in the Twenty-first Century
 1. McGivering, J., 'Mao still powerful in modern China', *BBC News*, Friday, 6 January 2006.
 2. Xinran, *The Good Women of China*, London: Chatto & Windus, 2002.
 3. Jiang, Y. and Ashley, D., *Mao's Children in the New China*, London: Routledge, 2000.
 4. Ibid., p. xv.
 5. 'China's Children too busy to play', *Women of China* website, 17 May 2007.
 6. On 1 June 2007, International Children's Day, China's central government introduced new laws to reduce the pressure upon children.
 7. Zhang Li, *Strangers in the City*, Stanford: Stanford University Press, 2001, p. 25.
 8. *China Human Development Report* (CHDR), 2005, p. 27.
 9. *The World Bank's Rural Sector Strategy for China*, 1 November 2006, p. 3.
10. Perry, E. J. and Selden, M., *Chinese Society*, 2nd edn, *Change, conflicts and resistance*, London: Routledge, 2002, p. 160.

11. Story from BBC News: http://news.bbc.co.uk/go/pr/fr/-/2/hi/ programmes/5086754.stm (published 12:17:48 GMT, 19 June 2006).
12. *New York Times*, 15 January 2006.
13. *Women of China* website, 22 May 2007.
14. Becker, J., *The Chinese*, London: John Murray, 2000, p. 374.
15. Chang, Gordon G., *The Coming Collapse of China*, London: Arrow Books, 2002.
16. Gelber, H. G., *The Dragon and the Foreign Devils*, London: Bloomsbury, 2007, p. 441.

Chapter 16. The Future of Religion in New China
1. Xing Funzeng, 'The Church-State Relations and Protestant Christianity', *China Study Journal*, December 2003.
2. Harrell, S., *Cultural Encounters on China's Ethnic Frontiers*, Seattle: University of Washington Press, 1995.
3. Ibid., p. 27.
4. 'Dalai Lama rejects Tibetan Buddhist praise of China', Reuters, Wednesday, 28 December 2005, 4:48 p.m.
5. Berlie, Jean A., *Islam in China*, Bangkok: White Lotus Press, 2004, p. 3.
6. Beech, Hannah, 'Henan's Ethnic Tensions', *Time*, Thursday, 4 November 2004.
7. Graham-Harrison, E., 'Muslim Uighurs left behind by China's tourism boom', Reuters, 27 December 2006.
8. Ibid.
9. Yao, Xingzhong, *An Introduction to Confucianism*, Cambridge: CUP, 2002, p. 274.
10. Guo Shipeng, 'Anxiety fuels Confucius craze in China', Reuters, 9 May 2007.
11. Ibid.
12. Law, Pui-lam, 'The Revival of Folk Religion and Gender Relationships in Rural China: A Preliminary Observation', *Asian Folklore Studies*, Vol. 64, 2005.
13. Ibid.
14. Berlie, Jean A., *Islam in China: Hui and Uyghurs between Modernization and Sinicization*, Bangkok: White Lotus, 2004.
15. Beck, Lindsay, 'China's Muslims look to Middle East as ties grow', Reuters, 27 November 2006.
16. Berlie, op. cit., p. 151.
17. *China Daily*, 30 May 2007.
18. Yang Huilin, 'Christian Faith Amongst Chinese University Students', reprinted in *China Study Journal*, December 2002.
19. Tang, Edmond, *China Study Journal*, March 2007.

INDEX

Printed in Great Britain
by Amazon.co.uk, Ltd.,
Marston Gate.